BUBBLEBALL

BUBBLEBALL

INSIDE THE NBA'S
FIGHT TO SAVE A SEASON

BEN GOLLIVER

ABRAMS PRESS, NEW YORK

Library of Congress Control Number: 2020944916

ISBN: 978-1-4197-5553-8
eISBN: 978-1-64700-364-7

Printed and bound in the United States
10 9 8 7 6 5 4 3 2 1

This book is based on reporting for the *Washington Post* during the
2019–2020 NBA season.

Abrams books are available at special discounts when purchased
in quantity for premiums and promotions as well as fundraising
or educational use. Special editions can also be created to
specification. For details, contact specialsales@abramsbooks.com
or the address below.

Abrams Press® is a registered trademark of Harry N. Abrams, Inc.

ABRAMS The Art of Books
195 Broadway, New York, NY 10007
abramsbooks.com

To Grandma Pat and all librarians.
To Mom and all teachers.

Contents

1

Welcome to the Bubble

My first steps back into the Central Florida sunshine, with squinting eyes and a deep-seated paranoia, were cautious.

Even under normal circumstances, I would be headed into stimulus overload. Disney World's grounds were dotted with tall palm trees and bright tropical flowers; tiny geckos circled my ankles and egrets launched off the grassy banks of blue lakes.

But these were the most abnormal circumstances of my lifetime. Security guards were watching my every move. I had agreed to always wear a face mask and an identification credential in public. I had been issued a Kinexon proximity alarm that would beep like a smoke detector if I stood too close to anyone else. I had listened to detailed security briefings informing me that I would be confined to a small portion of the Coronado Springs Resort and that I wouldn't be allowed, at first, to get a haircut or walk to the hotel gift shop, let alone drive a car or visit the nearby amusement parks.

While the jarring restrictions were straight out of dystopian fiction, I realized quickly that I had stepped into basketball's Garden of Eden. Within minutes, I stumbled across NBA players, award-winning executives, and well-known referees. They mingled by the pool, power-walked along a simple oval path, and fished from three bridges that converged at a central lake. The players' main hotel, the Gran Destino Tower, glimmered just beyond the bounds of the access allowed by my credential.

Donovan Mitchell, the Utah Jazz's All-Star guard, provided my official greeting to this hot, humid, and hectic new world: "Welcome to the bubble."

I was glad to be there. I was nervous to be there. I was still getting my bearings. OK, I was tripping out a little bit.

For a full week, I had been strictly confined to a hotel room with two queen beds, a long desk, a big-screen television, and a simple bathroom. Once a day, I was allowed to step onto my front porch for a few minutes so that medical professionals in full scrubs could swab my nostrils and throat. Prepackaged meals were left at my door by scurrying staffers who wore face shields and medical gloves. I could faintly hear my neighbors through the walls, but we weren't acquainted and didn't communicate. My room's only window didn't open. Visitors were forbidden.

To pass the time during my quarantine, I paced back and forth for hours: eight steps toward the bathroom, heel turn, eight steps away from the bathroom. Each morning, I diligently completed a health checklist that required me to take my temperature, measure my blood oxygen level, and fill out a detailed health questionnaire through an iPhone app. I strapped my MagicBand, complete with an NBA logo and Mickey Mouse ears, to my right wrist; Disney's electronic hotel key doubled as my facility access pass and tracked my movements around campus. I slid an Oura tracking ring on the middle finger of my right hand to gauge my temperature in real time.

On long, empty afternoons, I stared out my window at a lake fountain that shot water high into the air, a taunting mirage. The isolation made me a little loopy, and I started to feel like a circus performer or a reality television show participant. With nothing else to do and nowhere else to go, I filmed myself pacing and uploaded it to Twitter. Nearly 100,000 gawkers watched the sad sight of a sportswriter turned into a caged hamster.

The social media buzz led to dozens of interviews with media outlets from around the world, and they all seemed to be enjoying my suffering a bit too much. Their rubbernecking was understandable: I was a hostage at "the Happiest Place on Earth."

Well, that's how the sports talk hosts liked to phrase my predicament, but it wasn't quite true. I had volunteered for the assignment, a basketball obsessive eager to get a courtside view for the NBA's ambitious and unprecedented restart. The *Washington Post*, my employer, had paid more than $50,000 for my golden ticket as one of the few independent media members to live and work entirely inside the bubble. And I was technically free to leave at any time, although bailing out was an unthinkable proposition given all the money, energy, and stress required to get to Disney World in the first place.

How did I get here? The answer was simple and yet so big that it defied comprehension. All aspects of my new life in Orlando were shaped by the novel coronavirus pandemic, which spread from China to the United States in early 2020.

When I arrived at Disney World on July 12, 2020, Americans had been dying and American businesses had been struggling for months. This specific coronavirus, named COVID-19, caused a disease with a range of symptoms: fevers, fatigue, cough, shortness of breath, aches, and the loss of taste and smell. COVID-19 was deadly, especially among vulnerable populations like the elderly, and it spread rapidly. A widely available vaccine was still months away, and there was no sweeping federal game plan for confronting the virus or limiting its spread, only conflicting public health recommendations, shifting timelines, and a false hope, expressed repeatedly by President Donald Trump, that it would magically go away.

These invisible, unexpected killer germs rocked the American people and presented an existential threat to businesses. Twenty-two million Americans lost their jobs during the early stages of the pandemic, and the NBA wasn't spared. Thanks to a decade-long financial boom and a lucrative media rights deal, the NBA was an $8 billion-per-year business before the pandemic. Then, with little warning, the league had to shutter its arenas and indefinitely suspend its season when a player tested positive for the mysterious new virus on March 11, 2020. "Our revenue has essentially dropped to zero," NBA commissioner Adam Silver admitted on an April 17 conference call.

Less than three months after Silver delivered the direst statement of his six-year tenure, nearly 350 players on twenty-two teams arrived at Disney World. Considerable planning and extensive negotiations between the league and the National Basketball Players Association had produced a radical and ambitious solution to the pandemic. By strictly limiting contact with the outside world and enforcing public health best practices, the NBA hoped to play hundreds of games inside a "bubble" environment. Walled off from the rest of society, the NBA could attempt to complete its regular season and hold the playoffs.

While the plan made sense in theory, basketball was especially vulnerable to the coronavirus. Experts were still grappling with how the virus spread, but it appeared that indoor gatherings presented a higher risk and that close-contact situations should be avoided. Basketball, of course, was a full-contact sport played indoors. If one player unknowingly contracted the virus and played in a game, he could easily expose teammates, coaches, opponents, referees, and, possibly, media members.

But the NBA was intent on generating television money and crowning a champion, and I was intent on being there to see it succeed or fail.

Raised in the shadow of Nike's world headquarters in Beaverton, Oregon, I became enamored with basketball at a young age thanks to a steady diet of Michael Jordan propaganda and the Portland Trail Blazers' "Rip City" runs to the 1990 and 1992 Finals. Since I began covering the NBA in 2007, I had structured my life around the league's schedule, covering games on Christmas, hitting the road every spring for the playoffs, and taking brief vacations during the late-summer dog days.

My typical week involved writing five basketball stories and appearing on five basketball podcasts. When the arenas went dark, my life got dark. If I needed to sacrifice the comforts of home and hand over my private medical information to see the 2019–20 season's biggest names—LeBron James, Kawhi Leonard, and Giannis Antetokounmpo—compete for a title, so be it. The three leading contenders—the Los Angeles Lakers, Los Angeles Clippers, and Milwaukee Bucks—had to settle things on the court, and I was up for just about anything the NBA thought it needed to do to finish the season. Small price to pay.

Memphis Grizzlies guard Ja Morant said that he quickly settled into bubble life because he was "not a silver spoon guy." Clippers guard

Patrick Beverley noted that "the bubble is what you make it." I sought to channel Morant's low-maintenance approach and Beverley's pragmatism, but there was no preparing for any of this, no helpful reference point.

I had covered the nine previous NBA Finals, but none were played in nearly empty gyms typically used for high school tournaments. I had interviewed hundreds of players, but none had disclosed the excruciating details of their brushes with a deadly pandemic. I had spent nearly 1,000 nights in hotel rooms, but none of those stays had mandated a weeklong quarantine period.

My solitary confinement ended after I passed COVID-19 tests on seven consecutive days, and I did my best to make up for lost time. Like any new captive, I sought to test the fences by taking a full lap around the media's restricted area. I weaved through a series of four-floor hotels known as the Casitas. The five Spanish-style buildings were simple and a bit tacky, looking and functioning like dormitories at a warm-weather college. I lived in room 4432, on the top floor of the fourth building away from the players' hotel.

Everywhere I turned, I ran into noteworthy NBA figures. Mitchell smiled easily in his unofficial role as bubble ambassador, although the mandated mask covered his mouth and nose. Members of the Lakers cast fishing lines into the lake. Boston Celtics coach Brad Stevens nodded politely as he completed an evening walk. Longtime referee Scott Foster, one of the league's most well-known and polarizing officials, bobbed and weaved around a makeshift pickleball court. My new dormmates were media luminaries like Rachel Nichols of ESPN and Marc Stein of the *New York Times*.

Stations with free hand sanitizer, disinfecting wipes, and masks were placed at regular intervals, and signs stressing the importance of masks and social distancing were ubiquitous. Meanwhile, sets of Casitas rooms were transformed into BioReference Labs testing clinics. Every day, teams of four contracted employees would administer the daily tests and scrub the room clean after each attendee passed through the rigorous system. Results were communicated via email within a day.

The central lake, and its warning signs about alligators, ran along the entire front side of the campus; a long parking lot made up the back side. Decorative fountains were located in between the Casitas buildings, and the grounds were green and well maintained. In addition to the pool, the campus included a small fitness center, an outdoor activities area, and a shipping warehouse to receive packages.

I had no interest in Disney movies and I didn't have children, but I could see why minivan caravans descended upon Orlando year-round. Visitors were guaranteed a suntan or sunburn, there was a family-friendly vibe, and the major attractions were only a few miles away. Even if afternoon temperatures reached ninety-five degrees and thunderstorms rolled through almost every day, there were worse places to be stuck.

My exploratory walk ended abruptly near Casitas 1 thanks to a Disney security guard named Reymundo. As I headed toward the players' hotel, he looked at my credential and held up his hand. My badge, which included my headshot, name, and company affiliation, was green with red stripes. All-access badges were green only. From behind his face shield, mask, and sunglasses, Reymundo calmly but firmly let me know that I had to turn around. "I'm making sure the media is within your boundaries," he said, with a walkie-talkie ready in case of trouble.

That same scene repeated near Casitas 5. Joshua, another security guard, surveyed my credential and prevented me from walking any farther along the lakeside path. The boundaries of my new pen were established within a 0.8-mile perimeter. Walking all the way around my new stomping grounds took less than fifteen minutes, and video surveillance cameras were spread about the property.

It struck me then that fourteen of the twenty-two teams invited to the bubble were being housed at other nearby hotels—the Grand Floridian and the Yacht Club—that were beyond my sightlines and access. At least I could see the Gran Destino Tower and occasionally run across its inhabitants.

I had assumed that I would be able to go for morning walks with a friend staying at the Grand Floridian, but the hotels operated as independent bubbles. Cross-contact was strictly limited. NBA officials also advised that extended conversations with players and coaches, even if they walked through the Casitas, were prohibited outside of official media access periods. We had to stick to hand waves and head nods.

When they first left their families and arrived at the bubble, Lakers forward LeBron James and Portland Trail Blazers guard Damian Lillard said they felt like they were going away to prison. Philadelphia 76ers forward Tobias Harris jokingly referred to the experience as "luxury jail," and more than one bubble attendee compared the Coronado Springs Resort to a white-collar prison.

I had never felt less free and more monitored than I did while living in the bubble, but some perspective was in order. We were not inmates. We were working professionals making "extraordinary sacrifices"—Adam Silver's apt phrase—who also happened to be privileged to live in one of the country's safest places during the pandemic.

Still, this tiny, controlled space, with its clear borders and relative lack of amenities, was to be my home for the next ninety-three days. I did my best not to ponder past tomorrow.

"I've had numerous nights and days thinking about leaving the bubble," James said in late August, when the entire experiment nearly imploded amid tension and exhaustion. "I think everyone has, including you [media] guys. I don't think there's one person that hasn't had a mind to say, 'Oh, I've got to get the hell out of here.'"

2

Shutdown

Four months before I landed at Disney World for the NBA's attempted restart, I watched in horror as basketball came to a screeching halt. The historical record will show that the NBA was the first major American professional sports league to stop playing due to the coronavirus, and that Commissioner Adam Silver suspended the 2019–20 season before receiving a government mandate. It wasn't quite that simple. March 11, 2020, the day the balls stopped bouncing, unfolded in a frenzied panic.

While the NBA knew that the coronavirus was coming, no one was completely prepared. I certainly wasn't. In mid-February, I had attended All-Star Weekend in Chicago. Silver briefly mentioned the coronavirus during his annual address, expressing regret that Chinese media members weren't able to be in attendance and pledging the league's support for international relief efforts. Otherwise, the virus was a nonissue.

That changed quickly over the next few weeks. By early March, the country was beginning to familiarize itself with terms like "essential workers" and "mass gatherings." I was receiving emails from overseas fans who were sounding the alarm about the virus and its possible impact on sports. NBA games seemed to be nonessential and especially high risk because they were held indoors and drew 20,000 or more fans. How long could business continue like usual?

On March 6, LeBron James came out strongly against the idea of playing games in empty arenas as a precautionary measure. "I play for the fans," he said. "That's what it's all about. If I show up to the arena and there ain't no fans there, I ain't playing." Still, I received the green light from my *Washington Post* editors to travel to Minneapolis on March 7 for a story on the Minnesota Timberwolves, a young team with a first-time coach in Ryan Saunders and a first-time president in

Gersson Rosas. Their hope was to build a winner by carefully tracking all aspects of their players' lives, including their diet, sleep, workouts, practices, and games, I planned to let the team's executives, coaches, and trainers put me through the same gauntlet of tests they used on new players.

Los Angeles International Airport was a ghost town, and before departing I posted photos of the empty concourses to my Instagram followers. I arrived to find the downtown Minneapolis Marriott virtually empty, and I self-consciously made a beeline for the hand sanitizer stations. I stayed in my hotel room for most of the weekend because there was an eerie feeling in the air.

My time with the Timberwolves went as planned, and it was a blast. Their trainer tested and measured my flexibility, endurance, standing jump, and mobility. Their dietitian overhauled my daily food intake, their psychologist administered a personality test, and their coaches ran me ragged on their practice court. In a debrief, Dr. Robby Sikka, the Timberwolves' vice president of basketball performance, informed me that I had exerted more energy in my shooting workout than point guard D'Angelo Russell had in a light practice. Yes, it was basically an off day for Russell. Who cares? By one measure, for about one hour, I had outperformed an NBA All-Star. This was the greatest athletic achievement of my life.

I never got the chance to write that story, because a much bigger story was staring right at me. On March 8, I attended a game between the Timberwolves and New Orleans Pelicans. There, Timberwolves executives opted for fist pounds instead of handshakes, and they discussed the need to cut back on scouting trips. Players and staffers were encouraged to wash their hands regularly and to avoid shaking hands unnecessarily. Still, the game went on like usual. The arena was full of fans, with some sitting near the action in courtside seats. The postgame locker room scene was a little uneasy and tense, but I was still allowed inside.

The next day, March 9, I listened in as Sikka gathered the Timberwolves, including franchise center Karl-Anthony Towns, for a team meeting about the coronavirus. Minnesota was about to embark on a long road trip, and Sikka warned his team at length about the disease's risk factors. The short version of his speech: Don't go out and have fun on this trip, because we want everyone to come home in one piece.

The players needed this speech. I needed this speech. Sikka's words made me realize that James's commentary about emptying arenas was inadvertently dangerous. James later backtracked, but his sentiment reflected a lack of knowledge across the league. The players weren't alone. Fewer than twenty-five Americans had died of COVID-19 complications at that point.

That same day, the league office instituted protocols to keep reporters out of locker rooms and to maintain social distancing during interviews. Soon after, the text messages started coming in from other executives: The rest of this season could be compromised or canceled, and next season might be impacted too. "We aren't exempt," one executive told me. "I'm concerned for myself and my kids, and I'm scared for my parents. This is an unprecedented test for President Trump and our health care system, let alone the NBA. We don't know where this is going, and it could get really, really bad. That's not being alarmist. That's the truth."

The wheels were in motion now. Ohio governor Mike DeWine "strongly recommended" that the Cleveland Cavaliers empty their arenas on March 10. A day later, the City of San Francisco moved to ban indoor gatherings of at least 1,000 people, which included Golden State Warriors games at the Chase Center. Despite James's resistance, emptying arenas was an inevitable next step. Delays were getting harder to justify.

Even with those developments, my firsthand experiences in Minnesota, Sikka's expertise, and growing coverage of New York City's early outbreak, I still didn't get it. I flew home on March 10 and again posted airport photos. This time, two old college friends, who were now doctors, scolded me by text message.

"What are you doing?" one wrote. "Get home immediately. Cancel all future trips. Stay inside. Tell your parents to stay inside. This thing will KILL you." The other added: "Please listen to me. I don't want you to die. No story is worth that. Think about the message you are sending to people by getting on a plane."

On March 11, a Wednesday, I was back at home in Los Angeles when Silver convened a Board of Governors call to discuss the league's next steps amid the growing pressure. The majority opinion was that games should continue in empty arenas to protect the fans' safety, to protect the league's reputation, and to keep the show going in whatever form possible.

But a few owners felt differently, leading the NBA to table a final decision until Thursday, March 12. Houston Rockets owner Tilman Fertitta, for one, had made his stance clear in a March 6 interview with CNBC. "I would hope that we would just suspend for a week or two weeks," the billionaire restaurateur said. "But you don't want to play games with no fans. That's never going to work." While most owners had started to wrap their minds around the scope and immediacy of the coronavirus challenge, the lack of unanimity and of a federal mandate led to a delay.

"I was shocked by the number of teams that were clueless at the size that the coronavirus would get to," one team executive who participated in the Board of Governors call told me. "Some teams that hadn't faced an outbreak in their communities didn't think it was worth talking about. There were two teams that were adamant that games should continue like normal until there was government intervention. 'Why shut ourselves down?' We viewed that as completely irresponsible to our fans and community."

The first sign that something was amiss Wednesday night came when Dr. Donnie Strack, the Oklahoma City Thunder's vice president of human and player performance, ran onto the court shortly before an 8:00 p.m. EDT game against the Utah Jazz. This was a highly unusual sight. The Thunder and Jazz took the court in Oklahoma City expecting to play a normal game, just like the one I had attended in Minnesota a few days earlier.

Strack's dramatic entrance set into motion an unforgettable, alarming night. At center court, he huddled with the three referees to let them know that Jazz center Rudy Gobert, who was sidelined because he had felt ill, had just tested positive for COVID-19.

Gobert was a newly minted All-Star, a two-time Defensive Player of the Year, and a favorite of the basketball analytics crowd. But the seven-foot-one French center wasn't especially well-known among casual fans because he played in a small market, hadn't gone to college in the United States, and hadn't been a high draft pick. Now Gobert was about to become a household name as the Patient Zero of American sports.

There was no playbook for Strack and the referees, and they first sought to buy time by sending the Thunder and Jazz back to their respective locker rooms. The decision makers soon realized that trying to play the game without Gobert was an untenable proposition. He had traveled with, and been in close proximity to, his teammates before falling ill, meaning that everyone in the Jazz's travel party had potentially been exposed.

If the game continued, all sorts of further exposures were possible. The Thunder, the referees, the ball boys, the coaches, the team executives, the medical staffers, the scorekeepers, the courtside media members, the fans—everyone's health would be at risk. Meanwhile, the Jazz players, coaches, and staffers would need to be tested before they proceeded with their schedule or traveled back to Utah.

I was glued to the surreal scene in Oklahoma City, and my anxiety kept rising as the delay stretched to thirty-five minutes. The next night, I was scheduled to cover a high-profile game between the Los Angeles Lakers and Houston Rockets at Staples Center. I wanted to see LeBron James and James Harden go head-to-head, but those warning text messages were ringing in my head. If the Lakers' trainer went running onto the Staples Center court, I pictured myself grabbing my laptop, holding my breath, and sprinting to my car to get home as quickly as possible.

Oklahoma City's game operations staff stalled by letting the halftime act perform early. Finally, Mario Nanni, the Thunder's public address announcer, delivered bad news to boos from the confused crowd. No mention was made of Gobert's name or positive test. "Fans, due to unforeseen circumstances, the game tonight has been postponed," Nanni said. "You're all safe. Take your time in leaving the arena tonight and do so in an orderly fashion. Thank you for coming out tonight. We're all safe. Please drive home safely. Good night, fans."

Word of Gobert's diagnosis spread quickly. The Jazz, Thunder, and some media members were held at the arena and tested for COVID-19 by Oklahoma State Department of Health officials. Royce Young of ESPN.com reported that the Thunder were released by health professionals after having their temperatures taken, while members of the Jazz were held in the locker room until after midnight local time as they awaited their test results.

Meanwhile, four games continued to completion in other markets. A late-tip game between the Sacramento Kings and New Orleans Pelicans was called off because one of the referees scheduled to work the game had officiated a Jazz game two days earlier. Suddenly, everyone around the league was asking themselves the same questions: *When was the last time we played the Jazz? When was the last time we played someone who played the Jazz? Am I safe?*

At 9:32 p.m. EDT, the NBA issued a terse press release: "NBA TO SUSPEND SEASON FOLLOWING TONIGHT'S GAMES." The subject line made my hands shake. "The NBA announced that a player on the Utah Jazz has preliminarily tested positive for COVID-19," the release read, noting that the player wasn't at the arena. "The NBA is suspending game play following the conclusion of tonight's schedule of games until further notice. The NBA will use this hiatus to determine next steps for moving forward in regard to the coronavirus pandemic."

This was crushing news, but my first reaction was a deep sigh of relief. I was worried about the safety of my friends and colleagues around the league. Selfishly, I no longer needed to worry about getting sick at that Lakers game. I didn't need to mentally prepare for three months of cross-country plane trips during the upcoming playoffs. I could hibernate and wait to see how the virus shook out.

After rushing to file a story about the shutdown, I tried to collect my thoughts. The NBA owners had pushed off their decision, and the decision was made for them. It dawned on me finally that the season might not come back. I was heartbroken for the players, who were nearly five months into a season that might end before the playoffs could even begin. I was sick to my stomach at all the hours of practices, all the games, and all the anticipation that would go to waste.

The season's biggest story lines were evaporating before my eyes. James was chasing his fourth title, and the virus might impact his attempt to eclipse Michael Jordan as basketball's GOAT. Milwaukee Bucks star Giannis Antetokounmpo, the reigning MVP, was seeking the first title of his career after a disappointing 2019 playoff exit. Kawhi Leonard, the reigning Finals MVP, was eyeing his third title with a third team after leaving the Toronto Raptors for the Los Angeles Clippers in July 2019.

The NBA had crowned a champion every year since 1947. Seventy-three straight years! Was there now going to be an empty line in the record books thanks to this virus?

Sadness. Anger. Confusion. Helplessness. All those feelings swirled on March 11, as did a healthy degree of skepticism and cynicism.

Silver acted swiftly in response to Gobert's positive test, and his willingness to pull the plug on the season was cheered when the National Hockey League, Major League Baseball, and Major League Soccer all followed suit that week. Yet, in the heat of the moment, I felt strongly that the league should have moved more quickly.

Executives from multiple teams said that they expected Silver would have emptied fans from arenas beginning Thursday if Gobert hadn't tested positive. Others expressed their dismay that Wednesday's games had proceeded. "It's crazy they tried to play that game knowing that he was being tested," one told me. "Why did it take a positive test to shut things down? The players never should have been stuck in that locker room all night, and the fans shouldn't have been in the building."

Money was no small factor. NBA teams cleared $2 million per regular season game, on average, and roughly 40 percent of the NBA's $8 billion annual revenue came from game-related sources like ticket sales, parking, and merchandise. On March 11, the end of the 2019–20 regular season was about a month away, and some teams had already been effectively eliminated from the playoffs. Owners of non-playoff teams only needed to hold off the virus for a few more weeks.

Denial was also at play. People all over the earth, including NBA owners, held out hope that a deadly pandemic wouldn't touch them or their businesses. Recent pandemics had been deadlier overseas than in America, and the Spanish flu of 1918 was something that most people had only read about in textbooks. The Trump administration hadn't yet fully sounded the alarm. Indeed, President Trump told the famed journalist Bob Woodward in late January that he was intentionally downplaying the virus to avoid a "panic."

Wouldn't someone in a position of authority tell us—clearly, loudly, and repeatedly—if holding a basketball game or attending one might cost us our lives? Shouldn't such a warning take place before a doctor went running across the court moments before tip-off?

While I was frustrated that Silver and the owners hadn't acted more decisively during their March 11 call, I was also projecting. For weeks, I had read about the coronavirus and its deadly impact overseas. The top editors at the *Washington Post* had acted early to limit travel and, later, to empty the newsroom. I had plenty of access to good information about the virus, and yet I was guilty of hoping for the best and not fully preparing for the worst.

As with many Americans, the virus just didn't have a place in the stories I told myself about myself. I was in the middle of the NBA season, and nothing ever interrupted an NBA season. I was still shaken up from covering the tragic death of Lakers legend Kobe Bryant in January, and the playoffs were just around the corner. I was "busy" and living day to day, deadline to deadline.

The NBA was fortunate that the Jazz were able to acquire a test for Gobert and that he tested positive. Tests were extraordinarily difficult to come by in early March, and fewer than 5,000 were performed across the country on March 11. Gobert's positive result prevented future NBA games from being potential super-spreader events, and it prompted further testing inside the league, including fifty-eight members of the Jazz and their traveling media on Wednesday night. All-Star guard Donovan Mitchell tested positive that night.

The Jazz issued statements that confirmed two positive tests without naming Gobert or Mitchell. Other positives followed around the league, including Detroit Pistons center Christian Wood, who had had direct contact with Gobert in the days before his positive test. Members of the Brooklyn Nets and the Lakers, who had played each other in Los Angeles on March 10, also tested positive. If I hadn't traveled to Minneapolis, I would have attended that game. If Gobert hadn't tested positive on March 11, I probably would have talked myself into attending the Lakers' game against the Rockets on March 12. In theory, I could have been exposed at both games.

Those close calls don't haunt me as much as the frightening scene in Oklahoma City, which I still wish had never happened. Silver and the owners should have done better. President Trump should have done better. I should have done better too.

3

Data, Not the Date

Once I realized that I had been too slow in recognizing the coronavirus's ability to impact the NBA and touch my life, I did everything in my power to make up for lost time. My new mission was overcompensation.

I started by counting my blessings: I showed no symptoms after my trip to Minneapolis, I was accustomed to working from my home in Los Angeles, and I could cover the league's shutdown without traveling anywhere. The *Washington Post* was one of the most stable media companies in the country, and my other employers were on solid footing. From those facts alone, I knew I was lucky.

Still, I was worried. I could hardly sleep in the first days after the NBA went dark, getting up before sunrise to burn off stress in empty, dark streets. I feared the virus's lethal potential, a global economic collapse, and widespread unemployment, among other nightmare scenarios. I wondered how long the NBA could remain on hold before I would need to get a new beat. What else did I know enough to write about?

My life and most of my major relationships revolved around a sport that wasn't guaranteed to return anytime soon. I quit drinking alcohol in 2007, but going cold turkey with basketball seemed far, far worse. Basketball was one of the few things that made me happy and fulfilled. I never dreamed about retirement; I always dreamed about being the oldest guy in the press box.

Did I even have any hobbies? Well, I liked road trips, national parks, and the University of Michigan football team. Great. The coronavirus made traveling impossible, and the college football season, if there even was a season, was a long way off. How was I going to fill my days?

Simplicity seemed like the key to pandemic life. I mentally catalogued all my social interactions and sought to cut out as many as possible. No more trips to the coffee shop, grocery store, pharmacy. No visits with family, friends, or acquaintances, except on Skype. I went to the bank once a month to pay rent. I took laundry to the cleaners every two weeks. I had all my groceries delivered, and I started washing my hands about fifteen times per day.

To pass the time, I built elaborate Lego sets, experimented with origami, downloaded TikTok, and called my parents more often in April than I had in the previous year combined. I walked at least eight miles per day, chasing butterflies, examining snails, and marveling as smaller animals became more adventurous with no traffic on the streets. One afternoon, I did a double take as a wild peacock strutted by. On another, I watched bug-eyed as a heron stabbed a mole to death with its beak. My residential neighborhood in West Los Angeles was turning into the set of BBC's *Planet Earth*.

I paired the new exercise routine with a more disciplined diet, courtesy of the Timberwolves' experts. Proteins and fruit replaced carbs and sweets. By May, I weighed less than I had at any point since college. The pandemic was only two months old, and I already felt like a different person.

My regimen was a little intense, but it kept me balanced without basketball. The NBA is a twelve-month sport, as off-season rumors generate as much interest as the games. That nonstop cycle ceased during the hiatus, and the basketball community was quieter than it had ever been during the social media age.

Players were barred from working out at team facilities, and many quickly fell off the map. Team officials were waiting for directions from the NBA league office and mostly stayed out of the public eye. A few owners, including Tilman Fertitta of the Houston Rockets and Mark Cuban of the Dallas Mavericks, gave noncommittal interviews on cable television.

During the first days of the shutdown, the only news that really mattered came from Adam Silver, and it was almost always bad. On March 12, the commissioner said the hiatus would last at least thirty days. He added soon after in an interview with TNT that the Finals could still take place in late July, even if the hiatus extended six weeks. He added that "of course it's possible" the season and postseason would be canceled. By March 15, the Centers for Disease Control and Prevention (CDC) recommended that all gatherings of fifty or more people should be "canceled or postponed" for at least eight weeks.

That guidance seemed to put the NBA's return in grave jeopardy. Even if the NBA skipped the remaining month of its regular season and proceeded directly to the postseason, it would need about two months to hold its standard sixteen-team, four-round playoff format. If play couldn't begin until mid-May at the earliest, the NBA would need to scrap its summer calendar, which included the NBA Draft in late June, free agency on July 1, the Las Vegas Summer League in mid-July, and the Tokyo Olympics, which were still scheduled for July and August. If the NBA pushed out any further than that, the start of the 2020–21 season, set for October, would likely need to be delayed too.

Difficult questions abounded. Was it ethical to attempt a return during a pandemic that was wreaking havoc across the globe and accelerating in the United States? Could the NBA really hope that the situation would significantly improve in two months? Would teams with no chance of making the playoffs or winning a title even want to come back? Did the NBA plan to fly players around the country like a typical postseason?

How would the NBA protect its players from the virus if they did resume play? How much time would teams need to ramp up after a layoff? How long could they delay a restart before it felt like a new season rather than a continuation of the current one? Would the players be paid if games had to be scrapped? Should all parties look ahead to next season instead?

My wheels were turning on how to answer some of those questions even before Silver officially pulled the plug on March 11, and I laid out the basics of my plan in a March 14 column. The NBA would need to employ a neutral site to eliminate all travel. Fans would be barred. The rest of the regular season would be scrapped to cut the number of teams and players involved. The playoffs would be an entirely made-for-television event. Players would be housed nearby, and their contact with non-NBA personnel would be limited as much as possible. Teams would play every other day, and multiple games would run concurrently at nearby gyms. I imagined Las Vegas as the host, primarily because its annual Summer League utilized two adjacent gyms. I noted that a scaled-down, eight-team playoff format would take only six weeks.

In truth, I wanted to believe that my plan could happen more than I believed it would happen. Everything sounded good in theory, but the nagging health questions remained. Wouldn't a single positive test require the whole thing to be shut down? How much would this cost? Would fans view the eventual champion as legitimate? Would the players buy in? Could it come together in time? Would Silver and the owners be willing to bet their reputations and long-term profit-making potential on an unprecedented proposal?

It wasn't hard to poke holes in the plan, and plenty of fans, even diehards, told me that it wasn't worth seriously discussing until the pandemic subsided. On that front, things were only getting worse for the country and for the league.

On March 19, the *Washington Post* published an investigative story about COVID-19 testing that I worked on with Juliet Eilperin. While more than fifty members of the Utah Jazz had received immediate access to COVID-19 tests from the Oklahoma State Department of Health despite showing no symptoms on March 11, an emergency medical technician with serious symptoms lay in a hospital bed in nearby Tulsa and was still unable to get tested.

A similar scene played out in New York City, where the Brooklyn Nets paid a private company to test their entire team. Star forward Kevin Durant and three of his teammates tested positive. Meanwhile, a Brooklyn educator spent eleven days seeking a test only to finally receive one after he was admitted to a hospital and placed on oxygen.

COVID-19 tests were in short supply across the country, and the NBA was on the wrong side of the access crisis. Politicians took note. "An entire NBA team should NOT get tested for COVID-19 while there are critically ill patients waiting to be tested," New York mayor Bill de Blasio tweeted. "Tests should not be for the wealthy, but for the sick."

Silver and various team officials sought to add nuance to the conversation. The commissioner noted that the players should have been tested because they were potential "super-spreaders" due to their frequent travel, while the Nets issued a statement saying that testing their roster was "the right thing to do for our players and their families and the responsible thing to do from a medical and epidemiological standpoint."

Other teams pledged not to test players unless they showed symptoms. "We've been told that testing is in short supply," Golden State Warriors general manager Bob Myers said. "We're not better than anybody. We're not worse. We're just a basketball team, like any company."

The outrage aimed at the NBA was real and justified. Money and fame weren't the right criteria to determine who got a test. Yet the NBA's position was only a tiny sliver of the wider problem. Even if the NBA used zero tests, there weren't nearly enough tests to go around. Easy-to-obtain, affordable, and effective tests with quick turnaround times weren't universally available even six months later. And testing only people who exhibited symptoms wouldn't help to stop a virus where more than 20 percent of infected people are asymptomatic.

As the NBA found itself caught in the crossfire of a massive public health failing, it realized that any restart efforts would need to be messaged carefully. The league couldn't be seen to be using public resources or otherwise impeding the average citizen's ability to receive health care. It was simply too toxic for a league that prided itself on its decency and played to a younger, often left-leaning fan base.

A similar firestorm erupted in late April when the federal government launched a small-business aid program with more than $300 billion in funding. The Paycheck Protection Program (PPP) was designed to provide financial relief for companies with fewer than 500 employees to pay their workers during the pandemic, but the program was rife with administrative delays. Many qualified companies in need were left on the outside because the program was set up on a first-come, first-served basis.

The Los Angeles Lakers, perhaps the NBA's glitziest and highest-profile franchise, admitted that they had applied for and received $4.6 million under the first round of PPP funding. Despite quickly promising to return the money once the news became public, the Lakers drew intense criticism. Why was a professional sports organization valued by Forbes at $4.4 billion receiving aid that could have been better used by the program's intended recipients?

And then there was the case of Karl-Anthony Towns and his mother. Just two weeks after I had chatted with the Timberwolves' All-Star center during my visit to Minnesota, Towns announced that his mother, Jacqueline, was in a coma after contracting COVID-19. In a public service video released March 25, the twenty-four-year-old Towns urged viewers to take the virus seriously and called his mother "the strongest woman I know."

Jacqueline had gone to a New Jersey hospital for a COVID-19 test, but her results were delayed and her symptoms, which included a cough and a 103-degree fever, kept worsening. "I felt she was turning a corner," Towns said. "I knew there were more days to come, but we were heading in the right direction. [Then the doctors] said she went sideways. She went sideways quick. Her lungs were getting extremely worse. She was having trouble breathing."

Doctors told Towns that his mother needed to be placed on a ventilator. "I told her I loved her," Towns said. "Every day, I told her how much I loved her. She was telling me things I didn't want to hear."

The Towns family announced on April 13 that Jacqueline died after spending weeks in a coma. Jacqueline Towns was fifty-nine. "She was an incredible source of strength; a fiery, caring, and extremely loving person, who touched everyone she met," the family said in a statement. "Her passion was palpable, and her energy will never be replaced."

Timberwolves president Gersson Rosas said that he was "heartbroken," and condolences poured in from across the NBA. The Timberwolves organization grieved openly, and Towns remained out of the public eye for months. "The severity of this disease is real," Towns said in the video. "This disease needs to not be taken lightly. Please protect your family, your loved ones, your friends, yourself. Practice social distancing. Please don't be in places with a lot of people. This disease is deadly."

Towns' brave, wrenching words reframed the NBA's coronavirus conversation for me. Two weeks earlier, he had been laughing at the team's practice facility and yelling at the referees during the game against the Pelicans. I had photographed him leaning on D'Angelo Russell, his longtime friend and new teammate, and walking off the practice court flanked by his coaches. I had even watched Towns listen intently, his head resting on his wrist, as Timberwolves executive Robby Sikka gave his coronavirus safety address.

Now Towns was confronting the loss of his mother, who had been a regular presence at his games throughout his decorated high school career, his one-and-done season at the University of Kentucky, and in Minnesota. Sikka was devastated. "To be honest with you, I cried," the thirty-eight-year-old executive said. "I knew how heartfelt he was. He has an EQ that people don't always recognize. He felt so strongly about doing something positive for the community and helping others."

Sikka channeled his anguish into a message of unity and awareness. "This is only going to be tougher," Sikka warned Timberwolves staffers in late March. "It's going to impact more and more of your loved ones. Are you prepared? Are you going to communicate? Are you going to come to us? If you do, we'll do anything and everything we can to help. We're a family."

I knew Sikka's warning was accurate, and I wondered how much more the NBA could take. The 2019–20 season had opened with the biggest international crisis of Silver's tenure. Houston Rockets general manager Daryl Morey had tweeted in support of Hong Kong protesters seeking freedom, and the Chinese government, Chinese media companies, and Chinese sponsors had cut ties with the Rockets and the NBA in response.

Former commissioner David Stern—Silver's mentor, close friend, and predecessor—died at age seventy-seven on January 1 after suffering a brain hemorrhage. Later that month, Lakers legend Kobe Bryant and his thirteen-year-old daughter, Gianna, were among nine victims of a fatal helicopter crash.

In four short months, the NBA had lost hundreds of millions of dollars in revenue from its most important global market, perhaps the most influential executive in league history, and a beloved basketball icon who was so young that he hadn't even been inducted into the Hall of Fame yet. The weight of the coronavirus shutdown and Jacqueline Towns's death felt too great for a staggering league to bear.

After a month in isolation, I wasn't sure that I wanted the NBA to pursue a return anymore, even if it adhered to the logical steps that I laid out in my half-baked, neutral-site concept. Other major events like the NCAA tournament and the Coachella music festival had been canceled. For the NBA, this had become a matter of life and death, not wins and losses. Towns and the Timberwolves deserved time to grieve properly. Maybe American society needed some time and space to process everything that was happening.

Placing that series of events—from China to the coronavirus— into the NBA's historical context wasn't particularly difficult. Nothing could compare emotionally, psychologically, or financially. Labor stoppages had delayed the starts of multiple seasons, but the NBA always recovered to crown a champion. The 2007 gambling scandal involving referee Tim Donaghy had rocked the credibility of Stern's NBA, but the league moved on in relatively short order. Racist tapes of Los Angeles Clippers owner Donald Sterling had been a major test for Silver in 2014, but the new commissioner navigated the crisis with precision.

There was only one conclusion to be reached in April 2020. I came back to it night after night as I walked my neighborhood's empty streets, trying to process Jacqueline Towns's death and wondering what horrors the coronavirus had in store next.

This was the worst season ever.

* * *

The NBA's road back to the court was gradual, exhausting, and tense. More than anything, it was wary.

Commissioner Adam Silver kept a low profile during the first month of the hiatus, limiting his appearances to occasional video interviews with the league's television partners. He had good reason for that strategy. By April 1, the United States had more than 200,000 confirmed cases—tops in the world—and 4,300 deaths related to the coronavirus. Silver's early, hopeful forecasts for a quick return unraveled in the face of that rapid spread, and there was little to be gained by trying to predict the path of the coronavirus or to issue projected timelines.

The NBA had closed its arenas and practice facilities to its players and staffers when the hiatus began, and it wasn't clear how or when they would be able to reopen those buildings, given stay-at-home orders issued by state and local authorities that temporarily closed many businesses and public places. There wasn't much hope of holding games, let alone an entire postseason, if a player couldn't even shoot hoops in his team's otherwise empty gym.

There was no option other than to delay. Silver finally addressed reporters on an April 17 conference call, noting that the league was not yet "seriously engaged" on a return-to-play plan like the one I had imagined in March. Rumors were percolating about basketball's interest in a single-site "bubble" environment where games could be held more safely, but Silver avoided inflating expectations.

A "bubble" scenario would be outside the bounds of the NBA's Collective Bargaining Agreement, and such an unusual restart would be subject to negotiations with the National Basketball Players Association. Like any union, the NBPA would do everything in its power to protect the health and safety of its members. Even if Silver and the owners could construct a relatively safe playing environment, they would have to sell it to the players, many of whom were worth tens of millions of dollars and could afford to ride out the pandemic in relative comfort.

Quoting a line delivered by Disney chairman Bob Iger to the NBA's Board of Governors in a recent meeting, Silver explained that the NBA would let the progress of the virus dictate the NBA's return plans. "It's about the data and not the date," Silver said. "There's too much unknown to set a timeline. There is no appetite to compromise the well-being of our players. In terms of priorities, you begin with safety. We're not at a point yet where we have a clear protocol and a path forward where we feel like we can sit down with the players and say we can resume the season. Human life trumps anything else you could possibly be talking about."

That sentiment reflected the raw fear that many Americans felt toward the virus, which was confounding health experts. Mixed signals from the government—about everything from how long it would last, to how deadly it was, to how it spread—only made the situation worse. Did masks help or not? Was this a three-month problem or an eighteen-month problem? Was this a disease that primarily killed older citizens, or was everyone at risk? Should beaches and parks be closed, or were indoor restaurants the real culprit?

Without clear and consistent answers to those questions, Americans were left reading stories about overwhelmed emergency rooms, morgue trucks temporarily housing thousands of dead bodies, medical professionals without sufficient personal protective equipment, and political disputes between the federal government and state governors. In New York City, field hospitals were set up at Central Park and the Javits Center to handle the rising caseload. Outbreaks were being traced to birthday parties, weddings, and nursing homes. It wasn't difficult to imagine how vulnerable a basketball team would be, given all its shared time together in locker rooms, on planes and buses, at meals, and in hotels.

The nightmare scenarios unfolded from there, shaped largely by Rudy Gobert's positive test and the subsequent positive tests by Donovan Mitchell and Christian Wood. If one player tested positive and it went undetected, the virus could spread to dozens or hundreds of people, even if fans were barred. Infections could theoretically occur during gameplay, huddles, dead-ball arguments, pregame meetings, postgame dinners, and road trips.

Jacqueline Towns's death proved that the virus could touch the NBA community, and a bubble wasn't guaranteed to be a perfect solution. Were Silver and the owners really prepared to risk the death of a player or coach? Some high-profile coaches like the San Antonio Spurs' Gregg Popovich and Houston's Mike D'Antoni were senior citizens and therefore at higher risk. Even if players in their twenties and thirties were less likely to die, were they willing to risk the possibility of a career-altering illness with unknown long-term side effects? Would players' families be allowed to live in the bubble? If so, what would happen if they got sick? If not, how would players view the separation and isolation?

Aside from the health concerns, there were plenty of looming logistical challenges. If an outbreak occurred, would a team have to forfeit games or be sent into quarantine? Could the schedule be delayed? If television revenue was driving the league to fast-track a return, would there be special rules to accommodate a star player if he tested positive?

To me, these seemed like impossible questions. I wanted basketball back, but the worst-case scenarios led me to assume a return would be untenable in the short term. Of course, my pocketbook wasn't being directly impacted like those of the owners and players. It was easy for me to err on the side of absolute caution.

When the virus first hit, there was a thought that it might recede during summer's warm-weather months and return with a second wave in the fall. Silver's statement about following the data seemed to open the door for such a possibility. If the NBA remained patient and then acted when the virus receded, perhaps an unconventional salvage attempt could be possible. Playing through the summer would mean delaying the following season, but there was more than $1 billion of television revenue at stake with the playoffs.

Still, the virus was disrupting every aspect of life, and it seemed unlikely that things would return to normal in three to six months, like many hoped in March. If parks departments were removing basketball rims to prevent pickup games in cities across the country, how exactly would the NBA hold roughly one hundred playoff games?

According to Silver, three key data points would guide the NBA's return: new COVID-19 case counts, access to testing, and government guidelines. If the first wave receded, testing became more available to the public, and orders by local and national government bodies allowed the NBA back into its facilities, perhaps play could continue.

The World Health Organization reported that there were 28,711 new cases in the United States on April 17, the date of Silver's speech. That was in line with April's typical rate, which consistently ranged from 24,000 to 32,000. Those figures represented massive increases compared to March, and there was no end in sight. Much of the country had yet to experience a major outbreak, and President Trump wanted to lift stay-at-home orders and reopen the country to boost the economy, complicating efforts to predict the virus's progress in the months to come.

As a hedge against a possible cancellation of the season, the NBA and NBPA agreed on May 15 to withhold 25 percent of each player's remaining paychecks for the 2019–20 season. The agreement was intended to "provide players with a more gradual salary reduction schedule" to ease the hit to their pocketbooks if play never resumed. Silver also announced that he, Deputy Commissioner Mark Tatum, and other top NBA executives would take a 20 percent salary reduction. A league spokesman cited the "unprecedented times" for the league's need to "take short-term steps to deal with the harsh economic impact."

Silver was blunt about the ethical bind facing the NBA: Health and safety were the stated top priorities, but that wasn't the only consideration. "Our revenue has essentially dropped to zero, which is having a huge impact on our team business and arena business," he said. "There's a strong recognition that there are thousands of jobs impacted by the NBA, not just the ones the fans see. While this virus is a dire public health issue, so is shutting down the economy. I think that's why the league sees it as our obligation, to the extent we can resume play in a safe way, to look at every potential way of doing so."

That statement carried no promises, yet it was easy to read between the lines and conclude that the NBA was highly motivated to return. The financial fallout from the pandemic had already started nationwide, with 20 million lost jobs in April, and basketball was taking its lumps. The NBA increased its credit line from $550 million to $1.2 billion in March, and numerous teams laid off employees and part-time arena staffers.

Houston Rockets owner Tilman Fertitta, who said before the hiatus that playing in empty arenas "would never work," was especially vocal about his money woes. Fertitta, the chairman of the Landry's restaurant corporation, furloughed 40,000 employees in his casino and restaurant businesses in March. He then took out a $300 million loan at an eye-popping 13 percent interest rate in April to help weather the pandemic.

In mid-May, Fertitta visited the White House and appealed to President Trump and Secretary of the Treasury Steven Mnuchin to "add a category" to the Paycheck Protection Program to help larger companies like Landry's instead of directing the aid solely to small businesses. Fertitta acknowledged that he, like the Los Angeles Lakers, had received PPP money but added that he had returned it because he didn't want to be painted as "that billionaire who took the money from the little business."

Yet he plunged ahead with his hat-in-hand request. In response to questions from Trump, Fertitta noted that he was paying maximum contracts to James Harden and Russell Westbrook. "Russell and James both make $40 million a year and they were still getting paid, so a lot of my employees really wanted that PPP money," Fertitta said.

Trump, who noted that Fertitta's restaurants had "paid me rent for a long time," seemed open to the entreaty. Mnuchin sounded a bit bewildered and recalled the "backlash" generated by the Lakers' attempt to secure PPP funding. "We realize the issue, how it impacts your workers, and we're sympathetic to that," Mnuchin said, but he added, "This was a program for companies that were not necessarily quite as big."

Trump had been pushing the major professional sports leagues to pursue return plans, telling their commissioners on an April 4 call that he hoped they could return by late summer and that the National

Football League season would open like usual in the fall. Six weeks later, the president couldn't resist asking Fertitta for the latest on the NBA's plans.

"I think what they're doing is waiting to see what happens in certain states and if we're going to be able to play," Fertitta said. "Making sure the virus continues to go in the right direction in the next few weeks. If things keep going the way that it's going, I think the NBA, the commissioner, Adam Silver, who has done an unbelievable job through this, and the thirty owners will make the decision to try to start the season up again.

"I think we would play some games to get it going again and create the interest. Then go right into the playoffs. I think it would be great for America. We're all missing sports. Everyone wants to see these great NBA teams."

There was no denying that America was missing sports. The *Washington Post* decided to do away with a stand-alone Sports section in the daily paper, folding whatever we could come up with during the content drought into the back of the Style section. ESPN's television programming schedules were completely erased by the virus overnight. The major sports companies' social media accounts made do by posting reheated memes. NBA players hosted a virtual H-O-R-S-E tournament, to unenthusiastic reviews.

Michael Jordan always had impeccable timing, and he saved the day one more time when basketball fans were at their lowest point during the pandemic. Now fifty-seven, he had been retired since 2003 and had moved into an ownership role with the Charlotte Hornets. Other than his 2009 Hall of Fame induction, a couple of magazine profiles, and his moving tribute to Kobe Bryant at a public memorial in February, Jordan had kept a low profile. He cherished his privacy and was raising a family with his second wife.

Yet Jordan's legacy remained strong in basketball culture and on social media. His well-worn highlights were guaranteed to draw huge numbers of clicks, and the major sports accounts circulated them constantly. LeBron James's continued greatness fueled debates about who was the GOAT, and the Los Angeles Lakers star was filming a remake of *Space Jam*, Jordan's 1996 movie.

Even so, when I visited my mother's elementary school class and made a reference to Jordan, I got mostly blank stares. If they could place Jordan's name, it was because of his shoes, not his game. The achievements that I had spent my formative years memorizing—six championships, five MVPs, six Finals MVPs, two gold medals, ten scoring titles—were a foreign language to them. They had no idea about The Shot, The Shrug, or The Last Shot. I left the class visit wounded.

Jordan and his close circle of advisers were aware of the growing generation gap. They had been working on a legacy project called *The Last Dance*, a documentary built around exclusive, behind-the-scenes video footage shot by an NBA Entertainment camera crew during Jordan's sixth and final title run, in 1997–98.

Director Jason Hehir had prepared his first script in 2016 and conducted 106 interviews in the years that followed. He and his staff cast a wide net, digging through 500 hours of exclusive footage and more than 10,000 hours of archival material. They interviewed President Barack Obama, President Bill Clinton, and a host of NBA luminaries and other celebrities. Jordan sat for hours of interviews in which he cried, relived his greatest moments, lashed out at old rivals, and cursed like a sailor.

"I shook everybody's hands two years in a row when they beat us," Jordan said, disgusted that Isiah Thomas hadn't returned the favor after the Chicago Bulls defeated the Detroit Pistons in the 1991 Eastern Conference finals. "There's a certain respect to the game. That's sportsmanship, no matter how much it hurts. Believe me, it fucking hurt. They didn't have to shake our hands. We knew we whooped their ass already. To me that was better in some ways than winning a championship."

As a child, I worshipped Jordan. Jordan sneakers. Jordan basketball cards. Jordan posters. Jordan Valentine's Day cards. Jordan VHS tapes. All of it. I begged my parents to name our female golden retriever "Michael Jordan." We compromised on Emmy Jane (M.J.).

I watched the ten-hour project in eighteen hours—pausing only to sleep—and then rewatched it two more times. I couldn't believe my luck. Jordan was attacking Bulls general manager Jerry Krause, trash-talking with Hall of Fame guard Gary Payton, and playing a hotel room piano after slaying the 1998 Jazz. This was heaven, a documentary capable of carrying five straight Sunday nights and providing fodder for hundreds of hours of debate shows. With nothing else to write about, I spent a month recapping episodes and writing columns about the side characters.

The Last Dance was a smash hit, averaging more than 5 million viewers per episode. NBA players who weren't old enough to remember Jordan's career received a thorough indoctrination to the cult of MJ, and *The Last Dance* was a rare communal moment at a time of social distancing and isolation. Jordan even fought through the flu—the flu!—to gut out a tough win in the 1997 Finals.

"Young fans that never got to see Michael play now understand why he's the [GOAT] of basketball," Lakers legend Magic Johnson wrote on Twitter. "For me? Michael Jordan, Michael Jackson, and Beyoncé are the three greatest entertainers of my lifetime; and you could probably throw Muhammad Ali in there."

ESPN's original plan had been to air *The Last Dance* on off nights of the 2020 NBA Finals, which were scheduled for June. In its dream scenario, Jordan's story and LeBron James's title pursuit with the Lakers would alternate nights for two straight weeks. The coronavirus spoiled that plan, but it was better for all parties. Jordan's Bulls got their month in the sun, reminding basketball diehards like me not to give up. James and the Lakers would eventually get their day too.

As my heart swelled with Jordan nostalgia, I still struggled to wrap my mind around how the NBA might salvage its season during the pandemic. By mid-May, case rates and death rates had leveled off compared to their April peak. Testing access remained a problem, and there were still regularly more than 20,000 new cases and 1,000 deaths per day, but hospitals and medical systems had survived the worst of the virus's early onslaught. Trump, who was in a presidential election campaign, and his conservative allies were eager to pitch this as progress and get the country back to work.

The NBA began taking reluctant steps in that direction to accommodate players who had been locked out of their team facilities and cooped up for nearly two months. In states like Georgia that were among the first to reopen, league and team executives feared that players might turn to public gyms for their workout needs. The coronavirus risk would no doubt be higher in such settings, leading the NBA to inform its teams in late April that they would be allowed to reopen their practice facilities for individual workouts if their local governments loosened stay-at-home orders.

The Cleveland Cavaliers and Portland Trail Blazers were the first to welcome back players, on May 8. With direction from the league, teams reopened with strict health guidelines. The Toronto Raptors, for example, allowed only one player and one coach into their facility at any given time. Everyone who entered the building had to wear a mask and undergo a temperature check. Only the practice court was opened to players, with the rest of the facility and the weight room remaining shuttered. The court was cleaned before and after every workout. Despite the new rules and isolated conditions, the players celebrated the symbolic first step. Alongside an Instagram photo from the Cavaliers' facility, forward Cedi Osman wrote, "Great to be back!!!"

Still, Silver struck a measured tone on an hourlong phone call with the National Basketball Players Association that same day. The commissioner told the players that the league hoped to resume its season that summer, but he ruled out the possibility of playing in front of fans. He indicated that the league would need to utilize a single-site location to reduce travel and create a safe environment. If games resumed, players would undergo daily coronavirus testing and some teams might be left out if they were far outside the playoff picture.

"The questions and the concerns are about what if another player tests positive," said one player on the call. "Are we going to take the same precautions? I think they're optimistic that the season will resume. From a personal standpoint, I don't think that it will be smart just to run the season back and there's no vaccine."

A final decision on whether to play might not be made until June, Silver told the players, and there was no official word yet on where the restart might take place. Speculation, however, was rampant. On April 16, Keith Smith, a former Disney employee turned sportswriter, wrote a column for Yahoo titled "Why Walt Disney World would be the ideal spot for the NBA to salvage its season."

Smith pointed to Disney World's abundance of hotel options and the expansive sports facilities at the nearby ESPN Wide World of Sports Complex. He noted the close relationship between Silver and Iger, the clear business ties between the NBA and Disney, and the fact that Disney World was private property and therefore easier to transform into a protected bubble.

There was predictable backlash to the column, which was framed as an informed proposal rather than a sourced report. Millionaire NBA players staying at Disney World hotels? NBA games held inside high school gyms? To many, it seemed like a fantastical dream. Professional athletes went to Disney after they won a championship, not for three months away from home while trying to avoid a deadly virus.

Slowly but surely, the concept gained traction behind closed doors and in public. Back in March, I had assumed Las Vegas would be the favorite to land a restart because of its successful history hosting Summer League, the high volume of luxury hotel options, and the fact that tourism had dried up almost completely during the early stages of the pandemic.

Sin City had some obvious complications, though. The NBA would need thousands of hotel rooms, and it would be hard to locate them without utilizing the Las Vegas Strip. How feasible would it be to create a protected living environment in that type of location? Would players and staffers be able to stick to a strict health and safety protocol if the city reopened and its ever-present temptations were accessible? What safe activities would be available for those living inside a Las Vegas bubble? Going outside to golf or exercise in Nevada's desert heat, which regularly topped 110 degrees in the late summer, wasn't realistic.

Silver finally unveiled the NBA's plans on May 23 with a simple statement noting that "exploratory conversations" were taking place between the league and Disney for a restart at Disney World. For the first time, the NBA was ready to provide a timeline: late July. Plenty of other details, like which teams would be invited, where they would stay, how many games they would play, and what the playoff format would look like, remained unanswered.

Disney's interest in hosting the restart was obvious: Disney World and the Wide World of Sports Complex had been shuttered during the pandemic. With so many aspects of its business directly impacted by the virus, Disney announced plans to lay off 28,000 employees in September. The NBA's arrival would provide needed revenue, utilize otherwise unused facilities and hotels, and create hundreds of hours of television content for Disney's television networks, ABC and ESPN.

While the NBA hoped that COVID-19 case rates would slow over the summer, it could count on a business-friendly local government in Florida. Republican governor Ron DeSantis, a Trump ally, had been one of the loudest voices downplaying the severity of the pandemic and pushing for a reopening of the economy. On May 18, well before most states, DeSantis launched phase one of Florida's reopening, allowing restaurants, gyms, barbershops, and other businesses to operate at limited capacity.

Planning an expensive, large-scale event in advance was a tricky proposition, but the NBA didn't need to worry about DeSantis suddenly shutting down the whole thing. In fact, he was openly campaigning for teams and leagues to temporarily relocate to his state. "All these professional sports are going to be welcome in Florida," DeSantis said on May 13. "If you have a team in an area where they just won't let them operate, we'll find a place for you here in the state of Florida. We think it's important, and we know it can be done safely."

I had mixed emotions: I wanted basketball back, but I worried that the Disney World proposal might be too much, too soon. The debate over the NBA's return mirrored wider national discussions about reopening and returning to work, which had become heavily politicized. The NBA, which had often fashioned itself a progressive league with respect to LGBTQ rights and diversity issues, was now contemplating a bold action that aligned with right-wing politicians.

Trump had famously argued in March that the American economy needed to reopen during the pandemic because "we can't have the cure be worse than the problem." DeSantis said a shelter-in-place order meant "consigning probably hundreds of thousands of Floridians to lose their jobs" and "throwing their lives into potential disarray." Texas lieutenant governor Dan Patrick said the economic damage of a shutdown could be worse than the deaths caused by the virus, adding that he and other seniors were "willing to take a chance on your survival in exchange for keeping the America that all America loves for your children and grandchildren."

To many observers, the constant focus on economic arguments rather than public health concerns was callous, misguided, and unenlightened. Although the NBA had found itself with some unexpected bedfellows, at least the data was somewhat on its side. New cases had dropped from 28,711 when Silver first addressed reporters on April 17 to 20,475 when the league unveiled its Disney World plan on May 23. If the virus kept declining at a similar rate, the league would be in the clear, or close to it, by its late July target date for the bubble.

Unfortunately, that logic would prove to be wishful thinking.

4

Two Challenges

The NBA's selection of Disney World didn't guarantee that there would be a restart. Because the league's Collective Bargaining Agreement hadn't laid out explicit plans for a global pandemic, any resumption of play required approval from the National Basketball Players Association. If the owners and players couldn't agree to terms, the owners couldn't force the players back to the court. That said, the owners held a nuclear option called the force majeure clause, which could be triggered in response to a cataclysmic event like a pandemic. Exercising the force majeure clause would nullify the previous agreement, halt player salaries, and trigger a labor war.

No one wanted that. With NBA commissioner Adam Silver and NBPA executive director Michele Roberts overseeing talks, the two sides had enjoyed a collaborative and productive relationship that included an early agreement during their most recent negotiations, in 2017. Silver had long sought to cast the players and owners as "partners," in sharp contrast to David Stern's more bombastic and confrontational approach. That partnership, and the trust between the two sides, would be tested by the bubble negotiations, given the scope of the financial losses and the obvious health concerns.

As May ended, Roberts said that most players preferred resuming play safely to canceling the season, but numerous questions lingered. Silver and the owners needed to pitch the players on the Disney World concept. But the players were otherwise occupied, consumed by rage, disgust, and fear due to a white cop's knee on a Black man's throat.

The killing of George Floyd by Minneapolis police officer Derek Chauvin on May 25 sparked weeks of Black Lives Matter protests against police brutality across the country. Chauvin was captured on video pressing his knee onto Floyd's neck for more than eight minutes during an arrest, as three other police officers watched. Floyd, who had been detained and handcuffed before his death, called out for his mother and told officers that he couldn't breathe before he lost consciousness. While Floyd's death was later ruled a homicide, Chauvin and the other officers were not immediately arrested.

Prominent NBA players had decried police brutality for years, organizing protests and calling for justice following the deaths of Eric Garner and Tamir Rice, among other cases. Floyd's death hit close to home because he had been childhood friends with Stephen Jackson, a fourteen-year pro who retired in 2014. Jackson, who referred to Floyd as "Twin" due to their shared physical resemblance, immediately traveled to Minneapolis to lead protests and call for the arrests of the officers. NBA stars, including LeBron James, expressed their support for Jackson, and Karl-Anthony Towns and Josh Okogie joined Jackson at a Minneapolis City Hall demonstration.

"I'm here because they're not going to demean the character of George Floyd, my twin," Jackson said. "A lot of times when the police do things they know is wrong, the first thing they try to do is cover it up and bring up your background to make it seem like the bullshit they did was worth it. When was murder ever worth it? But if it's a Black man, it's approved. You can't tell me, when that man had his knee on my brother's neck, taking his life away with his hand in his pocket, that that smirk on his face didn't say, 'I'm protected.'"

With millions unemployed and much of the country still on lockdown due to the pandemic, Floyd's killing set off perhaps the most sustained racial justice protest movement since the 1960s. For weeks, protesters took to the streets and occasionally clashed with police. NBA players marched in California, Georgia, North Carolina, Oregon, Pennsylvania, Wisconsin, and everywhere in between.

Jaylen Brown of the Boston Celtics and Malcolm Brogdon of the Indiana Pacers livestreamed a march through Atlanta. "I'm a Black man and a member of this community," Brown said. "I grew up on this soil. This is a peaceful protest. We're walking. That's it. We're raising awareness. Some of the injustice we've been seeing is not okay. As a young person, you've got to listen to our perspective. Our voices needed to be heard. I'm twenty-three years old. I don't know all the answers, but I feel how everybody else is feeling."

Brogdon noted that his grandfather marched alongside Dr. Martin Luther King Jr., and that he "would be proud to see us" protesting again. "I have brothers, sisters, and friends who are in the streets," he said. "Who are getting pulled over, discrimination, day after day. The same bullshit. This is systematic. We don't have to burn down our homes. We built this city. This is the most proudly Black city in the world. Let's take some pride in that. Let's focus our energy. This is a moment. We have leverage right now."

Portland Trail Blazers forward Carmelo Anthony wrote on Instagram: "I Don't See An American Dream. I See An American Nightmare. The Greatest Purveyor Of Violence In The World: My Own Government. I Can Not Be Silent."

Numerous Black coaches issued statements, with Doc Rivers of the Los Angeles Clippers and Dwane Casey of the Detroit Pistons detailing the racism they had experienced. "I've personally been called more racial slurs than I can count, been pulled over many times because of the color of my skin, and even had my home burned down," Rivers said.

Casey added that he had felt "helpless" while attending a newly integrated elementary school in Kentucky. "I felt as if I was neither seen, nor heard, nor understood," he said. "I see how many people continue to feel those same feelings—helpless, frustrated, invisible, angry."

While NBA owners typically sought to avoid public discussions of race, most teams issued statements in response to Floyd's death that condemned discrimination and police violence. Michael Jordan, known for remaining tight-lipped about non-basketball matters during his playing days, pledged $100 million over ten years to promote racial equality and social justice. "I stand with those who are calling out the ingrained racism and violence toward people of color in our country," said Jordan, now the owner of the Hornets. "We have had enough."

Indeed, many Americans felt that enough was enough after Floyd's killing, viewing the horrific video of his death as clear evidence of broken systems and ingrained hatred of Black people. The NBA community's response reflected those feelings, and it marked new territory for a league that hadn't reacted to previous incidents with such shared public force.

Four days after Floyd's death, Chauvin was arrested, and later he was charged with second-degree murder. The protests continued for weeks afterward, leading some cities to institute mandatory curfews on top of existing stay-at-home orders due to the pandemic. In Los Angeles, which hadn't yet reopened, there were numerous clashes between protesters and police officers. Mayor Eric Garcetti ordered everyone inside by as early as 6:00 p.m., often sending text messages and notifications with little prior notice. My evening walks had to be rescheduled on a few nights, and for the first time during the quarantine, I felt boxed in by the walls of my one-bedroom apartment.

Tensions were so high—both inside the basketball community and nationwide—that it wasn't clear how Floyd's death would affect the NBA's bubble plans. One thing was clear: The overwhelmingly white NBA owners needed the overwhelmingly Black NBA players to put their lives at risk to work during a pandemic and to live a restricted and isolated existence.

Michele Roberts said in an ESPN.com interview in early May that the possible presence of armed guards to enforce the bubble "sounds like incarceration to me." Floyd's killing brought to the surface the racial overtones of the bubble proposal and the demographic disparities between the NBA owners and players. The partners needed to thread a needle through two holes simultaneously to save the restart proposal.

"Just as we are fighting a pandemic, which is impacting communities and people of color more than anyone else, we are being reminded that there are wounds in our country that have never healed," Silver wrote in a memo to staffers. "Racism, police brutality and racial injustice remain part of everyday life in America and cannot be ignored."

Even before Floyd's death, these were not simple negotiations. The NBA hoped to generate roughly $1 billion in television revenue and crown a champion, and the players were warming to the idea despite the health risks, because of the financial stakes. Yahoo reported that LeBron James, Kawhi Leonard, and Giannis Antetokounmpo all participated in a May 11 conference call with other superstars, and that the faces of the NBA's top three contenders shared a desire to restart the season. An informal poll of players conducted by the union in June showed that a strong majority preferred to play rather than cancel the season.

While the two sides had decided on the where for the bubble, they still needed to hash out the who, what, when, and how. The good news: Everyone had an idea for what the restart should look like. The bad news: Everyone had a different idea for what the restart should look like.

That was true among NBA teams and players as well as idling journalists and fans. I belonged to the cautious camp, in part because it dawned on me that I was likely going to cover the event if media members were invited. The *Washington Post* served a global audience, and we were one of the largest and most stable media organizations covering the NBA.

I felt a professional obligation to cover the NBA restart if given the chance, but I was sticking to my strict home quarantine and wasn't taking any chances with the virus. I believed strongly that the NBA had an ethical obligation to protect its players, and I didn't want my love of basketball to lead me stumbling into a high-risk environment. I knew that any bubble would only be as good as its weakest link. I could limit my contacts with other bubble inhabitants, but there was no way I could replicate my isolated existence while covering hundreds of professional basketball players 3,000 miles from home.

It bothered me that the NBA hadn't released its full health and safety protocols. I felt like the players and the public should know what the NBA was walking into, and I wanted to make the most informed decision possible. As the two sides began to negotiate the playoff format and schedule, it felt to me like they were putting the cart before the horse. Would there even be any games if the bubble couldn't hold?

My view was that the NBA should bring only sixteen teams to Disney World and proceed directly to the playoffs rather than restart the regular season. This would limit the scope of the event to roughly two months and limit the size of the bubble by leaving the worst fourteen teams at home. First-round upsets are rare in the playoffs, and I felt like the top contenders could shake off the rust against weaker teams before the competition heated up in the second round.

I wanted a champion crowned as simply, quickly, and cleanly as possible. Adding layers to the format or bringing additional teams might wind up looking penny-wise and pound-foolish. More teams would mean more television content, but the margin of error seemed microscopic. If one high-profile player got sick or a top contender suffered an outbreak, the bubble's credibility and viability would be shot. Why take unnecessary risks if most casual fans were tuning in to watch a select group of superstars and a few storied franchises?

The NBA owners, understandably, cared more about maximizing television revenue. The bubble would end up costing nearly $200 million to build and maintain, and they wanted to squeeze as many dollars from the project as reasonably possible. Some argued for bringing all thirty teams, even basement dwellers that were practically eliminated from the playoffs. The bubble was only going to be a bridge solution, and the significant financial damage caused by the coronavirus would likely extend into the 2020–21 season.

Others thought that twenty or twenty-two teams should come, in large part because Zion Williamson played for the New Orleans Pelicans, who were just outside the playoff picture when the shutdown began. The hyped rookie's January debut had drawn 2.36 million viewers, and he figured to be one of the bubble's top television draws with stars like Stephen Curry, Kevin Durant, Kyrie Irving, and Klay Thompson expected to miss out due to injuries. Williamson was such a magnetic presence that the NBA had scheduled the Pelicans to play on national television on opening night, Christmas, and Martin Luther King Jr. Day. I had flown to New Orleans for his dazzling debut, and then changed my itinerary twice so that I could watch his second and third career games. I couldn't get enough Williamson, and neither could millions of fans.

The NBA's contracts with regional sports networks—the stations that aired each team's games in their home markets—required that they reach seventy games played. The league had fallen just short of that key benchmark due to the hiatus and could surpass it with a few weeks of tune-up games. This was a strong counter to my argument that the NBA would be penny-wise and pound-foolish if it brought more than sixteen teams.

There was no immediate consensus within the league about the playoff format either, although the top contenders generally had the most incentive to play, while the also-rans had the most incentive to stay home. Executives from multiple lottery teams told me that they hoped they would not be included. To them, the risk wasn't worth the reward because they had no chance of being competitive. Steve Kerr's Golden State Warriors were the worst team in the West, and the coach said as early as April that "it definitely feels like the season is done for us."

The teams in the middle of the standings were trickier to peg. Some, like the Portland Trail Blazers, embraced the opportunity and campaigned for a shot to move up into the playoffs. Others, like the Washington Wizards, Brooklyn Nets, and San Antonio Spurs, saw key players decide to sit out the bubble due to injury issues, coronavirus concerns, or contractual reasons.

NBA commissioner Adam Silver, NBPA executive director Michele Roberts, and the NBPA's executive committee, led by Chris Paul of the Oklahoma City Thunder, knew that no scenario would please everyone. Even some of the NBA's worst teams, like the Atlanta Hawks and Cleveland Cavaliers, expressed a desire to participate. They had no chance at the playoffs, but they wanted to develop their younger players. In a twist, the top contenders began angling for other competitive advantages. If they couldn't enjoy a true home-court advantage, could they at least receive superior hotel accommodations, pump friendly crowd noise during games, or import the hardwood court from their home arenas?

After weeks of fierce discussion, the terms were set on June 4: twenty-two teams, eight regular season games, the possibility of a play-in round for both conferences, and then the standard sixteen-team playoff field. The Warriors got their wish to stay home. The Blazers' calls to play were heeded. The national television networks would be able to extensively feature Williamson's Pelicans, and most of the NBA's teams would be able to reach their seventy-game threshold with the regional sports networks.

The plan, which required a three-quarters majority vote of the thirty owners, received twenty-nine votes. Portland was the lone dissenter, because it preferred a twenty-team format. The players union's executive committee tentatively approved the plan on June 5, pending further negotiations on health protocols and other unresolved issues. Players were advised that they would need to return to their home markets by June 22, which was less than three weeks away.

I was relieved that the conversation had reached a conclusion, yet nervous about the bubble's expanded scope. Playing eight regular season games and a typical postseason would take at least three months. Could the bubble really hold that long? Bringing twenty-two teams meant that more than 300 players would be heading to Disney World. Would every single one of them really follow the rules? And what, exactly, were the rules? Had the players just committed to playing without fully knowing how the league intended to keep them safe?

While the NBPA's executive committee had committed to the basic framework, individual players wouldn't be forced to participate. If anyone wanted to stay home, he could do so without penalty. Many players had expressed long-standing concerns about the coronavirus, but another faction now wondered whether the players would be harming the Black Lives Matter movement if they went to Florida. What message would it send if hundreds of mostly Black players were confined to a restricted bubble to play games that would benefit their mostly white owners? Wouldn't the playoffs potentially distract from coverage of the protests and change the national conversation away from systemic racism and police brutality?

Kyrie Irving, a vice president of the players union, became the face of such concerns. During a June 12 conference call with more than seventy-five players, the Brooklyn Nets guard said that he opposed the restart and suggested that the players could make a bigger statement against racism by staying home. The NBA was already bracing for select players to opt out due to the virus, but a wider opposition over social justice matters threatened to scuttle the bubble entirely.

"Some guys are going to say, 'I want to sit out [for health reasons],'" Indiana Pacers guard Malcolm Brogdon said on a Ringer podcast. "Other guys are going to say: 'The black community and my people are going through too much for me to be distracted with basketball. I'm not going to prioritize it over the black community.'"

Damian Lillard, who weeks earlier had pushed hard for the Blazers to be included in the bubble, was suddenly conflicted. "Our league is made up of so many African Americans. A lot of our hearts are with our people," Lillard said on ESPN. "Our minds are with our people. We feel we should be a part of that fight. I think that's what you're hearing a lot of guys saying. Maybe we should be focused on that instead of worrying about jumping into the season. On the other hand—I can only speak for myself—we are the financial support for our families and a lot of our communities. We bring a lot of that financial responsibility to support black communities and businesses."

The players' deliberations made me stop and think back on some of my own experiences with systemic inequality. When I first arrived at Johns Hopkins University after attending a suburban public high school in Oregon, I marveled at how ill-prepared I felt compared with many of my classmates, who hailed from elite boarding schools and well-known private academies.

It took one hour of volunteering as an English teacher in a Baltimore City elementary school for me to realize the real meaning of an education gap. My students there were raised by single parents or grandparents, and they wrote poems to family members who were incarcerated, dead, or lost to drug addiction. Their school didn't have a computer lab or a passable library, and the teachers I assisted were worried about the building's heating system holding up through winter.

Many NBA players had survived difficult childhood circumstances and beaten the odds. Even so, they weren't free to base their collective decision to play purely on ethical considerations. If they stayed home, the NBA owners could respond by terminating the Collective Bargaining Agreement and starting a labor war. What's more, the public had shown little sympathy for millionaire athletes during the NBA's previous labor disagreements. If the players walked away from the bubble, they would likely become targets of scorn.

Irving's role as an anti-bubble voice was fascinating because he, unlike many of his colleagues, was free to follow his heart. At twenty-eight, he had banked more than $100 million in salary; recently signed a four-year, $136 million max contract with the Nets; and held lucrative endorsement deals with Nike and Pepsi. Irving was also recovering from March shoulder surgery and wouldn't compete in the bubble. In short, he didn't need the money, he wasn't missing out on a title chase, and his health wouldn't be at risk in the bubble. He came at the conversation strictly as an activist, and his heart led him to the opposite side of money, power, and pragmatism.

Irving's status as the messenger quickly clouded his message. Reporters and fans noted his long history of conspiracy theories and assertions that the earth was flat to damage his credibility. Irving had disrupted the Boston Celtics' chemistry during an inconsistent and disappointing 2018–19 season, and skeptics warned that he was leading the NBPA right off a financial cliff. Others pointed out that he had the privilege of viewing the debate as a philosophical matter rather than a financial one because he wasn't a mid-tier veteran or low-paid rookie.

I was a critic of Irving's game and leadership persona for years because I thought he dominated the ball, didn't commit to the defensive end, sought highlight plays, and regularly made comments that were detrimental to his teams. Despite that history, I admired his principled stand.

There were plenty of other players who cared deeply about these issues but weren't in a position to take the amount of heat that Irving absorbed. His public position helped set the tone for the next round of conversations between the owners and the union on social justice matters. While Irving never took the court at Disney World, his fingerprints were visible for months to come.

Just as Irving was willing to be the bad guy with his opposition, Chris Paul thrived in his role as union president and consensus builder. Together with Roberts and other union leaders, Paul carried on weeks of conversations with Silver and Deputy Commissioner Mark Tatum to determine how the bubble could reflect the players' sentiments on social justice issues.

Playing and protesting didn't need to be mutually exclusive, the union eventually concluded. But if the players were going to commit to months of games, they should be able to shape what the bubble would stand for and how it would look to viewers. "The issues of systemic racism and police brutality in our country need to end," Paul said in a late June press release, adding that the players and league needed to "put a spotlight on those issues" during the bubble.

Silver and the owners moved quickly to assuage the players' concerns, establishing a ten-year, $300 million foundation aimed at economic issues in the Black community, like job training, post–high school employment, and career advancement. Yet the NBA's leaders knew that money alone wouldn't be enough, given the tense climate.

"I think there's an expectation that there's more that this league can do," Silver said. "Part of it is going to require a fair amount of listening, something we've been doing already, and then engaging on very deliberate behavior together with the players. How can we use our larger platform, together with our players, to effect change? There's an appropriate role for protests."

In the end, the most convincing rebuttal to Irving was simple: Sitting out to protest would be a front-page story for a day, and then the news cycle would move on as players scattered around the country. If the players protested while they were in the bubble, they would reach massive television audiences every night for three straight months during a presidential election cycle. Protesting while playing had the potential to touch millions of voters and to provide a collective voice on matters of racism and police brutality.

The bubble could be a showcase for Black anger, resolve, and political power.

5

Final Pitch

I was beyond exasperated, and I wasn't alone.

Nearly a month had passed since the NBA selected Disney World to host its restart, including two tense weeks of debate among the players. Yet the NBA had still not publicly revealed details about what life would be like in the bubble or thoroughly explained its health and safety plan. With less than a month before I might be flying to Orlando to cover the event, I had no clue what would be waiting for me.

"I'm still up in the air a little bit," Blazers forward Carmelo Anthony said, when asked by TNT whether he would play. "We don't have all the details. We don't know a lot of information. Until we have that, it's hard to commit to it 100 percent."

Getting buy-in from players like Anthony was critical. As a former star, he didn't need the money. As a role player on a team outside the playoff picture, he had no shot at winning a title. As an upcoming free agent, he did have some incentive to perform well to secure his next contract. But he also had a family and more than $260 million in career salary to his name. He could afford to sit out the bubble if he felt uncomfortable with the setup.

On June 16, after working with union leaders to keep the plan on track through the racial justice protests, the NBA released its pitch to the players about life in the bubble. One day later, I obtained a copy of the NBA's full health and safety protocols. I had been so anxious to see the health protocols that I raced home from an afternoon walk in a wetland to pore over the document. After all that agonizing and with so little time before play was set to resume, I wanted to see a comprehensive and logical plan, not a rough framework.

The quick pitch came in the form of a 2,400-word memo from Byron Spruell, the NBA's president of league operations, and a thirty-three-page handbook. First, the ground rules: players would undergo a thirty-six-hour quarantine in their hotel rooms upon arrival, wear masks and maintain social distance in public, and stay out of one another's rooms at all times. They would be free to leave the bubble at any time but would need to undergo a quarantine period of up to ten days upon their return.

Only thirty-five people from each of the twenty-two teams could travel to Disney World, no exceptions. That travel party could include up to seventeen players, the coaching staff, an equipment manager, a security official, and one designated front office member. Family members would not be permitted at first, and physical contact with the outside world would be prohibited.

These terms weren't surprising, but there were still likely to be grumbles. Star players wouldn't be able to bring their personal trainers, chefs, agents, and other support staffers. All players, coaches, and staffers would be separated from their significant others, children, and love interests for at least a month. Importantly, though, teams that advanced past the first round would be able to reserve a room for their family members to join them in the bubble.

Perhaps hoping to head off complaints, the handbook led with glossy photos of Disney World's luxury accommodations and perks, rather than the health rules. The top four seeds in each conference would be staying at the Gran Destino Tower, which was pictured with its lake view all lit up around sunset. The next four seeds in each conference drew the Grand Floridian, complete with large white porches and charter boat access to fishing spots. The six non-playoff teams would occupy the stately Yacht Club, which abutted another large lagoon.

The handbook went on to detail many other amenities: private lounges, workout gyms, pool access, laundry services, barbers, manicurists, hair braiders, movie screenings, DJs, Ping-Pong, card games, a twenty-four-hour concierge service, and organized golf, boating, and fishing outings. All meals would be prepared by Disney chefs, and meal delivery options from restaurants outside the bubble would be available. While players couldn't leave the bubble to shop, they could have items and care packages delivered to a massive shipping depot that would quickly disinfect and distribute them. The league had even agreed to suspend drug testing for marijuana.

The NBA's plans called for teams to arrive by July 9, for regular season games to begin July 30, and for the playoffs to run from August 17 through October 13 at the latest. Top contenders would be staying for more than ninety days. The twenty-two teams would utilize three stadiums—AdventHealth Arena, HP Fieldhouse, and the Visa Center—as well as seven makeshift practice facilities spread out across convention center ballrooms and hotel conference centers. The arenas and practice facilities would be thoroughly cleaned before and after each session to reduce the risk of coronavirus spread.

I was impressed by the attention to detail in the handbook but doubted that the players, many of whom were accustomed to living in mansions and staying at the Four Seasons, would be enamored with the accommodations. The Disney setup looked like a mid-tier resort where I might cash in some Marriott points for some rest and relaxation.

"It may not be for everyone," Adam Silver acknowledged in an ESPN special. "It will entail enormous sacrifice on behalf of those players and for everyone involved—the coaches, the referees. Listen, it's not an ideal situation. We're trying to find a way to our normal in the middle of a pandemic and a recession, or worse, with forty million unemployed and now with enormous social unrest in the country. As we work through these issues, I understand that for some players, this is not for them. It may be for family reasons, health reasons, or it may be that they feel that their time is best spent elsewhere."

If I had a bed, air-conditioning, and Wi-Fi, I knew I could get by. My real concern remained the health protocols, and there I found myself relieved and pleasantly surprised. The full 113-page document laid out a daily testing plan and a tiered access system that effectively created a second bubble inside the wider Disney World bubble by strictly limiting who had direct contact with the players.

Tier 1 consisted only of players, coaches, health staff, equipment managers, and referees—the only people who would have direct access to the court. Tier 2, composed of a select group of media members, the scorekeeper and sideline personnel, front office members, and team security, would have limited access to the players and could sit courtside while attending games in person.

Tier 3 represented Disney employees who would clean players' rooms but only when they were unoccupied. Tier 4 included sponsors, league employees, and union employees, while Tiers 5 and 6 were made up of other broadcast personnel. Everyone in the lower tiers was barred from having direct access to players.

In my view, the bubble's biggest vulnerability remained the game itself. There was no way to maintain social distance or wear a mask while playing high-level basketball, and players and referees often got into animated conversations while in close proximity. If an infected player took the court, a multi-team outbreak would be hard to prevent.

The protocols seemed to indirectly acknowledge these concerns with their strict treatment of the game experience. Instead of one row of adjacent chairs, the team benches were transformed into multiple rows of spaced-out chairs. Instead of one Gatorade jug, players had individual hydration stations. The scorer's table was placed behind a plexiglass wall, and ball boys wore masks and rubber gloves. The referees even attached little bags to their whistles to catch spittle.

Players were encouraged not to lick their fingers, play with their mouthguards, spit, share towels, clear their noses, or swap jerseys with their opponents, and inactive players were required to wear masks while sitting on the bench. The players would be allowed to high-five and celebrate like normal during games, but they were encouraged to limit "unnecessary physical contact" with opposing teams at all other times. Once the game was over, players would immediately conduct socially distanced media interviews and then return to their individual hotel rooms to shower, rather than use a shared facility at the arena. Reporters and other nonessential staffers were barred from locker rooms.

This all sounded encouraging, but one ominous paragraph jumped off the page. "It is possible that staff, players, or other participants in the resumption of the 2019–20 season nonetheless may test positive or contract the coronavirus," the document read. "The occurrence of a small or otherwise expected number of COVID-19 cases will not require a decision to suspend or cancel the resumption of the 2019–20 season."

This was a realistic, sober, and necessary admission. There was no way to guarantee that the bubble would be perfect, and if the NBA was going to invest nearly $200 million into the bubble, it would need to keep its options open if a superstar tested positive right before the Finals or an outbreak crippled a team's roster during a tight series. The whole experiment would come down to how well the protocols were designed and upheld. Dr. Anthony Fauci, the director of the National Institute of Allergy and Infectious Diseases and one of the country's top coronavirus experts, gave a thumbs-up to the plan, adding a layer of independent credibility and helping to ease tensions.

Still, reading the language about positive tests was chilling. I tried to ponder what it would be like to live in an environment that I couldn't easily leave, knowing that one of its other inhabitants had contracted a potentially deadly virus. I imagined receiving a phone call from an unknown doctor telling me that I had tested positive or reading a text from a colleague who said he or she had tested positive.

I went to Twitter to see what the NBA community was making of the long-awaited news, expecting to see vigorous debates about the health protocols or hand-wringing about the league's stated willingness to play through positive tests. Instead, I found joke after joke about the Yacht Club.

For whatever reason, NBA Twitter had seized on the hotel that would host the six non-playoff teams as a source of relentless ribbing. The Yacht Club looked nice enough to me, and indeed it proved to be somewhat swanky in person. NBA Twitter treated it like a third-class destination or a backyard guesthouse compared to the Gran Destino Tower, which was home to top contenders like the Bucks, Lakers, and Clippers.

While the hotel-shaming baffled me, the light chatter was a rare reprieve from months of gloomy conversations. It felt like a turning point. The lack of information about the bubble plans created a vacuum for worriers like me, as well as critics who believed the NBA was being greedy by pursuing a return. This rush of details opened a new lane of discourse for fans who were desperate to watch basketball and wanted to regain a slice of normalcy. Even if the bubble later folded, it had succeeded in capturing the imagination of an otherwise barren sports world.

The players were ready to let the show go on. They mounted no coordinated public pushback to the health protocols, and on June 26 the NBA and the players association finalized their plans for the bubble. It was officially a go.

"We never pictured ourselves playing like this," Chris Paul said on a joint conference call with Silver and Michele Roberts. "When people hear health and safety, a lot of times people think about injury or they just think about COVID-19. While both are important, I think mental health is the biggest thing that a lot of us players think of first."

Miami Heat forward Andre Iguodala, a union vice president, added that the players felt "well-informed" about the state of the pandemic and their potential to protest on behalf of the social justice movement. "Everyone is making some type of sacrifice," he said. "A lot of people in America don't have jobs right now. We have the opportunity to be a beacon of light and show our sympathies."

Although the players' messages were directed elsewhere, the coronavirus threat mounted in Florida. Back when the negotiations began more than a month earlier, new COVID-19 cases in the state had been hovering below 1,000 per day. By June 22, that number reached more than 4,000. By June 25, more than 5,500. By July 4, more than 11,000. The bubble's home state and surrounding counties were experiencing an unmistakable spike.

Suddenly, the "data" that Silver said would drive the NBA's decision was clearly no longer on his side. "We are left with no choice but to learn to live with this virus," Silver said June 26, marking a clear shift in tone and framing. "No options are risk-free right now. And if we can't sit on the sidelines indefinitely, we must adapt. My ultimate conclusion is that we can't outrun the virus. While [the bubble] is not impermeable, we are in essence protected from cases around us. For those reasons, we're still very comfortable being in Orlando."

Red warning lights were flashing all over Florida, where numerous professional and college teams were starting to ramp up. So many teams sustained positive tests in late June that it was hard to keep track, including the MLB's Philadelphia Phillies, NHL's Tampa Bay Lightning, NFL's Tampa Bay Buccaneers, and National Women's Soccer League's Orlando Pride. Efforts to play team sports, even outdoor sports, were encountering challenges without help from a restrictive bubble. The Pride had to withdraw from a tournament after ten positive tests among players and staff members that were traced to a visit to an Orlando bar, which was opened at reduced capacity. As the MLB ramped up for a July 23 opening day, numerous teams had to close their facilities after positive tests, and some players complained publicly about delays in the testing results that were likely contributing to spread among teams.

Meanwhile, 16 NBA players (5.3 percent) tested positive when more than 300 reported to their teams in their home markets in late June. Roberts said she was "somewhat relieved" that the positivity rate wasn't higher, and Silver sought to cushion the bad news by noting that none of the players "were seriously ill in any way." The number of positive tests, he said, was in line with the league's expectations given that the players had been left to their own devices for more than three months.

By July 2, a total of 25 out of 351 players (7.1 percent) had tested positive, including All-Stars Nikola Jokic and Russell Westbrook. "We ultimately believe it will be safer on our campus than outside it," said Silver, who left open the possibility that a "significant spread" of the coronavirus could shut down the whole thing. "We're not saying full steam ahead no matter what happens."

Nevertheless, some players decided to stay home. Avery Bradley of the Lakers pulled out because one of his children had a health condition that elevated his coronavirus risk. Trevor Ariza of the Blazers couldn't play due to a custody arrangement involving one of his children. LaMarcus Aldridge of the San Antonio Spurs, Domantas Sabonis of the Indiana Pacers, Bojan Bogdanovic of the Utah Jazz, and

Bradley Beal of the Washington Wizards all missed out due to injury. Wizards forward Davis Bertans sat out because he didn't want to get hurt before his upcoming free agency. Multiple members of the Brooklyn Nets stayed home after testing positive for COVID-19, and injured stars Kevin Durant and Kyrie Irving opted against traveling to support their teammates.

But virtually all the key players were in, including LeBron James, Giannis Antetokounmpo, Kawhi Leonard, Damian Lillard, and the other stars who had held the conference call that pushed along the bubble idea in May. Zion Williamson was in for the New Orleans Pelicans, as was Ja Morant, the Memphis Grizzlies' No. 2 overall pick. Anthony, one of many players to express hesitation about the concept, decided to suit up for the Blazers.

The health protocols specified that the 350 or so players who were ready to compete for the 2020 title—along with hundreds of coaches and staffers—would be transported to Disney World by charter planes and buses. Everyone would undergo a temperature screening before getting on board, masks would be mandatory, and there would be no stops before arrival at the bubble. Once there, the players would enter their hotel room quarantines.

Unfortunately, I still didn't know whether I was going to be there to cover it. The NBA opened media credential applications on June 26, seeking basic information like name and work affiliation while noting in an email that an "extremely limited" press contingent would be living in the bubble. Only ten reporters not affiliated with the league's television partners would be selected, with no more than one per outlet. I wanted in badly, but the next two weeks proved to be the most nerve-racking of the entire bubble experience.

The *Post* had also given me the green light to apply despite the exorbitant cost, estimated at more than $500 per night for lodging, food, transportation, and daily COVID-19 testing. For the projected ninety-two-night stay, the total tab was expected to be $54,000—more than many journalists make in a year, and far more than I had earned in my first few years covering the NBA. The *Post*'s decision to cover the

NBA bubble was influenced by two factors: We wanted to be an independent check on the proceedings, and we wanted to be on the ground in case something went wrong.

I submitted my application, which required me to agree to a seven-day self-quarantine at home, a symptom check before departure, a seven-day in-room quarantine upon arrival, and daily COVID-19 testing, temperature checks, and symptom screens throughout my stay.

I had talked through the health risks ad nauseam, knew the league's protocols front to back, and concluded that I could control much of my bubble experience. Writing and podcasting happened to be solitary activities that kept me busy and isolated from potential germ spread. More than anything, the adventure was calling. I had covered every Finals since 2010, and the idea that this one would probably be the most memorable reporting experience of my life weighed heavily on my mind. I couldn't miss this.

The tedium that concerned many of the players didn't really turn me off. What else did I have to do? I had been walking circles around my neighborhood and writing about Michael Jordan's Bulls for the last three months. I felt confident I could handle walking circles around Disney World and covering the playoffs. I was prepared to treat it like a study-abroad semester. Go in with an open mind and come out with some great stories.

I consulted with my parents, my editors, other industry colleagues, my primary care physician, my cardiologist, and a psychiatrist. I was born with an aortic valve defect that required two surgeries, including an artificial valve implant in 2008, and a daily dose of blood-thinning medication. My doctors all agreed that I was fit to live in the bubble, and they generally supported Adam Silver's position that the Disney World campus would be much safer than most places in the outside world. Finally, I filled out an extensive health questionnaire, where I noted my heart surgeries and approvals from my doctors. Then I waited. And waited. And waited.

After a few days, Tim Frank, the head of the NBA's public relations department, called to double-check that I wanted to be in the bubble for the full time. I said that I did, and joked that I was unreasonably excited at the prospect. I spent the next few days comparing notes with other writers, trying to determine who else had applied and guessing how the NBA might divvy up the seats. I still hadn't heard back from the league heading into the Fourth of July weekend, and I was starting to sweat. Games were only a few weeks away, and it seemed like the window for a reasonable amount of advance warning had come and gone.

On July 4, a Saturday, Frank emailed: "Just wanted to drop you a quick note to let you know that you have been accepted to join us on campus in Orlando for NBA Restart 2020. Your arrival date is July 12, and you will be with us for the duration of the NBA season." I hurriedly informed my editors and plotted how best to handle the logistics of traveling during a pandemic.

My plan was straightforward: I would fly directly to Orlando and indulge in a first-class seat upgrade, arrange a private SUV service from the airport, and stay at the Ritz-Carlton near Disney World before I checked into the bubble. I would wear an N95 mask, a face shield, and rubber gloves throughout the trip. I would hide out in the Delta lounge before my flight, try to avoid using public restrooms, and handle my own bags with the help of disinfecting wipes. Hand sanitizer would always be with me.

That all sounded good enough. Prices for the flight and hotel were down 50 percent due to the steep drop in travel during the pandemic, which made it easier to justify the extravagant departure from my typical routine. Everything seemed on track until July 9, two days before my flight.

The NBA had asked us to sign an ungodly number of forms: a liability waiver, a COVID-19 warning and compliance agreement, a release of my likeness for future media projects, and various other health information forms. My note on the questionnaire about my heart surgeries caught the attention of one of the league's doctors, and I received a generic form email: "Based on the information provided, an NBA-designated physician has determined that you may not participate in activity related to the restart in Orlando."

My artificial valve works great, but my heart skipped more than a few beats as my face flushed red. This was my worst nightmare, akin to Charlie Brown trying to kick the football and having it yanked away at the last moment. I had been mentally preparing for the trip, had all my accommodations set, and had even packed most of my bags. I flat-out panicked.

I had been here before. Shortly after graduating college, I was accepted by the Peace Corps and assigned to serve in Jordan. My family had lived in Haifa, Israel, during my fourth-grade year, so I was excited about the possibility of returning to the Middle East and learning a new language. I was directionless at the time. Somehow, I hadn't put it together that if I loved basketball and writing, maybe I should try writing about basketball.

Late in the process, Peace Corps doctors sent me a form letter denying my placement due to my heart condition. They wouldn't consider an appeal. I was crushed then, and now it was happening all over again. I read through the email a second time and saw a brief "physician rejection" note: "Resubmit when you have the letter from your cardiologist. Thank you."

This represented hope, but I only had about thirty-six hours to track down the note before my flight, and cardiologists are notoriously difficult to reach. It was late in the week during the summer, and their offices were temporarily closed due to the pandemic. My only option was to call and beg.

On my third frantic call of the afternoon, Jenny, my cardiologist's receptionist, realized that I would just keep calling if she couldn't find a way to work a miracle. After some scrambling, she contacted the doctor on his day off, worked with me to draft the approval note on the appropriate letterhead, and got it on his desk first thing on Friday morning. By the time I woke up and called to triple-check the plan, the signed form had already been emailed to me.

I submitted the note to the NBA's online health portal and walked in circles around my computer for fifteen minutes, refreshing the site over and over. The NBA's doctors surely had hundreds of applications to process for the various personnel who were heading to Florida so I tried to wait it out, but I couldn't take it anymore and reached out to the league. That afternoon at 5:23 p.m., I received an email from the NBA's Jaralai Christiano: "You're all set!"

Mission accomplished, with eighteen hours to spare before my flight. All the worrying I had done about traveling to Orlando now seemed like child's play compared to this near miss. I was no longer fixated on my elaborate plan to navigate two airports and a hotel lobby with as few social contacts as possible.

I was still skeptical that the bubble would last to the end—it felt so long and so ambitious—but after two exhausting weeks, there were no more hoops to jump through. This wasn't going to be the sequel to my Peace Corps disappointment. I was in. I had been stuck at home and stuck without basketball for nearly four months, but now I would be covering practices, scrimmages, and games as soon as I cleared quarantine.

As Philadelphia 76ers center Joel Embiid prepared to fly to the bubble, he wore a full-body hazmat suit and posted a photo on Instagram with the caption: "Get rich or die trying." Nobody could top Embiid, but I did my best by donning my mask, face shield, rubber gloves, and a pair of sunglasses. I threw on an old, purple John Stockton jersey to complete the ridiculous look, treating my final morning in California like a rookie photo shoot.

My pent-up apprehension had subsided, replaced by pure excitement and a willingness to embrace whatever awaited me at Disney World, no matter how long my stay lasted. The Instagram caption for my CDC-approved Stockton outfit read: "Bubble bound."

6

Acclimation

Hurry up and wait, wait, and wait some more.

That was the story of everyone's bubble arrival. My plane landed on time, my driver was there to pick me up, my check-in process at the Ritz-Carlton was easy, and my ride from the hotel to Disney World pulled up as planned. I was one of the first media members to arrive at the bubble and was quickly assigned a room number and given a MagicBand, which functioned as my hotel room key. I was also given a green plastic wristband, which signified that I had not cleared quarantine and that I should be stopped by any security guards who saw me on campus.

I briefly mingled with a few other writers at check-in, but we didn't linger. The rules said that we needed to report directly to our rooms and wait for our first meal and COVID-19 test. I did a quick lap around the Casitas 4 building to get my bearings and shoot some video for the *Washington Post*, and then I dug in for the quarantine process. I couldn't leave room 4432 for seven days or my clock would restart.

What struck me most that first day was the intense global interest in the NBA's experiment. I uploaded an unremarkable video of my first visit to my hotel room, complete with a sweeping shot of its two beds, two chairs, long desk, nightstand, weird cactus painting, and bathroom. The fourteen-second clip drew more than 188,000 views on Twitter. A picture of my first meal, which included cold pasta, a few blocks of cheese, grapes, apples, a salad, and a bag of Doritos drew 148,000 impressions. I was floored.

I quickly realized that, in addition to the renewed excitement around basketball's return, some people were rooting for the bubble to fail. Media requests poured in from England, Germany, Australia, New Zealand, Canada, and plenty of other countries, and the reporters all asked essentially the same questions. Do you think someone will get sick? Will the NBA shut down the playoffs if there's an outbreak? What happens if someone dies? Do you feel safe? Is quarantine driving you crazy?

These were dark, but fair, questions. I didn't know most of the answers yet because I wasn't allowed to step foot outside. Instead, I tried to bring the outside world into my room by livestreaming on Instagram, doing at least twenty-five radio and television interviews, and hosting ten podcasts in the first seven days. By Day 2, I tried to entertain the rubberneckers by videotaping myself pacing back and forth in my hotel room and planking across my hotel beds. Tens of thousands of viewers watched. As interest mounted, the *Washington Post* ran my quarantine diary on the front page of the website with the tagline: "Cannot leave for any reason." Within hours, I received dozens of concerned messages from high school friends, former coworkers, and other acquaintances I hadn't heard from in years. It was all ludicrous.

But laughs were hard to come by during the pandemic, so it felt good to chuckle at the many responses on social media. I dubbed Casitas 4 the "Type House"—a writerly play on the "Hype House," which was a collection of well-known TikTok influencers who lived together in Los Angeles. The name didn't stick, largely because my colleagues were much older than TikTok's typical demographic. Oh well.

I spent a lot of time that week looking out my window, gazing at a lake fountain near three bridges in the distance, marveling at the afternoon thunderstorms, and trying to spot NBA personalities on the sidewalk below. Mostly I saw anonymous assistant coaches going for walks and hotel staffers hustling our prepackaged meals around campus. The quarantine made me appreciate technology: Twitter, Instagram, FaceTime, Netflix, and the exercise tracking apps passed the time and kept the isolation from feeling unbearable.

The quarantine food was on par with airplane meals. I braced for the worst because the players had complained so loudly about their fare, which consisted of sketchy chicken breasts, snack boxes, and way-too-small portions for professional athletes. The NBA adjusted by the time the media showed up, so there were plenty of options, even if they weren't always healthy or tasty. For a while, I saved all the junk food—sugary sodas and coffee drinks, endless bags of chips, all sorts of cookies and cakes—just to ogle the revolting pile.

NBA commissioner Adam Silver sent welcome emails to the reporters one afternoon, an unexpected personal touch that went a long way given the circumstances. I counted my blessings: I had daily access to COVID-19 tests that many Americans still couldn't receive easily, plenty of diversions, and a clear end to my short-term isolation. This wasn't even close to prison.

While unpacking my suitcases, I set aside my pair of black and red Jordan 11 sneakers and my three dress suits. Those Jordans were dubbed "the playoffs" by sneakerheads, and I planned to break them out if the NBA completed its regular season and opened the postseason. Casual dress would be the standard given Orlando's hot and humid summer weather, but the suits would be reserved for the Finals. Tradition dictated that even ink-stained wretches tried to look presentable for the biggest dates on the NBA calendar. Now that I was on the ground, I was gaining confidence that I would get to wear the Jordans. I still had no idea about the suits.

On Day 7, NBA communications director Mark Broussard came by to drop off my media credential and grant my freedom. "You all look very excited to get out and enjoy some sunshine and stretch a little bit," Broussard said. It was time to enter the bubble. "I've never been more excited to wear a badge in my life," I told him.

Stepping into the NBA bubble felt exactly like traveling to a foreign country, minus the language barrier, and I spent my first few days of freedom trying to catalogue the many differences from normal life. My initial survey of the Coronado Springs Resort campus didn't take long. I walked out of my hotel room door along the central lake to the right, running directly into Donovan Mitchell and the first security checkpoint within a quarter mile. Media and players weren't really supposed to interact, but a demilitarized zone had formed where brief conversations could take place. I located the Maya Grill, a converted restaurant where I could grab to-go containers of food from heated cabinets and coolers. I ran into more security when I tried to check out the Disney store. Players and coaches only. The Gran Destino Tower, home to the top contenders, was even further away. Total no-go.

I pivoted and walked back toward my room, encountering an activity area where Scott Foster and a bunch of other referees were playing pickleball. I knew nothing about the sport but took note of their high energy level under the beating sun.

Foster, a Maryland native known for his stern on-court demeanor, informed me that he was the self-appointed pickleball "commissioner" and planned to oversee two-on-two games all summer. The sport is a combination of tennis and Ping-Pong, played with hard paddles and a Wiffle ball. Games went to 11 points, and the referees filled their off days with marathon sessions.

The fifty-three-year-old Foster took his role as evangelist and judge so seriously that he ranked his colleagues' abilities every week and distributed his list via email. Invariably, he ranked first. "There's me, and then there's everyone else," Foster told me. "Is that cocky enough for you?" The competition got so heated that Foster trash-talked his opponents and scolded his teammates. Profanities were common. "If I were a referee watching myself play, I'd think, 'What a crazy guy,'" Foster added. "I would probably throw myself out of the game."

Past the pickleball court were the makeshift COVID-19 testing center, the pool, and a long and mostly empty parking lot for guests. Given that none of the bubble inhabitants were allowed cars, the only vehicles were owned by employees. I noticed a few pickup trucks with "Trump 2020" bumper stickers. That made sense because we were in Florida, but the messaging didn't exactly align with the players' politics.

Past the parking lot was a road that I had been told I couldn't walk on yet, so I doubled back toward my room and encountered another security station. In less than fifteen minutes of walking, I had gone everywhere I could. The bridges that I saw from my hotel room window were off-limits. I couldn't do much of anything except enjoy the fresh air and wait for practices to begin the next day.

I walked in circles for an hour, talked to a few security guards, chatted with my colleagues at a hospitality dinner, and retreated to my room to record my first impressions. As I wrote that night, I felt like "a kid in a candy store—only with all the best treats just out of reach and under lock and key."

The next round of culture shock came the following day when LeBron James and the Lakers met the media for the first time. I hopped on the Disney Cruise Line charter bus—complete with a large picture of Mickey Mouse on the side—and took a twelve-minute ride to the nearby ESPN Wide World of Sports Complex. There, the three arenas sat side by side on a large, protected campus that also included an unused baseball stadium and a long patch of soccer fields. The whole complex was a fortress: All vehicles had to pass through a security checkpoint, and police officers manned the main entrance at all hours. I had to swipe my MagicBand to gain access to the arena complex as Disney employees kept a watchful eye.

The Lakers were set to practice at AdventHealth Arena, the bubble's crown jewel. The 7,500-seat multipurpose stadium hosted everything from Amateur Athletic Union (AAU) tournaments to high school cheerleading championships, and the NBA had retrofitted it for use during its most important playoff games. Up a short hill to the left sat the HP Fieldhouse, a 5,000-seat basketball arena that felt like an oversized high school gym and would host games through the first two rounds of the playoffs. Directly across from the HP Fieldhouse was the Visa Center, a much smaller, 1,200-seat arena designed for basketball and volleyball that would be used as an overflow venue for regular season games before the playoffs started.

I hadn't seen James since March, and he struck a jarring pose with his arms crossed and his gray-speckled beard grown out. He didn't look comfortable. "Nothing is normal in 2020," he said. "Nothing seems as is. Who knows if it will ever go back to the way it was? It's 2020. It's different from the vision 20/20. It's not that clear."

James was unfailingly open with the media in the bubble. That began on the first day of practice, when he paid tribute to U.S.

Representative John Lewis of Georgia, the civil rights pioneer who had just died. Yet the scene was so odd. James was seated in front of a video camera mounted to a flat-screen television, and his answers were beamed out in real time to reporters who were participating in the press conference remotely from around the world. The writers in the room had to jockey for places around the television while remaining socially distant. If we got too close to one another, our Kinexon proximity alarms would start beeping until we moved apart. The beeps went off repeatedly in the early days, drawing sighs and groans as they interrupted interviews.

The setup felt high-tech but impersonal, especially because James was instructed to look into the camera when answering questions rather than making eye contact with reporters. "Maybe we should let Siri ask all the questions and we can go home," I joked to a colleague afterward. When James was done talking, an NBA staffer pulled out a giant roll of black tape and created a large box around the interview seat. We were told that we must stay outside the box to avoid infringing on the player's space. One more cold rule to add to an interminable list. This scene repeated outside countless practices, which were held in sprawling convention center ballrooms that might typically be used for large weddings or sales conferences.

The NBA had no interest in wasting anyone's time. Just three days after the media cleared quarantine, scrimmage games began. The players needed to get in shape, the NBA needed to put its facilities to the test, and the media needed to adjust to the new logistics and scenery.

On the plus side, the smaller arenas had an intimate feel. For years, I'd listened to writers like Bob Ryan of the *Boston Globe* gush about how close they sat to the action in the good old days. My first seats as a reporter were at the top of the 200 level at the Moda Center in Portland—not quite the nosebleeds but still well removed from the action. When I moved to Los Angeles in 2015, the media seating at Staples Center was far better, located behind a few rows of courtside seats in the baseline sections. I could occasionally hear the players chirping if they were animated.

The bubble seats were unlike anything I had ever experienced, and I was hooked from the first scrimmage. In the Visa Center, the smallest of the three venues, the media seats ran along the sideline at court level. I felt like Jack Nicholson or Rihanna at a Lakers game. With almost no one else in the building, I could hear everything—play calls, trash talk, and arguments with the officials. With the special lighting on the court, the viewing experience was so intense it felt like a virtual reality simulation or a futuristic video game. The action was right in my face, and I had never seen basketball look so fast, physical, and exhausting.

The seats were set back from the sideline just a bit at the HP Fieldhouse, but the NBA opened baseline sections as the bubble unfolded. During close games, I could walk back and forth between sections during timeouts to get closer to the action. If the Boston Celtics had the ball on the far end, I could walk down there and take a baseline seat. When the Toronto Raptors came back the other way, I could mosey back along with them. It was a diehard's dream.

During one game at the Fieldhouse, LeBron James drew a foul while backing down Chris Paul in the post. Paul, to no one's surprise, disputed the call with both officials. When he didn't get the answers he was seeking, Paul walked down the court and began making his case to Monty McCutchen, a former referee who was now the NBA's vice president of referee development. Sitting directly behind McCutchen, I listened as Paul executed the basketball equivalent of "Can I speak to your manager?" The conversation resumed during the halftime break before Paul finally dropped it.

Before long, I referred to the AdventHealth Arena as "The Set," because the basketball gym had been converted into a made-for-television stage. AdventHealth Arena would host the NBA Finals, and it had the most bells and whistles. A rail camera ran along the sideline to follow the action up the court, extra cameras were affixed to the backboard to provide new angles, and high-sensitivity microphones were deployed to capture sneaker squeaks and bouncing balls. The NBA's hope was to combat the fan-less feel with an immersive experience for the television viewer, adopting the "Whole New Game" marketing tagline.

Massive videoboards were the court's gaudiest feature. They ran along both baselines and behind the team's benches, covering up the empty seats and providing nonstop visual stimulation: player graphics, video highlights, dancing cheerleaders, and, in a polarizing twist, virtual fans. Through a partnership with Microsoft, the NBA essentially turned the court into a giant Teams call, allowing fans to cheer along from home. Images of the fans were beamed onto the boards with little lag. If a player missed a free throw, dozens of the opposing team's fans could be seen clapping.

"When I was watching the game for the first six minutes, I thought it was cool that when somebody scored they had their own graphics on the screen," Clippers guard Lou Williams said after an early scrimmage. "I heard the 'defense' chants. Once I was on the court, I didn't see it, hear it or feel it. I was locked into the game. I don't know who that experience was for, because there's no fans in the arena. But it definitely wasn't for us."

While I was convinced that the videoboards would be prone to glitches when I first heard Microsoft's pitch, they worked quite well. The whole experience was meta, but it was far better than the empty seats or cardboard cutouts that often filled the background of other sporting events during the pandemic. When celebrities like President Obama and Lil Wayne were slated for a videoboard cameo, I scanned the virtual crowd like I was reading *Where's Waldo?*

The seats at AdventHealth Arena were raised and set farther back from the sideline than in the other gyms, but it was still possible to hear the players talk on the court even with a DJ playing music and artificial noise pumped in. Mostly the players shouted, "And-one!" when they thought they were fouled, exclaimed, "Yeah!" when things were going well, and yelled profanities when things were going poorly. When Anthony Davis got the ball in the post, the Lakers' bench delighted in shouting out types of foods to mock defenders who were about to get eaten up by the All-Star forward.

Despite my up-close view of the court and the NBA's thorough efforts to provide a rich viewing experience, the best word to describe watching bubble games was *eerie*. All told, there were usually fewer than 200 people in the building for any given contest, including the players, coaches, team executives, media members, cameramen, ball boys, scorer's table crew, league employees, and union staffers. Viewers were instructed to remain quiet and composed throughout the games, so the hustle and bustle of a typical crowd was nonexistent.

"I played Division III ball, so I'm very used to playing in front of very small crowds," joked Milwaukee Bucks coach Mike Budenholzer, a Pomona College graduate. "We're a team that tries to be very steady from the start of the game to the end. Hopefully, the day-to-day routines that we put a lot of value in will carry over to the different environment."

LeBron James probably drew more fans as an Ohio fourth grader than he did in the bubble. Heck, I played in front of larger crowds during middle school tournaments, even when the Beaverton Runnin' Beavers traveled to rural Oregon. "It has that AAU feeling," James said. "That's a great feeling. It's all about the joy of the game and the love for the game."

This was both sad and sublime. Stars like James are geniuses, and their craft should be appreciated by tens of thousands every night. At the same time, I felt like I was getting private access to the Guggenheim or the Sydney Opera House night after night.

The players didn't know quite how to handle the weirdness. The Lakers tried to fill in the silence by shouting out defensive coverages every play and cheering constantly from the bench. Other teams pretended to wave to imaginary fans as they jogged onto the court for warm-ups. Without a crowd to rev up the players, there were fewer grandiose celebrations and verbal altercations.

"It's different when you walk out on the floor, but when the game starts it's just basketball," Clippers coach Doc Rivers said. "Once you get in between the lines, you can make the case that's as comfortable as the players will ever be or as normal as everything will ever be."

My head was spinning too. As the scrimmages started, I realized there were too many games and not enough writers on hand to cover all twenty-two invited teams. At one afternoon game, I snapped a photo of an otherwise empty media row, noting that there were more bottles of Clorox wipes in attendance than writers. I wondered: If a player had a career night in an empty bubble gym and no reporters were there to witness it, would he make a sound?

I spent a lot of time in the run-up to the bubble thinking about how the neutral site and empty arenas might impact the results. Would favored teams make easier work of weaker teams because there was no crowd to help narrow the talent gap? Or would favored teams be more vulnerable because they were accustomed to entering every play-off series with a baked-in advantage? Often, role players shot better at home than on the road. Would teams that were reliant upon three-point shooting fall back to earth in a neutral gym, or would they stay hot indefinitely?

Once I got to Disney World, chemistry seemed more important than pure talent. Living in the bubble was a chore, and playing in the empty gyms was a constant test of a team's internal motivation. If players weren't on the same page or if they weren't fully bought into the experience, the cracks were bound to show. A team couldn't hide its warts in an empty gym.

Adaptability was big too, as each aspect of game production was slightly different than normal. The ball boys wore gloves and masks, and the referees made a point to limit their physical contact with players as much as possible. Cleaning crews in white suits waited patiently before disinfecting the playing surface and hoops after every game. The television broadcasters sat removed from the court in restricted booths, and in-game interviews took place with an extended distance between the sideline reporters and coaches.

Working under such strict guidelines was oppressive at first. Security was always watching. My mask slipped off my nose while I drank an iced tea during one game, and within minutes I had received a text message from a public relations staffer that I needed to pull it up. Gray areas were cause for occasional alarm. During the first week of games, the basketball sailed into the media seats. We looked around at each other, unsure if we could touch the ball and return it to the official. Would that be a health protocol violation?

Not to be lost in the made-for-TV updates and the coronavirus accommodations was a major change to the hardwood. Three words appeared front and center on all three courts for every bubble game: Black Lives Matter. The phrase had initially referred to a particular organizing group, but it had come to represent the wider push for social justice, racial equality, and police reform. It had also become politicized, with conservative voices asserting that All Lives Matter and pro-police organizations coining Blue Lives Matter.

But the summer's many high-profile incidents of police brutality helped to dramatically reshape public opinion of the movement. The Pew Research Center found in June that 67 percent of adult poll respondents expressed support for Black Lives Matter. That was up from 43 percent when then San Francisco 49ers quarterback Colin Kaepernick began kneeling during the national anthem four years earlier.

NBA players occasionally donned warm-up T-shirts of support after high-profile deaths like those of Trayvon Martin and Eric Garner, but most of their activism remained on social media and at a distance from their places of employment. The bubble removed those barriers, and the players' desire to use the resumption of play to further their activist efforts led to Black Lives Matter appearing on the courts, arena signage, and T-shirts. The players also negotiated for the ability to wear Black Lives Matter and other league-approved slogans, like "I Can't Breathe," "Equality," and "Say Her Name" on the back of their jerseys. While some players felt the jersey slogans were overly anodyne, they became an inescapable part of the experience.

As the bubble's opening night approached, the players made a coordinated effort to back up the jersey slogans with messaging during their practice and postgame interviews. Philadelphia 76ers forward Tobias Harris called for the arrests of Louisville police officers who were involved in the killing of Breonna Taylor, a Black woman who was shot eight times when law enforcement served a no-knock warrant at her home. Taylor, a twenty-six-year-old emergency medical technician, was asleep when officers burst in, causing her boyfriend to fire his gun at what he thought was a home invasion. Clippers forward Paul George redirected every question during a postgame interview to social justice. "Breonna Taylor, Rest In Peace," he said. "George Floyd, Rest In Peace. There are so many others that have been brutally murdered by the hands of the police."

James, as always, was the loudest voice, joining Harris in calling for the arrests of the Louisville police and saying that Taylor's case was the top social justice issue for NBA players. On July 23, he lamented the lack of progress on racial issues in the years since Barack Obama's presidency and told a group of mostly white reporters that "you might feel for us, but you can never really, truly understand what it is to be Black in America."

Around the country, the pandemic had led many pretenses to be dropped: People dressed more casually and spent less time grooming when they worked from home, and online discourse seemed to sharpen as time passed and frustration with the virus mounted. I saw the same phenomenon in the bubble, where there were no crowds and no pomp and circumstance. The players didn't bother to mince words, dress up before games, or trim their beards.

This experiment was shaping up to be a combination of pure basketball and raw emotion at a moment of high tension and stress nationally. Before the regular season resumed, there was one person I knew I needed to interview.

7

Opening Night

No one would have blamed Rudy Gobert if he had skipped the bubble.

The Utah Jazz center's positive test had stopped the NBA season in its tracks on March 11, but that was only the beginning of his battle with COVID-19. As Patient Zero in American sports, Gobert became the face of a deadly virus at a time when few people in the country knew much about it. When he tested positive, the NBA had just started instituting limited social distancing measures between players and reporters. Fans were still in the arenas, and masks weren't yet viewed as a critical prevention step, inside or outside the league.

A few weeks before his positive test, Gobert had played in his first All-Star Game. This was a major milestone, especially for a franchise stalwart who had shed tears publicly when he was snubbed during the 2019 All-Star voting. Together with Donovan Mitchell, Gobert had led the Jazz to a 41–23 record and the West's No. 4 seed when the NBA shut down. The standings were tight, and Utah had a decent shot to climb to the second seed. While the balanced Jazz were viewed as a second-tier contender because they lacked a top ten player, they had advanced to the second round twice in the previous three seasons.

One day, Gobert was at the apex of a decorated career. The next, he had a serious disease and was a national pariah to boot. The coronavirus threw his ascendant life off course.

When I caught up with Gobert for a lengthy interview in late July, he still hadn't fully recovered his sense of smell after his COVID-19 battle. He also hadn't been able to see his mother, Corrine, who was stuck in France because of international travel restrictions. Gobert was still smarting from his four-month marathon in the spotlight too.

"The media portrayed it like I caused the NBA to shut down, instead of saying that it's a pandemic and Rudy Gobert tested positive," he said. "For a lot of people who don't think further than what's put in their faces, they really thought I brought the coronavirus to the United States."

Gobert made a regrettable mistake a few days before his positive test, a decision that came back to haunt him. As he finished a media interview, he stood up from his chair and reached out to touch the phones and microphones that were laid out on the table in front of him. His action was intended as a lighthearted jab at the NBA's new coronavirus rule, which required that he be interviewed in a press conference setting rather than a tight locker room space. The devices were on the table to ensure that there was physical distance between reporters and players.

Video of the incident went viral following his positive test, leading many to view him with scorn rather than sympathy. As Gobert's cold-like symptoms worsened and he experienced tingling toes and sensory loss, he heard from countless social media users who thought he had been reckless and blamed him for ending the season.

"I looked like someone who doesn't care about other people's safety or lives," Gobert acknowledged. "It was hard for me to see so many people question my character based on one video. That was a big learning experience. I know who I am. People around me know who I am. Everyone is going to have a different perception and opinion of you. If I start putting my energy into that, I'm going to be living a very painful life."

Gobert did what he could to reclaim his reputation, issuing an extensive apology, taping a public service announcement for the NBA, and donating $500,000 to coronavirus relief efforts. He spread the money around to his home country of France, Utah, and Oklahoma, where he had tested positive.

Ranting strangers online were one thing, but Gobert's fractured relationship with Mitchell, his most important teammate, was another. After the twenty-three-year-old Mitchell tested positive in Oklahoma City, he initially severed contact with Gobert and went on *Good Morning America* to air his frustrations. Teammates argue all the time over playing time, shots, card games, and even romantic interests, but a coronavirus split was uncharted territory. From afar, I wondered in a column whether the Jazz would be able to repair this relationship or if they would need to trade Gobert or Mitchell. As cold as that sounded, the root of their tension was deeply personal.

Some time passed, and cooler heads slowly prevailed. There was no way to determine whether Gobert had infected Mitchell, whether Mitchell had infected Gobert, or whether someone else had infected both of them. Gobert was the one caught on tape acting childishly, but the entire country was caught off guard by the pandemic. Remember, I had been on a crowded flight from Minneapolis to Los Angeles one day before Gobert tested positive. Not many people had standing to throw rocks in this glass house.

Gobert was in a tough spot during those first few weeks: sick, isolated from society, at odds with Mitchell, on the receiving end of national criticism, and cut off from his mother. "The toughest part was that I was away from my mom," Gobert said. "I didn't want her to come over, because I didn't know if I was still contagious or not. I still haven't seen my mother since everything happened. It's something I don't really like to talk about, but she's supported me a lot since I was very young. Just knowing how worried she was and knowing she wasn't able to be with me, it was pretty tough mentally."

I could relate. I was a mama's boy who hadn't seen my mother since February. Gobert and his mother were in the middle of the longest separation of their lives; I hadn't been apart from my mother for this long since college. Our cases were hardly unique, as the coronavirus was breaking family bonds across the globe.

Gobert danced around another question: Had he been depressed? He told me that it was "hard to be vulnerable," adding that he was impressed by players like Kevin Love and DeMar DeRozan who had gone public with their mental health stories. Still, Gobert was struggling in April when the NBA first started discussing a summer comeback.

"I was still not in the right state of mind to play basketball," he said. "I didn't think it could happen at that point. As things went by, we had meetings and learned more about the virus, I started feeling better mentally and physically. The main concern for most of us was to make sure they weren't just putting us out there to play and generate money and not care about our health."

His path back to the court included some key checkpoints. Most of his symptoms subsided, he and Mitchell had heart-to-hearts "like men" and put aside their differences, and he took a long look in the mirror. While Gobert had been Utah's best player for years, Mitchell was rising fast and the roster around them had matured. Gobert concluded that he was "too honest" with his teammates sometimes, and that he might have come off as overly negative when demanding the basketball or organizing the defense.

For the Jazz to move forward together, he needed to strike a balance between telling his teammates "things you don't want to hear" and "putting myself in other people's shoes." This new approach was reflected in his plans to wear the word "Equality" on the back of his jersey during the bubble.

I had expected candor from Gobert but not like this. Rarely do All-Stars directly acknowledge their faults in public. Understandably, he seemed to be searching for a clean slate and was intent on preaching a positive message heading into the restart. Gobert said that he was now in a "great place" mentally and that his life had felt "kind of empty" during the hiatus. He wanted to prove that he, Mitchell, and the Jazz would survive their trial.

"People were seeing this as something that could destroy the group," Gobert said. "I see it as something that could make the group even stronger. If you're able to come back from that, we won't be worried about a team beating us or a bad defensive quarter. It gives perspective."

To no one's surprise, the NBA scheduled Zion Williamson, the television ratings magnet, and his New Orleans Pelicans in the opening game of the bubble. But the other half of the matchup raised eyebrows: Gobert's Jazz.

Utah had been a model small-market franchise for more than three decades of ownership by the Miller family, but they were rarely given premier television placement. Indeed, the Jazz had appeared on Christmas Day just once since 1998. Their headlining placement here seemed to be orchestrated. Utah had been at the epicenter of the March 11 shutdown, and it would be at the epicenter of the July 30 comeback.

If the NBA bosses wanted a full-circle moment, they got it. Gobert won the opening tip. He scored the bubble's first points just eighteen seconds into the game. He scored 14 points, grabbed 12 rebounds, and blocked three shots in thirty-three minutes. To top it off, he stepped to the free-throw line with six seconds left and the score tied at 104.

Like many centers, Gobert was an unreliable free-throw shooter, making fewer than half of his attempts as a rookie and hitting just 63 percent for his career. After four months of sickness, anguish, and recovery, he stepped to the line and hit both to deliver a 104–102 win. One game into the Disney World experiment, and I had already witnessed a movie script that felt too good to be true.

What stuck with me most about my time with Gobert was his high level of personal accountability. He was wounded by critical words, he endured difficult personal circumstances, and his structured life was upended at a moment's notice. Gobert had so many easy paths available to him: He could have made excuses, blamed others, gone into hiding, skipped out on the bubble, demanded a trade, resented everyone, or refused to discuss any of this stuff publicly.

Gobert didn't need the bubble for his career: He was plenty wealthy, in his prime, and under contract through 2021. But I came away thinking that he needed the bubble to move on with his life. He was back on the court together with Mitchell. He did his best to control his moments of anger and lead positively and inclusively. He tried to show anyone who was watching and tell anyone who was listening that he was a person, not Patient Zero or Public Enemy No. 1.

"We all have the tendency to judge people without knowing them," Gobert said. "You watch us play basketball every day, but you don't know who we are, what we've been through, what we're going through. Get to know people. Go deeper. You can spread a lot of positive messages, but you can also spread hate and judgment. You've got a choice."

When players make mistakes during games, coaches often stress "Next play" so that they move on quickly and don't dwell in the moment. There's plenty of time for a deeper review and corrective advice during film sessions the following day. To me, it felt like Gobert had put himself through an all-encompassing film session after his infamous viral video. Who did he want to be? How did he want to communicate? How could he make things right? How could he heal?

My lasting image of Gobert was the first thing that I saw when I entered the Jazz's practice gym for the interview. As his teammates cleared the court, Gobert was doubled over a chair quietly eating a rice bowl. After he was done, he grabbed a Clorox wipe and painstakingly cleaned his makeshift table. He wiped side to side. Front to back. His hand moved like a riding lawnmower through a field of grass.

This man had learned his lesson.

As captivating and tidy as it was, Gobert's triumphant comeback wasn't the biggest story of the bubble's opening night. Not even close. NBA players had spent months waiting to get back on center stage, and they were intent on delivering a loud statement on social justice.

Opening night began in the dark: The arena lights were cut off so that all eyes could turn to a two-minute social justice video. Jaylen Brown, Damian Lillard, and other players who had protested in the wake of George Floyd's killing were shown first, as demonstrators shouted, "No justice, no peace!" between their brief interviews.

"Things aren't going to change until we make them change," union president Chris Paul said, imbuing the bubble with a mission statement that arose during the extensive debate about whether the players should take the court or stay at home. Black and white players appeared in the video, with Donovan Mitchell lamenting Breonna Taylor's death and JJ Redick describing his anger at the country's racial climate. Carmelo Anthony bemoaned the "ongoing cycle" of violence against Blacks, and a chorus of players declared that they "would not be silent."

The presence of Gregg Popovich, Doc Rivers, and other coaches lent weight to the production. "We can still play basketball, but at the end of the day social justice has to be had," Rivers said. The NBA and

NBPA logos flashed alongside each other at the end of the video in an intentional sign of unity.

As the lights came back on in the building, every player from the New Orleans Pelicans and Utah Jazz locked arms and knelt to the court in a nod to NFL star Colin Kaepernick's famous and polarizing protest of police brutality. The players, who were wearing Black Lives Matter T-shirts, were joined by both coaching staffs and the referees. Collectively, they took a knee for the national anthem near the Black Lives Matter sign on the court, while the videoboard behind them flashed a giant American flag and the NBA logo.

It was a stark and unforgettable visual, and photographs and video of the protest quickly spread online. NBPA executive director Michele Roberts led the applause from her courtside seat. That scene repeated for the second game of the night, between the Lakers and Clippers, with LeBron James, Anthony Davis, Kawhi Leonard, and Paul George all taking a knee with their teammates. Indeed, the scene repeated before every game of opening weekend and before every game for the duration of the bubble.

"I hope we made Kaep proud," James said after the Lakers' opener. "We thank him for sacrificing everything he did to put us in a position today, even years later, to have that moment that we had tonight."

James's reference to "years later" was worth noting because of the NBA's long-standing rule that required players to stand during the national anthem. WNBA and soccer players had followed Kaepernick's lead by kneeling, but NBA players had complied with the league rule for four years. As the star quarterback took immense criticism for allegedly disrespecting the flag and suddenly found himself without any job offers, NBA players voiced their support in interviews and on social media but never staged protests of their own. "Kaep was someone who stood up when times weren't comfortable, when people didn't understand, when people refused to listen to what he was saying," James said.

By the time the NBA players held their protests, public opinion had shifted. Support for Black Lives Matter was reaching new heights in the wake of Floyd's death, and most observers now understood that the target of the national anthem demonstrations was police brutality, not the flag or the military. The various sides had staked their positions long ago: Proponents of the protests viewed them as patriotic acts of self-expression, while opponents felt they were unpatriotic acts of defiance.

The act of kneeling was still divisive, but it was no longer radical. What's more, NBA teams issued a flurry of statements in support of the players' actions, and Adam Silver said the league wouldn't be punishing the players. "I respect our teams' unified act of peaceful protest for social justice and under these unique circumstances will not enforce our long-standing rule requiring standing during the playing of our national anthem," the commissioner said in a statement.

The NBA community was so aligned in its support for kneeling that the conversation briefly shifted to the few players, coaches, and referees who decided to remain standing. Miami Heat center Meyers Leonard, who is white, stood to honor his brother's military service and issued statements of support for those who knelt. Orlando Magic forward Jonathan Isaac, a devout Christian who is Black, said that he stood to take the conversation "out of the realm of skin color" because "racism isn't the only thing that plagues our society."

This was a remarkable turnaround. Whereas Kaepernick's protest had been unsanctioned and largely unscripted, the NBA players had prior approval and had orchestrated every beat. These would prove to be key distinctions when tensions increased a few weeks later. Like many protest movements, there were players who felt the urge to push harder against the system and to be more radical in their actions. Their time would come.

If nothing else, the opening night demonstrations succeeded in triggering President Trump. "When I see them kneeling, I just turn off the game," Trump said. "I have no interest in the game. Let me tell you, there are plenty of other people out there [tuning out], too. The ratings for basketball are way down."

James quickly fired back, saying that basketball "will go on without his eyes on it" and that the NBA community "could [not] care less" about Trump's criticism. NBA players had spent most of Trump's presidency in a cold war with the administration. The 2017, 2018, and 2019 NBA champions had all passed on making traditional White House visits, stars like James and Stephen Curry had dabbled in anti-Trump commentary, and coaches like Popovich and Steve Kerr had lambasted Trump's leadership approach and caustic tone.

The entire league was out on a tree limb together now, battered by political winds. Conservative critics parroted Trump's critiques, arguing that the players should "stick to sports" because their activism was turning off some viewers. With racial tensions already high, Black NBA players had become a wedge issue in the ongoing presidential campaign between Trump and Democratic nominee Joe Biden.

James understood the dynamics, telling reporters that "November is right around the corner, and it's a big moment for us as Americans. We want better, we want change, and we have an opportunity to do that." Trump saw the same stakes.

"We have to stand up for our anthem," the president told Fox News. "A lot of people agree with me. Hey, if I'm wrong, I'm going to lose an election."

8

Title Chase Commences

Through all the protests, activism, and political barbs, there were still NBA games to be played. My head was spinning nonstop with so much off-court activity, but I sensed a refocusing as the start of the playoffs drew closer.

Entering Orlando, the basketball pundits and Las Vegas oddsmakers agreed that the top tier of title favorites included three teams: the Bucks, Lakers, and Clippers. I was still clinging to my preseason pick of Clippers over Bucks in the Finals, believing that the Clippers were the deepest and most versatile team in the twenty-two-team field. There were healthy debates to be had, though, because the Bucks had been the league's winningest team and the Lakers had cruised along at the top of the West standings all season.

The 2019–20 season stood in stark contrast to the previous half decade, when the Golden State Warriors had won three titles, reached five straight Finals, and established themselves as overwhelming favorites time and again. This year had real intrigue thanks to a rock, paper, scissors dynamic. The top three contenders were led by the league's top three healthy players: the Bucks' Giannis Antetokounmpo, the Lakers' LeBron James, and the Clippers' Kawhi Leonard.

At the start of the season, I had agonized over how to rank the three of them in my annual Top 100 NBA Players list, ultimately settling on Leonard at No. 1. James had held the top spot for years, but he was coming off a lottery trip and the first major injury of his career. Leonard was in his prime and had proven to be a more reliable postseason performer than Antetokounmpo.

The three superstars circled one another all season. During a December victory over the Lakers, Antetokounmpo celebrated a 3-pointer by placing an invisible crown on his own head. When the

Lakers got a revenge victory in March, James received an invisible crown from teammate Kyle Kuzma. Meanwhile, New Balance released an ad for Leonard that declared Los Angeles to be "his city" and featured a crown key chain. The imagery was as plain as it gets.

All three had claims to the throne. Antetokounmpo was the reigning MVP. James was the sport's top talent throughout the 2010s, and he still had a strong case as the best all-around player. Leonard was the reigning Finals MVP. Each had played brilliantly throughout the 2019–20 season in his own distinct way.

The twenty-five-year-old Antetokounmpo was the youngest and most powerful of the three. His offensive game and shooting ability were less refined, but he was a fearsome dunk machine who punished smaller opponents. Although Antetokounmpo functioned as a lead playmaker on the perimeter, he drew comparisons to Shaquille O'Neal by averaging 29.5 points, 13.6 rebounds, and 5.6 assists. He was also arguably the sport's best defensive player, given his ability to protect the rim and force turnovers by roaming around the court.

Milwaukee had painstakingly crafted its systems to accentuate Antetokounmpo's strengths. Under coach Mike Budenholzer, the Bucks spread the court with shooters on offense and played big, physical lineups defensively. They were bruising and efficient, and they racked up double-digit victories with ease. Antetokounmpo had to play only 30.4 minutes per game, an insanely low figure for an MVP in his mid-twenties.

The biggest question facing the Bucks was how they would respond to their 2019 playoff disappointment. In a stunning Eastern Conference finals collapse against the Toronto Raptors, Antetokounmpo had been bottled up by Leonard, and Budenholzer had struggled to adjust. For Antetokounmpo, the bubble represented a possible revenge tour and an excellent shot at his first ring. The East was clearly weaker than the West, giving the Bucks an easier path.

James, at thirty-five, was the league's elder statesman and most visible superstar. His contemporaries were largely retired or reduced to role players, but he continued to defy Father Time in his seventeenth season.

He averaged 25.3 points, 7.8 rebounds, and a league-leading 10.2 assists per game, forming a dominant duo with Anthony Davis after the Lakers landed the All-Star forward in a 2019 blockbuster trade. While James wasn't as quick or as high-flying as he had been during his athletic prime, he remained a brilliant tactician and a poised leader.

The Lakers weren't as deep as the Warriors had been, and their roster aside from James and Davis was full of unproven role players and low-cost free agency pickups. Their team defense and chemistry had been superb under new coach Frank Vogel, even as they endured the tragic death of franchise legend Kobe Bryant in January. In truth, the Lakers still faced a healthy degree of skepticism. Most analysts had pegged them as a middle-of-the-pack team in the West's playoff picture before the season, and they still appeared top-heavy when they entered the bubble.

James's legacy as one of the NBA's all-time greats was secure. He had already won three championships, three Finals MVPs, and countless individual awards. Of course, he viewed the bubble as a chance to add a fourth ring, thereby narrowing the gap in his chase of Michael Jordan in the GOAT conversation. But would James be able to hold up to heavy minutes in the postseason? Would he still have his legs late in games? Would the Lakers' supporting cast be able to provide enough help? And was Davis, who had won just one playoff series in his seven seasons with the New Orleans Pelicans, ready for prime time?

The Clippers loomed like sharks below the surface thanks to Leonard, the NBA's most enigmatic superstar. Leonard had little interest in the media, and he played by his own rules. In 2018, he forced his way out of San Antonio, abandoning legendary coach Gregg Popovich under perplexing circumstances. After leading the Raptors to the 2019 title, he bolted for the Clippers not long after Toronto's championship parade.

Moving to Los Angeles returned Leonard to his Southern California roots and allowed him to team up with Paul George, another talented two-way wing. The Clippers' vision under coach Doc Rivers was to field an elite defense filled with tough, physical, and versatile players, and to surround Leonard and George with trusted veterans on offense. It all looked great on paper, and it played out according to plan in two early season victories over the Lakers in which Leonard outshined James.

Still, the Clippers hadn't reached the conference finals in their fifty-year franchise history, much less won a title. They naturally faced chemistry questions in the players' first year together, and there had been midseason scuttlebutt that some of Leonard's teammates took exception to his managed workload and special treatment.

Picking the Clippers was a bet that the twenty-nine-year-old Leonard, who averaged 27.1 points, 7.1 rebounds, and 4.9 assists, would step up his game in the playoffs just as he had for the Raptors. Leonard and George were an ideal tandem to guard James and Antetokounmpo, and both the Lakers and Bucks seemed to lack high-level wings to counter the Clippers' duo. Steve Ballmer, the former Microsoft CEO, represented another advantage for the Clippers. The NBA's richest owner had invested heavily in his roster shortly before the shutdown, adding a host of veterans to Leonard's supporting cast.

Heading into the bubble, I was fully convinced that one of these three teams would win it at all. With the long layoff, no home-court advantage, and the possibility of positive tests, many of my media colleagues began predicting there would be upsets and unpredictability.

Others broached the possibility of applying an "asterisk" to the champion if there were an outbreak or if the favorites didn't respond well after the hiatus. The top three teams all shot that down, with Antetokounmpo saying that the bubble title would be "the toughest championship you could ever win" and Vogel arguing that winning "deserves a 'harder than ordinary' asterisk" because of the added adversity.

"Adam Silver said the team that wins this will deserve a gold star, not an asterisk," Clippers coach Doc Rivers said, citing a recent chat with the commissioner. "Whoever comes out of this, it's going to come down to [mental toughness]. There's going to be so many things that are thrown at us that we don't even know yet."

Most of the upset talk centered in the Eastern Conference, where the Bucks were viewed as potentially vulnerable due to their 2019 playoff collapse. The Boston Celtics were a popular pick because Jayson

Tatum, one of the league's rising superstars, had been on a roll before the shutdown. The Raptors were the defending champs, and they had nothing to lose after Leonard's exit the previous summer. The Philadelphia 76ers were loaded on paper and had scored a convincing win over the Bucks on Christmas, but style-of-play questions loomed large. The Miami Heat were a dark horse at best, although coach Erik Spoelstra's disciplined coaching style was a natural fit for the bubble and center Bam Adebayo was a strong matchup for Antetokounmpo.

Out West, a conference finals showdown between the Lakers and Clippers seemed inevitable, although the Houston Rockets with James Harden and Russell Westbrook were intriguing spoilers. Houston had adopted a micro-ball approach at the trade deadline, moving Clint Capela and playing center-less lineups that featured only players six foot seven or shorter. They bombed 3-pointers like crazy and hoped to throw off their opponents with philosophical chaos. The West's other second-tier contenders—Denver and Utah—lacked good matchups for the star-powered L.A. favorites.

Shortly after the season resumed in Orlando, I started to reconsider my position. The three favorites had every reason to coast through the eight extra regular season games, but I was troubled by their lackluster early results.

The Bucks lacked joie de vivre. Antetokounmpo sent a big message with 36 points, 15 rebounds, and 7 assists in an opening win over Boston, but he seemed out of step with his teammates, particularly late in games. Multiple Bucks had tested positive for COVID-19 before arriving in Orlando, and the entire team had to play in the shadow of their dominant regular season and adjust to life without home-court advantage. After leading the league with 19 wins by 20 or more points during the regular season, the Bucks struggled to execute down the stretch of close losses to Houston, Brooklyn, and Dallas.

"It's amazing to beat teams by ten, twenty, thirty," Antetokounmpo said after the Houston loss. "We learned from this. It's good to play close games. We didn't play a lot of close games in the other sixty-five games that we played. We've got to be consistent and do it every night. The most important thing is to get shots. We can't turn the ball over. We've got to find the open man and get shots up."

Antetokounmpo got off to an erratic start, as he regularly dealt with foul trouble and then headbutted Moe Wagner of the Wizards in a meaningless game. He expressed regret for the headbutt, which he called a "terrible action," but the inexplicable display of frustration earned him an ejection and a one-game suspension. Things had come so easily during the season, and now Antetokounmpo was pressing as he sensed something was amiss.

In important moments, he committed turnovers, ran into defensive walls, and missed free throws. His trust in his shaky 3-point shot wavered, even as he followed the coaching staff's instructions to keep hoisting. Make no mistake, Antetokounmpo was still the most dominant force virtually every time he stepped on the court. But the Bucks needed their superstar to play his best basketball if they were going to live up to their lofty expectations, and Antetokounmpo wasn't quite there.

The Lakers had a different problem: an anemic offense. LeBron James and Anthony Davis both arrived in Orlando focused and ready. Who would step up to help them? During the eight regular season games in the bubble, the Lakers ranked twenty-first out of twenty-two in scoring and dead last in 3-point percentage. Their offense was down 8 points per game compared with before the restart, and their depth was stretched by the losses of Rajon Rondo to a broken thumb and Avery Bradley to concerns about the coronavirus.

I wondered whether the lack of 3-point shooting would prove to be a fatal flaw, given that Golden State and Houston, the West's dominant powers in recent years, had both built their offenses around the outside shot. In theory, the Lakers might need to beat four superior shooting teams—the Blazers, Rockets, Clippers, and Bucks—to claim the title. That felt like a big ask if a third dependable source of offense failed to emerge.

James's first impressions of the bubble struck an ominous note, like when he chalked up an ugly loss to the Oklahoma City Thunder to "some things that you can't control that's here, that I really don't want to talk about, that's off the floor." He repeatedly sought to distance the bubble Lakers from the boisterous group that had romped through the West prior to the shutdown. "This is a totally different season," James said. "A totally different, drastic situation."

The Clippers had their own issues, which began in a loss to the Lakers on the bubble's opening night. After twice outplaying James in late-game situations earlier in the season, Leonard froze up on the Clippers' final possession. Instead of driving past James or shooting over him, Leonard dribbled indecisively before passing out to Paul George as the clock ticked down. George only managed to get up a hopeless heave. In a subsequent loss to the Phoenix Suns, Leonard chose not to double-team Devin Booker on the final play of a tied game. Everyone in the gym knew Booker would shoot, yet Leonard backed off and watched as the All-Star guard drilled a game winner.

These were split-second decisions by Leonard, precisely the type of coin-flip scenarios that get overanalyzed by pundits. But the Clippers had catered to Leonard all year, trading a boatload of draft picks to acquire George, carefully managing his minutes, and allowing him to live in San Diego and commute to games by helicopter. Their entire strategy was to put Leonard in position to deliver in close games, and he had come up short twice in the opening week.

The Clippers were also dealing with a major lack of lineup continuity. Remarkably, Rivers wasn't able to play his best five-man group together for a single minute during the bubble's eight regular season games. Patrick Beverley suffered a calf injury that kept him out of multiple games. Ivica Zubac was late arriving after contracting COVID-19. Lou Williams landed himself in a ten-day quarantine after he was spotted at Magic City, a well-known Atlanta strip club, when he left the bubble to attend a funeral. Montrezl Harrell missed the Clippers' first eight games after leaving the bubble to attend his grandmother's funeral.

Rivers juggled his rotation well enough, plugging in backups like Reggie Jackson and Joakim Noah to bide time. Despite all the roster turnover, the Clippers scored early blowout wins over the Pelicans,

Mavericks, and Denver Nuggets that fueled their tendency to talk trash and aggravate opponents.

During an August 8 win over the Blazers, the Clippers took things too far when Damian Lillard missed a pair of late free throws that nearly cost Portland its shot at the playoffs. Beverley's voice echoed around the gym as he mocked Lillard's well-known wrist-tapping celebration and "Dame D.O.L.L.A." nickname, shouting, "Dolla time!" and "Dame time!" as Portland's usually clutch guard came up empty. Then Beverley and George waved Lillard off the court after the final buzzer. That gesture was payback for Lillard's series-clinching 3-pointer against George's Oklahoma City Thunder in the 2019 playoffs.

Lillard was unfazed by the Clippers' cockiness, unloading on Beverley and George through glaring eyes during a postgame press conference. He brought up his dagger over George and a series-clinching jumper against Beverley and the Rockets during the 2014 playoffs.

"He experienced getting waved at last year," Lillard said of George. "Patrick Beverley, I sent him home before at the end of a game. Paul George just got sent home by me last year in the playoffs. They know. The reason they're reacting like that is what they expect from me. That's a sign of respect. It just shows what I've done at a high clip more times than not. I'm not offended by it. If anything, it should just tell you how much it hurt them to go through what I put them through in those situations previously."

The Clippers fired back on Instagram. George wrote that Lillard was "getting sent home this year." Beverley replied with "Cancun on three"—an age-old reference to what a team would cheer when it knew its season was over. Lillard, still seething hours later, got the last word: "You boys is chumps."

The ferocity of Lillard's personal attacks left reporters laughing in the hallway after Portland packed up its bus. I suspected that the bubble might be fertile grounds for verbal confrontations, given the frustrating lifestyle restrictions, and here was the first major blowup involving superstars.

It was hard to remember the last time a high-profile player like Lillard had so thoroughly undressed a team like the Clippers, who were viewed as the title favorite once they landed Leonard. The best recent comparison was a series of tense exchanges between James and the Warriors during the 2016 Finals. No one had bashed the Warriors like that since they landed Kevin Durant and became nearly unbeatable. James's peers revered him and wouldn't dare call him a "chump" in public.

To me, the incident revealed that the Clippers thought more highly of themselves than their opponents did—a red flag for a team whose main pieces hadn't won big together. It also confirmed my growing suspicions that the top three contenders shouldn't expect a cakewalk once the postseason opened.

* * *

The resumed regular season was a blur, too much basketball for anyone to consume.

All told, the NBA held eighty-eight games over a sixteen-day period, using all three gyms to hold as many as seven games in a day. There were no days off, and tip-offs began as early as noon and as late as 9:00 p.m. This was the Las Vegas Summer League type of schedule that I had envisioned all the way back in March, except instead of watching fringe pros fighting for roster spots I was gorging on All-Star players.

The NBA's media rules required that I submit my requests for games in advance, and I decided within the first few days to put myself on a hoops diet. I was worried about burning out. At Summer League, I would watch four or five games every day, but that event lasted only two weeks. I needed to pace myself for three months, so I would try to stick to two games per day.

I wanted to catch as many Bucks, Lakers, and Clippers games as possible to get an early feel for the title chase. After that, I found myself drifting toward the West's playoff race, which had a new wrinkle in the bubble thanks to the play-in round.

The play-in round had been floated for years as a method for injecting interest into the dog days of the NBA season and discouraging teams from tanking. Typically, the playoff teams have largely separated themselves from the pack by late March, leading many teams that fall out of the postseason picture to angle for better odds in the draft lottery by resting their top players and developing their young prospects. Often, that meant weeks of ugly basketball.

To counter this practice, the play-in round would open a new pathway into the playoffs. Instead of simply taking the top eight seeds from both conferences into the postseason, only the bubble's top seven seeds would advance automatically. The eighth seed would be treated differently.

If the eighth seed held more than a four-game lead over the ninth seed, it would automatically advance like normal. If not, the eighth and ninth seeds would square off in a head-to-head play-in round. In that round, the eighth seed would need to win only once to secure its playoff spot, while the ninth seed would need to win twice in a row to steal the final spot. The winner of this play-in would then face the conference's top seed in the first round of the playoffs.

All things considered, this was an equitable, if somewhat convoluted, solution. I wasn't convinced it would amount to much. The Washington Wizards, the East's ninth seed, entered the bubble without two key players, Bradley Beal and Davis Bertans. I figured they would bow out with a whimper unless the Brooklyn Nets, who were missing half their rotation due to injuries and positive COVID-19 tests, somehow collapsed. The horse race never developed, as the Wizards lost seven of their eight games and failed to force the play-in.

But the league's new plan worked brilliantly in the West, where six teams were vying for the right to face the top-seeded Lakers in the first round. The pack included Zion Williamson's Pelicans, Damian Lillard's Blazers, Devin Booker's Suns, and Ja Morant's Grizzlies, and the race was so tight that a play-in round was a virtual certainty. Eighth seeds rarely upset top seeds in the playoffs, but the restart's many unknowns and the Lakers' early inconsistency in the bubble raised the stakes.

I had been against expanding the bubble field from sixteen teams to twenty-two because of the added coronavirus risk, but the league's gamble set up a thrilling race for the eighth seed. Williamson, who had missed much of his rookie season due to a knee injury, was a source of constant intrigue thanks to his high-flying dunks and unconventional physique. Lillard was an all-NBA talent trying to carry an injury-ravaged roster into the playoffs. Booker was an electric scorer and first-time All-Star hoping to reach the playoffs for the first time in his five-year career. Morant was named Rookie of the Year after turning the Grizzlies into arguably the league's biggest overachievers.

While many viewed Portland as the favorite to claim the eighth seed, given Lillard's experience and clutch moments in previous post-seasons, the twenty-year-old Williamson was the center of attention. The prospect of a first-round series between the Lakers and Pelicans was enticing to television executives, media, and fans alike. Almost imme-diately, though, Williamson and the Pelicans seemed overwhelmed by their new surroundings and their position at center stage.

The Pelicans got their first taste of Zionmania when Williamson made his long-awaited debut after missing three months due to knee surgery. ESPN hyped Williamson's debut for the better part of a week, and one of the network's reporters joked that they were treating the event like a combination of Donald Trump's impeachment and the moon landing. I flew to New Orleans to see it in person and was enthralled by his combination of size, quickness, force, and leaping ability.

In his last game before the shutdown, I watched Williamson score 23 points and throw down two jaw-dropping dunks in an easy win over the Timberwolves. He was flourishing, and I couldn't wait to see him take the court in the bubble. The networks couldn't either, deciding to air seven of the Pelicans' eight bubble games on national television.

Unfortunately, Williamson didn't pick up where he left off. On July 16, while I was still stuck in my hotel room quarantine, the Peli-cans announced that Williamson would be leaving the bubble, citing "an urgent family medical matter." No additional details were given in the statement, and the full story never emerged.

Williamson returned to the bubble on July 24, with enough time to clear a second quarantine period before the Pelicans' July 30 opener against the Jazz. Everyone expected him to play, but he was listed as a game-time decision by the Pelicans because he had barely practiced in two weeks. New Orleans appeared to be trying to lower expectations and telegraph its intention of limiting his minutes for the first few games.

The Pelicans' opaque explanation of his departure and curious handling of his return only raised more questions. When Williamson finally met the media on July 29, he smiled nervously and largely avoided eye contact. He spoke vaguely about his "emergency" absence and tried to toe the party line about easing back onto the court. "Me and my team are going to look for what's best for me and my future," Williamson said. "Being safe. But if you know me, I want to hoop."

By that point, Pelicans coach Alvin Gentry and the team's other players had spent a week answering questions about Williamson. This was the NBA's version of the old *Brady Bunch* line: "Marcia, Marcia, Marcia." Zion. Zion. Zion. Was he healthy? Was he in shape? How much would he play? Did the Pelicans want to make the playoffs or protect his future?

The Pelicans acted like a pack of groomsmen trying to cover for a groom who had mysteriously disappeared on the wedding day. Williamson's relative youth compared with his teammates only made the dynamic trickier, and things got worse once they took the court. Williamson was limited to fifteen minutes in the opener and fourteen minutes in an ugly blowout loss to the Clippers two nights later. Within days, their playoff hopes evaporated after demoralizing losses to the Kings and Spurs.

Williamson looked heavy, slow, and out of sync, and he expressed frustration with his minutes limit, which required that he play in short bursts and sometimes sit during crunch time. The player who had flown around the court and sailed through the air before the shutdown now struggled to sustain his energy level and keep up with the action on the perimeter.

"It just hits different in a bad way when I'm on the bench in the fourth quarter and there's nothing I can do to help my team win," Williamson said, after finishing off a win over Memphis. "I was just glad the training staff and my team trusted me to be able to close the game out."

As Williamson softly aired his grievances, his teammates seemed to be doing everything they could to ensure that they would soon depart the bubble. Even in must-win games against other playoff hopefuls, the Pelicans often looked checked out, jogging nonchalantly through warmups, committing careless turnovers, and not responding to Gentry's postgame criticisms. I had spent weeks looking forward to watching the next chapter of Williamson's career, and within five games I just wanted the Pelicans to pack up and head home. They were wasting everyone's time.

The Pelicans left as the biggest disappointment, going 2-6 and resting Williamson for the final two games because they were already eliminated from the playoffs. Gentry, who said there was "no explanation" for his team's uneven effort, was fired two days after the Pelicans' bubble exit. New Orleans's trials offered an important early lesson: If a team wasn't on the same page and fully invested in competing hard together, the bubble experience would eat it alive. They were the first team to succumb to the powerful and ever-present temptation to return to a more normal life, but they wouldn't be the last.

To my great surprise, the Suns emerged as the anti-Pelicans. They entered the bubble as the West's 13th seed with a 26-39 record, six losses back of the 8th-seeded Grizzlies. Even with the addition of the play-in round, I figured they were in for a brief and forgettable run. If they lost their opener against the Wizards, they would practically be eliminated from the playoff chase.

Phoenix won that opener and then kept winning and winning, eking out narrow victories over the Mavericks and Clippers. Booker's picture-perfect game winner, which exploited Kawhi Leonard's defensive lapse, was the difference against Los Angeles.

Booker, twenty-four, drove hard to his left on the final play, faking away from Leonard and spinning back toward a tough jumper. He launched over the top of Paul George, one of the league's best perimeter defenders, and fell to the court, landing on his back just as the shot swished through the net. Booker remained prone on the ground and tilted his head back with his arms to his side, almost as if his body were resting in a coffin.

Although Booker's lackluster defense and ball dominance rankled me at times, his shot was an awesome payoff after five straight losing seasons. He looked exhausted and satisfied as he lay on the ground, and his teammates raced over to dogpile on top of him. "Not a big celebration guy," Booker said. "They caught me on the ground so I couldn't get away from them. I want a reputation in this league as a winner. Through five years, I haven't got to that part of my career yet, but I'm working extremely hard to get there."

Suns coach Monty Williams lauded his team after the last-second win, saying that "our guys just grew up tonight" against a Clippers team "that could possibly win a championship." Indeed, if the Pelicans had struggled to find their fits around Williamson, the Suns were eager to hop on Booker's back. The empty arenas didn't seem to bother Booker, a pure bucket-getter and summer pickup game regular. Plus, the young Suns had dubbed themselves the "Valley Boyz" during the regular season. Living at Disney World was working out just fine for a group that wasn't too far removed from the AAU circuit and dorm life.

After scoring 35 points against the Clippers, Booker had 35 in a win over the Heat. Then he scored 35 in a blowout over the Thunder. Then 35 again in a commanding win over the Sixers. He closed the bubble with 27 points in a blowout win over the Mavericks. While some of those victories were aided by opponents dealing with injuries or resting key players, Booker carried Phoenix to a perfect 8-0 record in the bubble and its first eight-game winning streak since 2010. All that winning brought the Suns into a tie for the ninth seed with the Grizzlies heading into the final night of the regular season. If Memphis won, it would land a spot in the play-in round against Portland. If not, Phoenix would claim the spot.

The Grizzlies were riding high entering the bubble thanks to Morant, a skinny and electric point guard with a brash confidence that is rare among rookies. Lightning quick off the dribble and blessed with excellent leaping ability, the twenty-one-year-old Morant quickly racked up an impressive collection of almost-dunks. Every other night, Morant would spring off the hardwood, take off eight feet from the hoop, and attempt to posterize a power forward or center by trying to leap over or through them. His attempts often caught the back rim or ricocheted out near half-court, but they went viral all the same.

I was high on Memphis's chances because of Morant's game and no-nonsense personality. As some veterans complained about Disney World's accommodations, he was one of the first prominent players to push back. Morant looked like a 2021 All-Star in the making, but the Grizzlies lost starting forward Jaren Jackson Jr. to a knee injury in their third game and sputtered to a 1-6 start.

If the NBA had brought only sixteen teams to Orlando, the Grizzlies would have faced the Lakers in the first round, a huge showcase with valuable postseason repetitions for Morant. Their bubble regression was somewhat expected, given their youth and Jackson's injury, but they would crash out of both the postseason and the play-in round if they couldn't get a win in their bubble finale.

Their last game was against the Bucks, a nightmare matchup on paper. When the two teams faced off in December, Milwaukee had scored 127 points in a blowout win and Giannis Antetokounmpo had posted 37 points and 11 rebounds in only twenty-six minutes. Memphis lost that game despite a career-high 43 points from Jackson, who got red-hot and hit nine 3-pointers.

As it turned out, fate was smiling on the Grizzlies. Two days before the big game, Antetokounmpo was ejected for his headbutt of Moe Wagner. The NBA decided to suspend him for the game against Memphis. Even better, the Bucks had already locked up the East's top seed, so they had nothing to play for and could rest their key players before the playoffs. The icing on the cake: Taylor Jenkins, the Grizzlies' first-year coach, was a former Bucks assistant. If Bucks coach Mike Budenholzer went deep into his bench, he could help lift the Grizzlies into the play-in round.

That's exactly what happened. Budenholzer played twelve guys and limited his key starters to about twenty minutes apiece. Morant shot poorly, but both he and center Jonas Valanciunas managed to post triple-doubles against their undermanned opponents. At the same time, in the gym next door, the Suns blew out the Mavericks to complete their magical 8-0 run through the bubble. Yet Phoenix was going home anyway.

For the Grizzlies, the win brought a brief sigh of relief and the need to refocus on its upcoming play-in round with Portland. For the Suns, it was a bitter pill to swallow. They did everything in their power to climb in the standings—leaping over San Antonio, Sacramento, and New Orleans—only to come up one result short. Both Memphis and Phoenix finished the regular season with 34-39 records, and the Grizzlies won the tiebreaker because they had defeated the Suns three times in December and January. Those games were ages ago, and it was clear which team had more momentum now.

Williams, in his first season as Suns coach, called his team together in the locker room after its final game. Four years earlier, he had lost his wife, Ingrid, at age forty-four in a tragic car accident. After delivering a moving speech at Ingrid's funeral about the importance of forgiveness, Williams stepped away from coaching for multiple years so that he could raise his children.

"This was therapeutic for me to be around you guys," Williams told the Suns. "I love you. It has been cool for me to be with y'all. To watch you guys work and battle and gain the respect of your peers on this trip. We're not the Suns of old. We've been through a lot. It's hard to play the way you played every single night. Nobody believed we'd come in here and go 8-0. This is special."

The setting of Williams's speech reflected the fortitude that powered the Suns' bubble run. The team was gathered in a converted equipment storage room. The bells and whistles of a typical NBA locker room—wood-paneled lockers, high-tech video screens, catered postgame spreads, personalized nameplates, stacks of sneakers—were all nonexistent. As Williams talked, his players and coaches squeezed together in a plain concrete space decorated only with hand sanitizer dispensers.

No one expected the Suns to make their run, because of their rough recent history, like Williams noted, but also because most teams would have rolled over in their position. An ESPN.com projection by Kevin Pelton in early June saw Phoenix reach the play-in round just once out of 500 simulations. The Suns entered the bubble with the second-worst record out of twenty-two teams, topping only the Wizards, and they left as the only team to complete the regular season with an 8-0 mark. Williams was right: Their consistent effort demanded the league's respect.

Lillard made sure that the Blazers got the same treatment from their peers. The thirty-year-old point guard got off to a 3-1 start in the bubble, netting 45 points in a win over Denver and helping reintegrate center Jusuf Nurkic and forward Zach Collins after long-term injuries. Lillard had won playoff series with buzzer-beaters in 2014 and 2019, and his meditative style seemed like a perfect fit for the bubble. Even during the peak moments of his career, Lillard was famous for remaining expressionless. When he knocked out the Thunder in 2019, he waved Paul George off the court and then stared directly into a television camera with a blank face as his teammates mobbed him on the court. He was a quintessential basketball assassin with a fearless aura and an unwavering desire to have the ball in his hands for the last shot.

That clutch reputation was flung back in his face during the August 8 loss to the Clippers, which saw Patrick Beverley and George mock him for missing two free throws. As a longtime Lillard viewer dating back to my days living in Portland and covering the Blazers, it was a stunning scene. With eighteen seconds left and the Clippers already playing their backups because they didn't need to win, Lillard missed twice while trailing by one point.

For his career, Lillard was an 89 percent free-throw shooter. In the playoffs, he was an 88 percent shooter. That was about as good as it gets. With a season hanging in the balance, Lillard was one of the top two or three most trustworthy players in the league. Yet the Clippers' heckling was more shocking than Lillard's misses. What were they thinking? Didn't they know better than to poke this bear?

After Lillard's seething press conference and harsh Instagram posts mocking Beverley and George as "chumps," everyone in the bubble braced for him to go off the next night. The stakes were simple: Portland needed to beat Philadelphia, Dallas, and Brooklyn in its final three games to clinch a spot in the play-in round. One loss and the Blazers were almost certainly headed home.

Lillard came out and dropped 51 points on the 76ers, leading the Blazers to a comeback victory by scoring 9 points in the final three minutes. The dust had barely settled on that spectacular performance when, two nights later, he played perhaps the best game of his career. In a back-and-forth contest with the Mavericks, Lillard scored 61 points and drained nine 3-pointers, with 10 points in the final five minutes to close out the win.

Lillard's latest classic moment came with less than two minutes remaining and Dallas leading 130–127. He stood roughly four steps behind the 3-point line with the ball, so far from the hoop that his feet aligned with the two t's in the Black Lives Matter decal that graced center court. The ball was at his waist as he let the shot clock tick.

Seeing no better options, Lillard raised up and launched a ceiling-scraping 3-pointer that clanged hard off the back rim. But instead of bouncing out toward the 3-point line, the ball ricocheted straight up, so high that it cleared the top of the shot clock and briefly left the field of vision for television viewers. As everyone on the court and on the sidelines watched with bated breath, the ball came back to earth and passed so cleanly through the rim that the net barely moved. Media members sitting courtside yelped. The shot tied the game and Portland never looked back, with cameras catching Lillard shouting, "Put some respect on my fucking name!" at the buzzer.

"I probably said about twenty pleases—please, please, please—repeatedly," Carmelo Anthony said, recalling the uneasy wait during the ball's upward carom. "It wasn't meant for us to lose when that shot went in."

Lillard credited divine intervention, dedicating the shot to Brandon Johnson, his cousin and personal chef who died in Portland during the hiatus. In a small interview room not much bigger than a closet, Lillard described how he had "prayed over his body" and cried with his teammate C. J. McCollum when they got the news. "I shot it real straight," he said. "I thought it was going to go in. When it hit back rim and went straight up, I kept watching it. I think that's going to go in. It dropped in. I think that was my cousin, Rest in Peace Chef B. I think that was him dropping that in for me. Losing him hurt. It was tough. I just try to continue what I think he would want me to do. I've been dealing with it that way, on a path that I know he was proud of."

Blazers coach Terry Stotts was never one to take credit, but he laughed off the notion that he had played any major role in Lillard's latest explosion. "The season was on the line," he said. "The best way I can help him is to put him in good situations. I help where I can, but that was Dame's night."

Portland's work still wasn't done. To clinch a spot in the play-in game, they needed to beat the undermanned but scrappy Nets. Although Brooklyn had little to play for, Caris LeVert threw a big scare into Portland by scoring 37 points. Lillard countered with 42 points of his own, but this time he got major help from McCollum and Nurkic, plus a clutch 3-pointer from Anthony. The Blazers, through a team effort, narrowly held off the Nets and clinched the 8th seed and their play-in date with the Grizzlies.

The numbers from Lillard's three-game closing push were staggering. After the Clippers heckled him, Lillard averaged 51.3 points and 9 assists. He made twenty-one 3-pointers and shot 48.8 percent from beyond the arc. He played more than forty minutes in each of the three games, which Portland had won by a combined 7 points. Perhaps most remarkably, he made 41 of his 43 free-throw attempts since his two misses against the Clippers—95.3 percent.

Lillard channeled a few slights from Beverley and George into the bubble's most outrageous scoring display. "When I first came here, I said I didn't come here to waste my time," Lillard told TNT in a post-game interview, his face as blank as ever. "The job still ain't done."

Per the terms of the play-in round, Portland, the 8th seed, would get two chances to beat Memphis, the 9th seed. Lillard needed only one, leading the way with 31 points and five 3-pointers. Morant acquitted himself nicely with a game-high 35 points in defeat. The Grizzlies were outworked inside by Nurkic, who found out earlier in the day that his grandmother had died after a long battle with COVID-19.

"I didn't want to play," Nurkic said, fighting back tears after scoring 22 points and grabbing 21 rebounds. "She made me play, I guess. Personally, I thought I wasn't going to play tonight. I didn't want to shoot any balls during warmups. I already came and made the decision to stay here to be with the team. I think she wanted me to play. I'm glad we won and are in the playoffs. That's what we came for."

Stotts summarized his team's physical and mental exhaustion, quipping that the Blazers had "just played a nine-game playoff series" simply to reach the real playoffs. "It went the full nine," he said, proud of Portland's 7-2 jaunt.

Later that night, the NBA hosted members of the media for dinner at Ale & Compass, a steak and seafood restaurant, to mark the end of the regular season. Ale & Compass was located at the Yacht Club, which had been home to the Blazers and the five other teams that had been outside the playoff picture when they entered the bubble.

The Yacht Club was the subject of so many Twitter jokes back in June when it was first announced as the home of the bottom six teams, but those wisecracks were now a distant memory. Two lobby signs bearing Portland's pinwheel logo and "Rip City" nickname welcomed the Blazers back to the hotel as conquering heroes.

The Pelicans embarrassed themselves. The Suns did everything they could. The Grizzlies put up a great fight. But the Blazers were the last team standing in the chase for the West's 8th seed. Their players and coaches spread out around the bar nursing drinks and toasting what had been a two-week marathon. They could have chosen to pack it in plenty of times, and a missed shot here or a turnover there could have spoiled their strong closing push. One off night from their franchise player would have spelled doom.

Instead, Lillard delivered his seventh straight playoff appearance in memorable fashion. A date with James and the formidable Lakers was just around the corner, but that Saturday night was all fun and games at the Yacht Club.

I returned to my hotel room with a belly full of pasta. At dinner, the media contingent sat two to a table that might typically seat eight, spaced out much farther than six feet apart, and the waitstaff all wore masks. The Blazers, wary of the league's health protocols, greeted reporters but remained at a safe distance. It was the first time I had been in a restaurant since March, and it was my first real meal since entering the bubble more than a month earlier. It felt like a major milestone.

There was one thing I had to do before I drifted off to sleep: I pulled out my black-and-red Jordan 11s and wiped the dust off the patent leather. The bubble had made it to the playoffs.

9

No Positives

The look of pure hurt in Jusuf Nurkic's eyes as he processed his grandmother's COVID-related death was unforgettable. The Blazers center was hollowed out by grief, present physically in a cramped interview room but somewhere else entirely from a mental standpoint. He was hurting so badly that he no longer cared if anyone could tell, a rare sight in professional sports, where athletes do their best to shield and deny their vulnerabilities.

In 2017, I spent a long afternoon chatting with Nurkic while writing an extensive profile of him for *Sports Illustrated*. He was in a contract year and relatively unknown on the national level, so he was motivated to speak candidly. He told me his famous basketball origin story, how his father, a six-foot-ten, 400-pound police officer, made headlines in Bosnia for beating up thirteen people in a bar fight. He told me how a basketball scout came calling after reading the story and sent him away at age fourteen to play in Slovenia, where he endured terrible homesickness. He explained how naive he had been when he first came to the United States for the 2014 draft. "My very first day, some guy asked me if I wanted drugs," Nurkic said. "My first experience in New York is a drug dealer! What's going on here? It was just like the movies."

Nurkic first landed with the Denver Nuggets, but the key turning point in his career was a 2016 trade to the Blazers. In Denver, he collected negative labels: lazy, overweight, selfish, and uncoachable. In Portland, he had a larger role and Damian Lillard to guide his development. Nurkic committed to losing weight, improved dramatically on defense, and took full advantage of his second opportunity. He played so hard and so well after the trade that Blazermaniacs caught "Nurk Fever," and he went from pariah to fan favorite in a matter of months.

In March 2019, Nurkic suffered a gruesome leg injury that ended his season. He missed out on Portland's improbable run to the Western Conference finals, cheering his teammates from the bench and providing emotional lifts when he could. Nurkic did not play a single minute in 2019–20 before the shutdown, but the four-month hiatus allowed him enough time to get back on the court. Portland struggled inside without him, and his bubble return raised hopes for the playoff push.

Nurkic played well but inconsistently as he worked his way back into game shape. Still, he came up big in Portland's must-win over Brooklyn to close the regular season, and he was dominant in the play-in victory over Memphis.

The death of Nurkic's grandmother was a reminder of the coronavirus's ability to devastate families. Seventeen months after his leg snapped, Nurkic was completing an amazing comeback story. That week should have been the happiest of his young career. Instead, he could barely keep his composure, and he agonized over whether he should keep playing.

Nurkic wasn't the first player I had seen play well through grief, and I knew some viewers would spin his response into an act of heroism. Such talk always made me recoil. I didn't know Nurkic that well, but I knew that he would trade his 22 points and 21 rebounds against the Grizzlies for one more phone call with his grandmother. Anyone would. The Blazers' win and his stellar performance, his face silently told reporters, were trivial.

That scene hit especially hard for two reasons: Nurkic had talked extensively about his family when I interviewed him back in 2017, and I had been living free of the coronavirus's grasp for more than a month. The bubble offered a trade-off. In exchange for constant annoyances and demanding rules, I received a pure piece of mind shared by very few people anywhere in the world. Nurkic's loss, much like Karl-Anthony Towns's back in April, pierced that sense of invulnerability.

Every morning, I took my temperature and blood oxygen reading as soon as I woke up. I inputted the results into the NBA's MyHealth tracking app and answered a symptoms questionnaire. Then I donned my mask, credential, and proximity alarm for the short walk to the COVID-19 testing center.

In the modified hotel rooms, I swiped my MagicBand to check in and signed a form confirming my identity at the first station. I then moved to a second seat, where I reconfirmed my name and birth date before a technician in full scrubs administered the test by sticking swabs down my throat and into each of my nostrils. As I proceeded out of the rooms in clockwise fashion, another staffer disinfected both chairs that I had sat in, any other surfaces that I had touched, and the pen that I had used to sign my name. The results usually came back by email before I went to bed that night.

The NBA took no chances enforcing its rules, which were overseen by David Weiss, the NBA's senior vice president, and designed in consultation with David Ho, a noted HIV/AIDS research pioneer, and former U.S. surgeon general Vivek Murthy. Ho's relationship with the NBA went back decades due to his treatment of Magic Johnson, who contracted HIV in 1991.

During the players' quarantine period, Rockets forward Bruno Caboclo was busted for leaving his room and forced to restart a ten-day isolation. Lakers center Dwight Howard was warned for not wearing his mask on campus. And Kings center Richaun Holmes was sent back into a ten-day quarantine period for leaving the bubble to meet his Postmates driver. Holmes's mother, Lydecia, jokingly scolded her son on Twitter: "You only cross the line for your MOMA's COOKING! AND I WAS NOT IN FLORIDA SIR!!"

Lou Williams's strip club foray was easily the highest-profile early violation. The 2019 Sixth Man of the Year left the bubble in late July to attend his grandfather's funeral. While in transit, Williams took a side trip to Magic City, an Atlanta strip club he frequented so regularly that they named their lemon pepper barbecue wings in his honor. The visit would have gone undetected if Jack Harlow, a Kentucky rapper, hadn't been at the strip club and posted a photo of Williams.

As the photo circulated, prompting an NBA investigation, Williams claimed he had only been at Magic City to pick up food. "Ask any of my teammates what my favorite restaurant in Atlanta is," Williams wrote on Twitter, explaining that his "in and out" trip to Magic City was to pick up food. "Ain't nobody partying. Chill out. Mask on."

Regardless, the NBA sent Williams back into an isolated quarantine for ten days and withheld his game checks, leading to roughly $150,000 in lost wages. Clippers coach Doc Rivers scolded Williams, saying that the photo was "something we obviously didn't enjoy seeing." As with the Holmes incident, Williams's indulgence prompted days of jokes on social media.

I didn't find Holmes's food run or Williams's side trip funny at all. I entered the bubble worried that an inconsequential player like Caboclo or Holmes would have less motivation to follow the rules than key players on contenders, and that their poor decisions could spoil everything. Williams had simply been reckless and selfish. His desire for comfort food was understandable, but all of Disney World's temporary inhabitants were stuck in this thing together. The bubble was only as good as its weakest link.

I was grateful that the security procedures worked and were enforced. I had been standing six feet from Williams during a postgame interview on the day before he left the bubble. What if Williams's trip hadn't been discovered and that same scene had repeated the day after his brief quarantine? It was easy to imagine myself smack in the middle of a nightmare scenario, masks or not.

Those incidents brought flashes of fear, but they passed quickly. The NBA held so many health meetings, issued so many reminder text messages, and watched us so carefully that I became more afraid of accidentally breaking the rules than of the coronavirus. After Suns center Deandre Ayton was held out for a portion of a game because he forgot to take his COVID-19 test, I kept second-guessing for days afterward whether I had gotten my morning test taken.

My mind was first put at ease by a July 20 email from the NBA headlined: "NBA and NBPA announce COVID-19 test results." I held my breath when I read the headline. The short email read: "Of the 346 players tested for COVID-19 on the NBA campus since test results were last announced on July 13, zero have returned confirmed positive tests. In the event that a player on the NBA campus returns a confirmed positive test in the future, he will be isolated until he is cleared for leaving isolation under the rules established by the NBA and the Players Association."

The NBA sent subsequent emails on July 29, August 5, August 12, and August 19 to report zero positive tests. By the time the last one came through, I didn't even bother to open it because I was so confident in the protocols. Shortly thereafter, the NBA decided not to send out the email updates unless someone tested positive. No news was great news.

Although regulations on media behavior remained strict, the league gradually allowed access to a 1.5-mile oval walking loop, an on-campus barbershop, and charter fishing trips once it became clear the bubble was holding. Media members also received access to hot food buffets served up at a station that resembled a Subway or Chipotle, rather than the prepackaged meals that had greeted us upon arrival.

The buffet food quality was noticeably better, but it was largely bland American fare that leaned way too heavily on potatoes. The media food paled in comparison to the fancier cuisine the players enjoyed, and I regularly salivated at their spreads when they were set up near the practice courts. Still, I couldn't complain too much because there were always vegetarian options and, later, a thin room service menu. The worst of the bubble food, though, was atrocious: I started randomly pranking friends by texting them photos of the veggie meat loaf, which arrived as a large, dark brown brick. Guaranteed puke-face emoji every time.

My favorite new perk was the expanded walking area. The oval loop was a flat, two-lane road that surrounded the entire Coronado Springs Resort. Covered fences and dense woods separated the bubble campus from nearby roads, officers patrolled the loop regularly and sat near the two main entrances, and signs warned bubble inhabitants not to leave the secured portions of the property. A second round of more ominous signs noted that there was twenty-four-hour video surveillance of the loop, and I spotted not-so-discreet cameras attached to light poles and street signs.

Walking clockwise from the back of the Casitas, where the media were housed, I passed the Ranchos and the Cabanas, a pair of empty vacation resorts. Then came the players' entrance to the Gran Destino Tower and the adjacent Convention Center, where teams practiced in ballrooms. The back side of the Convention Center featured a series of loading docks, including the bubble's shipping depot. Finally, there was a guarded side entrance and the Casitas just beyond the shipping depot. That was it. The whole loop took about thirty minutes to walk.

My favorite stop on the loop was the 28,300-square-foot shipping depot, and I checked in almost every day even if I wasn't expecting a package. The depot, which served as the central receiving area for all bubble inhabitants, felt like a combination of an airplane hangar and a Costco designed exclusively for millionaire professional athletes. According to NBA figures, the facility handled an average of 700 packages per day, topping out at 1,200. The FedEx, UPS, and DHL trucks were ever present, and I watched on numerous occasions as a full-size delivery truck unloaded all its contents at the depot's entrance.

No place in the bubble better reflected the wealth standard of the NBA community than the depot, which ran like clockwork thanks to dedicated staffers who worked long hours spraying every package upon arrival before sorting all of them alphabetically. Individual signs marked off large mounds of packages for the twenty-two teams near the front entrance. The media's much smaller piles were off to the left side, and dozens of pallets of disinfecting wipes, stacked ten feet high, were off to the right. While many online retailers suffered shortages of cleaning supplies during the early months of the pandemic, the depot was the Fort Knox of Clorox.

I have no way to prove this, but the total value of items shipped to the bubble surely ran into the millions of dollars. Flat-screen HDTVs, oversized mattresses, microwaves and other home appliances, Peloton bikes, pinball machines, and arcade-style video games sat untouched for weeks. There were full-size basketball hoops, barrels of free sneakers from Adidas, countless exercise machines, personal protective equipment, and daily alcohol deliveries. Sponsors and wanna-be sponsors sent free gear, hoping that the players would wear it on campus or show it off on social media. The Campbell Soup Company even sent more than 2,000 cans of Chunky soup to Udonis Haslem because the Miami Heat veteran had mentioned that he was eating a lot of it in the bubble.

This was the new routine: Wake up, get tested, do a morning round of work, eat lunch, go for a walk, check the depot, get cleaned up, go to the arena, watch a few games, attend a few press conferences, and stay up late writing about it. Rinse and repeat. In the middle of that scripted daily existence, it was easy to lose track of how the coronavirus was shaping lives outside the bubble and how it was influencing every aspect of life inside the bubble.

There was one big scare: A colleague living inside the bubble texted me to say that a media member had tested positive. According to my colleague, that media member had second-tier access: They could call games from the arenas but didn't live full-time in the bubble. Still, an outbreak was possible, and a confirmed positive test would be major headline news.

As I investigated the incident, the rush of paranoia that I felt when I first left quarantine returned. Should I ride the shuttle bus? Should I go to the arena? Should I just stay in my room? Within a few hours, I confirmed that the media member who tested positive had done so after leaving the bubble. The person had never tested positive while working at Disney World. No one else had tested positive in recent days. Disaster averted. I scrapped my half-written story and breathed a deep sigh of relief.

There was one day off before the playoffs, which gave me some time to think after attending two games a day for two weeks straight. I realized that the bubble had already survived its biggest test by holding up under the weight of twenty-two teams. The campus, down to sixteen teams in mid-August, would shrink to eight by Labor Day. Fewer teams meant fewer games, fewer people, fewer social interactions, and fewer potential weak links. Keeping everyone healthy was only going to get easier. I finally cracked open my 3,600-piece Lamborghini Lego set, which had sat untouched since I arrived, and thought about my compromised medical privacy and the byzantine regulations that shaped bubble life.

I concluded that the alternative was far worse. Florida averaged more than 10,000 new cases per day throughout late July, yet the bubble hadn't been penetrated once. We were all following best practices with regards to masks and distancing, and we were being tested daily. If the entire country could follow only those steps, the national response would be so much more effective.

In a way, the dystopian Big Brother elements of my new life represented a public health utopia. Deep in Central Florida, I was getting a taste of what life was like in Taiwan, New Zealand, and other foreign countries that had been hailed for their coronavirus response. The rules and routines bogged me down, but I felt thankful for my privileges. And guilty about them too.

On September 10, Greg Jaffe of the *Washington Post* published a lengthy feature about the Star Motel in Kissimmee, Florida. As Jaffe wrote, the motel was ravaged by the pandemic and subsequent economic downturn. The motel's owner abandoned the property, the residents lived without power, and drug abuse and crime were rampant. The piece, and the accompanying photos, painted a terrifying picture of how the coronavirus was pushing people and businesses past the breaking point.

The Star Motel was just eight miles away from the Coronado Springs Resort, where I was staying, and only a few miles past the arenas where I spent most of my days. The bubble and the Star represented the starkest, side-by-side divide between the haves and have-nots that I had experienced since teaching in Baltimore public schools while attending Johns Hopkins. What did it say about our national priorities that the wealthy could find a way to safely play games in pursuit of a billion dollars while, just down the road, the destitute were squatting in dark, unsafe, abandoned buildings with no access to health care?

This wasn't a new American story, but a grotesque distillation of an age-old one.

10

Swept Out

Other than the Bucks, Lakers, and Clippers, the two teams I was most curious to watch in the playoffs were the Philadelphia 76ers and Houston Rockets. Both had All-Star talent and past postseason experience. Both had coaches on the hot seat and questions about their chemistry. Most importantly, both played unorthodox styles that could potentially reveal how bubble basketball was different from normal basketball. The answers on the Sixers came almost immediately, thanks to a riveting collapse.

Philadelphia had an impressive roster on paper, and its collection of name players had convinced me before the season that a conference finals trip was possible. Joel Embiid was a bona fide franchise center with a massive frame that made him a force on both ends. Ben Simmons was a former No. 1 pick—a six-foot-ten point guard with impeccable vision and the ability to defend multiple positions. Tobias Harris was a floor-spacing forward who averaged nearly 20 points per game but didn't need to dominate the ball. Al Horford was the prized free agent acquisition, a heady big man plucked off the rival Boston Celtics. Josh Richardson was a quality two-way wing who could fit in as a fifth option and complete a well-rounded defense.

While the rest of the league was prioritizing shooting, Philadelphia built itself around Simmons, a total non-shooter, and Embiid, a willing but inconsistent one. While modern trends focused on downsized line-ups and interchangeable wings, Philadelphia loaded up on size and worried less about versatility. While other top contenders ran their offenses outside-in through perimeter playmakers, Philadelphia's attack shaded more toward an inside-out approach with Embiid.

The Sixers were zagging where others zigged, and it hadn't worked all that well. They entered the playoffs with a 43-30 record and the No. 6 seed, matched up with the Celtics, who had claimed the 3rd seed with a

48-24 record. Philadelphia had its moments during the regular season, including an impressive Christmas Day win over the Bucks in which Embiid had convincingly outplayed Giannis Antetokounmpo. For the most part, though, they underperformed with an average offense and a seventh-ranked defense that never fully lived up to expectations. Embiid and Horford weren't clicking, and Simmons's shooting woes led to constant spacing problems.

After hearing hot seat talk for years, coach Brett Brown was now facing a do-or-die postseason. The affable Maine native had been hired in 2013 to oversee a deep rebuilding effort known as "The Process," and his boundless optimism became the franchise's defining characteristic as it won fewer than twenty games in his first three seasons. But Brown's patience paid off when then the Sixers drafted Embiid and Simmons, beginning their gradual transformation into a perennial winner. In his seventh season, Brown now needed to prove that he was still connecting with his players and that he had the right skill set to oversee a deep playoff run. Turning around a losing program was a different task than lifting a good team to greatness.

The Sixers were a perfect bubble bellwether. They had played well at home and horribly on the road during the regular season, but now every game would take place at a neutral site. Would that help their raw talent shine through? Alternatively, would their lineup and fit questions be even more obvious in an empty gym? Would a team with several potential breaking points and chemistry concerns be able to keep it together while isolated from the outside world?

When making predictions, I tried to evaluate players and teams by setting aside their best days and their worst days in search of their baselines. That approach left me skeptical of the Sixers. I just wasn't convinced they could flip a switch and raise their game no matter how many times Brown insisted that his big and physical team was "built for the playoffs." I also worried about injury issues, given that Embiid and Simmons were often in and out of the lineup.

My suspicions deepened when Brown decided to shift Simmons out of the point guard role in favor of the unheralded Shake Milton once the

Sixers arrived at the bubble. This was a clear demotion for Simmons and a sign that Philadelphia didn't trust its own philosophical approach. Only a desperate coach would attempt such a radical move right before the playoffs.

The role shift became a footnote when Simmons suffered a knee injury midway through the third quarter of an August 5 win over the Wizards. There was no major contact or collision. Simmons simply grabbed at the top of his knee after landing hard on his left leg while rebounding. Within days, he left the bubble to undergo surgery to address a dislocated kneecap. He didn't return, ending his bubble stay after just three games.

For a player who missed his entire rookie year due to a foot injury and spent the hiatus rehabilitating from a back injury, this was another tough and untimely break. The Sixers were left shaken and in disbelief. "He really has worked physically to come back stronger," a disappointed Brown said of Simmons. "I feel bad for him that this situation has happened after all the hard work he put in. You're just numb to it. You coach who you have. I do genuinely believe that this can galvanize our group and bring us, in an inverted way, together."

Brown's spin was unconvincing. By the time the playoffs started, there were teams that had adjusted to their new environments and teams that hadn't. Philadelphia was in the latter category, dropping three of its first four games after losing Simmons.

Unfortunately for the Sixers, the Celtics had settled into bubble life nicely. Anyone could have predicted the winner of Game 1 of their first-round series simply by watching the two teams warm up. Boston jumped around, laughing and loose. Philadelphia sleepwalked, flat and tight. The Celtics looked like they genuinely enjoyed one another's company and were focused with playoff intensity. The Sixers looked like preteens forced by their parents to participate in a school play.

Embiid, the biggest and most respected player in the series, seemed like he was carrying the weight of the world on his shoulders. Brown was on edge, quick to leap from his seat to shout instructions or to berate a referee, while Boston coach Brad Stevens watched placidly.

All of Philadelphia's strategic bets backfired one by one in Game 1. Using big lineups left the Sixers struggling to keep up with the Celtics' perimeter trio of Kemba Walker, Jayson Tatum, and Jaylen Brown. Playing Embiid and Horford together led to poor spacing on offense and constant mismatches on defense, and the Sixers were outscored by 18 points in Horford's thirty-one minutes. Playing through Embiid on offense worked at times, but he struggled with turnovers and grew fatigued down the stretch. Boston's more flexible and potent lineups outlasted Philadelphia thanks to a strong fourth-quarter push. "I've got to do more," said Embiid, who finished with 26 points and 16 rebounds. "I've got one job to do: carry us."

This was the right leadership sentiment, but Philadelphia's issues were bigger than one man could fix. Boston had won Game 1 going away despite shooting the ball poorly and losing forward Gordon Hayward to a bad ankle injury. What's more, the Celtics' undersized front line, led by Daniel Theis, and active team defense had held up well against Embiid.

Game 2 saw Brett Brown replace Horford with rookie Matisse Thybulle in the starting lineup. This was a logical move: Thybulle was a disruptive and intelligent defensive wing who matched up better with Boston's stars. But like the Simmons shift, it also revealed Brown's lack of trust in his central players. Horford, who was signed away from Boston to help defeat his former team, was now relegated to a reserve role in a must-win game.

Boston got hot in Game 2, and Philadelphia never stood a chance in a 128–101 drubbing. Tatum hit eight 3-pointers to score 33 points. The Thybulle maneuver was of little help, as Philadelphia was outscored by a whopping 30 points in his twenty-four minutes. Embiid plugged away for 34 points and 10 rebounds, but he knew he was Sisyphus in sneakers with the game decided shortly after halftime. Harris was a nonfactor, Horford didn't offer much in his new role, and the Sixers' bench was badly outplayed.

"It got deflating when their shot-makers went bananas," Brett Brown said, careful to credit Boston rather than criticize his wavering team's effort. "If the planet were normal, we would be going back to Philadelphia. The message is some level of belief."

Embiid also yearned for the comforts of home. "We're in a bubble," he said. "Obviously, it would be a different story if we were actually going back to Philly because we never seem to lose in front of our fans."

It was only natural for their minds to be on the Wells Fargo Center. The Sixers went 29-2 at home before the hiatus, the best mark in the league. They were 4-2 at home during the 2019 playoffs, with all four wins coming by double digits. Without Simmons, with Tatum going nuts, and with younger players asked to step up into new roles, they needed the boost that comes from a home crowd in the playoffs. They were openly admitting they needed it too.

The Sixers were drowning, and their minds were on lifeboats that were never going to come. Embiid, who was becoming more demoralized with each loss, lamented Philadelphia's defensive approach on Tatum. "Jayson has been killing it," Embiid said. "You have to find a way to get the ball out of his hands. I know they want me to stay back on all pick-and-rolls to protect the basket. We've got to make adjustments. Something's got to change. It feels too easy. He's walking into those shots."

After Game 1, Embiid had accepted responsibility. After Game 2, he was laying blame at his coach's feet. Teams implode every year during the playoffs, but the bubble offered a zoomed-in look at Philadelphia's struggles. During a normal year, Embiid and Brett Brown would have sat on raised podiums with ten or fifteen feet of separation from the media. Here, they gave interviews in cramped hallways and in rooms that were the size of a small home office. As Embiid shuffled around in sandals, I felt his exhaustion and waning hope. When Brown, with his shirt collar unbuttoned, leaned back in his chair to dispute pointed questions about his future, a sense of dread was palpable.

Game 3 was Philadelphia's last hope to salvage some pride and make this a series. With Philadelphia clinging to a 94–92 lead, Embiid drew a double-team on the left block and eyed an open Harris in the right corner. Instead of passing to Horford, who was open cutting hard to the hoop, Embiid tossed a flat cross-court pass that Marcus Smart managed to intercept. The turnover reversed the game's momentum and launched the Celtics on a 10–0 closing run to win 102–94. Philadelphia could barely get a clean shot down the stretch, and Boston put away the game at the foul line.

Minutes later, the Sixers were back facing the media yet again. Brett Brown insisted he wasn't thinking about getting axed, and he artfully avoided singling out Embiid for his crucial turnover.

"If we had to do it again, there were other targets that were open," Brown said. "We made the wrong read and there's the game. Because it's exacerbated and more pronounced in crunch time, it stands out." Of course, Embiid—not "we"—had made the wrong read. But the last thing the Sixers could afford was another fault line between coach and superstar.

When Toronto's Kawhi Leonard hit a four-bounce buzzer-beater in Game 7 to eliminate Philadelphia from the second round of the 2019 playoffs, Embiid sobbed openly in the back hallway. That was a heartbreaking and improbable defeat, one that caught everyone off guard. Losing Game 3 to the Celtics triggered in Embiid a detached despair rather than a repeat of his emotional outpouring.

Embiid sat in a cutoff T-shirt, sounding anxious to leave the building as quickly as possible. When one final question came in from the Zoom monitor, Embiid covered his face with his hand, closed his eyes, stroked his temples, and pinched his fingers together at the top of his nose.

To me, this was one of the most enduring images from the bubble. Embiid looked like he had stepped in dog poop or spilled red wine on white carpet. Without much time to process the loss and without space to compose himself, Embiid was exposed and vulnerable just like he was after the Game 7 loss to the Raptors. Every part of his body was acting in concert to declare that he couldn't believe what was happening.

"You can't give up," he said, trying to gather himself. "I don't want to be swept. I don't want that in my résumé. I've been playing my butt

off. It's tough. Man, it sucks when you play super hard and do everything possible to win games and you come up short."

Boston had no interest in letting Philadelphia off the hook. In
Game 4, Tatum cemented himself as the best player in the series with
28 points and 15 rebounds, while Walker got loose for a game-high
32 points. Brett Brown, Richardson, and Harris received technical
fouls when their frustration boiled over at various points. The Celtics seized control in the third quarter and held off the Sixers' frantic
fourth-quarter rally.

It was too little, too late. Boston completed its sweep with a 110–106
victory, leaving Philadelphia to process the sudden end to its season. As
members of the Sixers media wished Brown well and said their good-
byes over Zoom, the coach lamented his team's injury issues and took
responsibility for their disastrous playoff result.

"The job of an NBA head coach is to take the team you have and
maximize it," Brown said. "I did not do that. We came in and talked
about smash mouth, bully ball, and that we're built for the playoffs. We
have a huge team, a big team. The thing I found the most challenging
as the season played out, space became an enormous issue. Effectively,
you had a mismatch every time down the court."

In that moment, Brown sounded exactly like every Sixers skeptic
from the past ten months. The doubts had proven true, decisively, and
there was no longer any point in denying them. If Brown seemed at
peace with what was to come, Embiid sounded confused, disappointed,
and defensive. He deflected a question about Brown's future, saying
that he was "not the GM," and offered a noncommittal response when
asked about his future with the Sixers. "I always say I want to end my
career here. If it happens, good. If it doesn't happen, well, you move on
and all that stuff."

Embiid's most interesting statement, by far, came in response to
critics who argued that he made life easier for his opponents by settling
too often for jumpers rather than dominating around the basket. TNT's
Shaquille O'Neal and Charles Barkley were two of the most prominent
NBA voices banging this drum. The talk clearly bothered Embiid, who

didn't have the luxury of playing in the 1980s and 1990s, when big men weren't expected to be as active, versatile, and quick as they are in the modern game.

"A lot of people always want me to be a big man, to be Shaq," Embiid said. "But this league, and this game, is completely different. They call a bunch of offensive fouls all the time. You can't use your elbow. You can't push people all over the place. You can't post up as much anymore. You've got to move the ball. I've just got to work on my game and fit whatever the team wants me to be. I can be dominant down low, but it's not always about me. It's about the team."

There was plenty of truth in what Embiid said, even if some perceived it as whining. The game was vastly different from previous eras, a fact made clear by the relative impact of Tatum and Embiid. The twenty-two-year-old Tatum was still years away from his prime, but his 3-point shooting and deep range created far more problems for Philadelphia's defense than Embiid's size did for Boston's defense.

Critics who wanted Embiid to tighten up his shot selection and reduce his reliance on low-efficiency midrange shots had a point, as did detractors who argued that the Sixers had gone as far as they would ever go under Brown. The biggest issue, though, was that Philadelphia general manager Elton Brand had constructed a roster in 2020 that would have been far more successful in 1990, 2000, or even 2010. Big changes were needed immediately.

Because of the bubble's condensed schedule, which saw teams play every other day early in the playoffs, the Sixers' postseason run was over in the blink of an eye. By August 24, exactly one week after the playoffs opened, Brown was fired. "Unfortunately, we fell well short of our goals this year and I believe it is best to go in a new direction," Brand said in a brief statement, acknowledging that the Sixers were entering an "important offseason" and that they needed to "get back on track" toward title contention.

The bubble had stripped the Sixers bare, forcing them to contemplate existential questions they had spent months trying to avoid.

11

Boycott

The morning after the Sixers were eliminated, I woke up bleary-eyed to face a new week. It was a Monday, but the days of the week were meaningless by that point. I had been living at Disney World for forty-three days, almost the halfway point. I was at the arenas covering multiple games seven nights a week. My life was an endless blur: podcast, story, game, postgame, story, podcast, game, radio interview. There were no days off.

Other reporters were heading home and getting replaced by their colleagues, but I was in it for the long haul. I didn't let myself imagine the end. One day, one game, one assignment, one step at a time.

I walked in the sun for at least an hour every afternoon, but otherwise my life was consumed by the playoffs. I was holding up well, all things considered, mostly because I was getting to see season-long story lines pay off from courtside seats and arm's-length interviews. I had already decided on a new goal: Once the second round of the playoffs began, I wanted to attend every remaining game. With a maximum of two games per day at that point, I figured I could handle the workload and leave the bubble with an accomplishment that might never be duplicated. To put it mildly, I was in deep.

With so much going on inside the bubble, anything that happened outside my small corner of Disney World might as well have taken place on the moon. I followed the latest election news and coronavirus headlines, but the bubble's physical and emotional isolation was intense.

One of my few regular contacts with the real world came on Monday mornings, when I checked in with Jason Murray, my *Washington Post* editor, by telephone. With the Sixers eliminated, I was ready to shift my focus to Dallas Mavericks sensation Luka Doncic and his first-round dogfight with the Clippers. Murray had more pressing business to discuss. "There was another shooting caught on video," he said. "The tape is bad. Really bad. You'll need to be ready to write once the players react."

Murray's grave tone sent me rushing to find the video of a white police officer shooting Jacob Blake, a twenty-nine-year-old Black man, multiple times in the back in Kenosha, Wisconsin. News reports didn't yet have all the details, but Blake was reportedly attempting to enter his vehicle following a domestic incident, and three of his children were present at the time of the shooting. Blake, who survived but was left paralyzed from the waist down, didn't appear to be acting aggressively on the video before he was shot.

I had spent a lot of time pondering how the bubble's inhabitants would react if there were a coronavirus outbreak or another George Floyd–like incident. Now it was here, during a moment of high tension. The players had been at Disney World for well over a month, and they had been playing every other day for weeks. The postseason stakes only added to the stress. What's more, they were separated from their friends and family, unable to comfort their loved ones or answer their children's questions. They wouldn't be able to join protests in the streets, a fact that some players had used months earlier to argue that they shouldn't compete in the bubble at all.

For those reasons, I expected anger, disgust, and coordinated activism from the players, who had regularly paid tribute to Floyd and Breonna Taylor while in the bubble. But I wasn't prepared in the slightest for what unfolded.

That night, after the Lakers beat the Blazers to take a 3–1 lead in their first-round playoff series, LeBron James reflected at length on the Blake shooting. He pointed out that Blake was shot while his children watched helplessly, and he questioned why the officers felt the need to fire seven times when they "could have tackled him or grabbed him." James said that Blake survived "through the grace of God," and he sent prayers to Blake's family and to Kenosha, a city with a population of roughly 100,000 located forty miles south of Milwaukee.

"We are scared as Black people in America," James said, noting that he and his childhood friends had hidden from police officers out of fear. "Black men, Black women, Black kids, we are terrified. You have no idea how that cop left the house. You don't know if he woke up on the good side of the bed or the wrong side of the bed. You don't know if he had an argument at home with his significant other or one of his kids said something crazy and he left the house steaming. Maybe he just left the house saying, 'Today is going to be the end for one of these Black people.' That's what it feels like. It just hurts."

Without hesitating, James then touched a third rail of American politics. "Guns are a huge issue in America," he said, returning to an issue he had raised following a 2018 school shooting in Parkland, Florida. "They're not just used for hunting, like a lot of people do for sport. For Black people right now, when you're hunting, we think you're hunting us."

James was hardly alone in expressing his outrage, but many of his fellow players began voicing a different message: that the bubble games shouldn't go on as scheduled. Toronto Raptors guard Fred VanVleet said that a boycott of playoff games was "being talked about" because "taking a knee is not getting it done."

"If we're going to sit here and talk about making change, then at some point we're going to have to put our nuts on the line," VanVleet continued. "What are we willing to give up? Do we actually give a fuck about what's going on or is it just cool to wear Black Lives Matter on the backdrop or wear a T-shirt?"

Celtics guard Marcus Smart added that sitting out was "something in the back of our mind" because "there's more important things than basketball right now." Bucks guard George Hill said that "we shouldn't have even came to this damn place, to be honest. I think coming here just took all the focus off what the issues are." On Twitter, Jazz guard Donovan Mitchell was as blunt as possible: "F THE GAMES AND PLAYOFFS!!! THIS IS SICK AND A REAL PROBLEM. WE DEMAND JUSTICE!"

From the start, I took seriously the conversations about a possible boycott because I knew it would only take one conscientious objector to trigger perhaps the biggest NBA story of the year. There was a lingering sentiment about the bubble distracting from the social justice cause dating back to Kyrie Irving's initial objections months earlier. Blake's shooting represented a crossroads.

There hadn't been an NBA boycott in my lifetime, although the Clippers had seriously considered the idea in 2014 after a tape of racist comments made by owner Donald Sterling leaked. The bubble boycott talk put the NBA league office in a bind. It was one thing for Adam Silver to waive an outdated rule about standing during the national anthem or to put the statement that Black Lives Matter on the court. It would be a much more difficult and delicate situation if players refused to take the court during the middle of the playoffs.

The commissioner's options weren't great. He could punish dissenting players by ruling that a boycotted game was a forfeit and by withholding their salaries to compel them back to the court. He could look the other way and cross his fingers that the players would return quickly and voluntarily. He could try to make a grand gesture of support in response to Blake's shooting and hope the players would accept his olive branch. He could theoretically postpone or cancel games if need be, but that might encourage players to pull the plug on the entire experiment.

Remember, any player was free to leave the bubble at any time for any reason. They just needed to go through a quarantine upon their return—if there was a return. If prominent players or even a full team decided to stop playing, the bubble's integrity would be in serious jeopardy just like if there had been a coronavirus outbreak. How many departures could the NBA withstand before the playoff bracket would collapse and the remaining games would be devalued? If even one team or one superstar left, wouldn't the eventual champion be viewed with an asterisk?

All of Monday's games went on like usual. Ditto for Tuesday's games, including the Clippers' 154–111 blowout of the Mavericks. Despite the victory, Doc Rivers, who had coached the Clippers during the Sterling incident, was overcome with emotion during his postgame press conference.

"Just watching the Republican convention, and they're spewing this fear," said Rivers, fifty-eight, who is Black. "All you hear is Donald

Trump and all of them talking about fear. We're the ones getting killed. We're the ones getting shot. We're the ones who were denied to live in certain communities. We've been hung. We've been shot. All you keep hearing about is fear. It's amazing why we keep loving this country and this country does not love us back.

"If you watch that video, you don't need to be Black to be outraged. You need to be American and outraged. How dare the Republicans talk about fear. We're the ones that need to be scared. What white father has to give his son a talk about being careful if you get pulled over? It's just ridiculous. It keeps going. There's no charges. Breonna Taylor: no charges, nothing. All we're asking is you live up to the Constitution for everybody."

Like James, Rivers's fear and pain resonated with people well outside the NBA universe. In that moment, it struck me that Rivers was perhaps the most qualified person to weigh in on a possible boycott. He had been in the locker room in 2014 when the Clippers had seriously considered the idea, he was as outraged as anyone now, and he was one of the most respected voices in the league.

I asked Rivers point-blank: "What is your advice for players who are mulling a boycott over the Blake shooting?" It was late at night, and he paused a moment to consider the hypothetical.

"My message is go after your dreams," Rivers said. "You don't allow anything to take you away from your dreams. During the Donald Sterling thing, Matt Barnes, Chris Paul, DeAndre Jordan, Blake Griffin and JJ Redick all pulled together. When we were little kids, in the backyard by ourselves and we had these dreams about winning a championship, Donald Sterling was not in our dreams and neither were these cops."

Playing, Rivers argued, was its own statement. Rather than boycott in 2014, the Clippers staged a protest by taking off their warm-up jackets at center court before a game, obscuring the team's logo by wearing their T-shirts inside out, and donning black wristbands and socks. Silver acted swiftly in response to Sterling's statements, banishing the longtime owner for life and facilitating the franchise's sale to Microsoft billionaire Steve Ballmer.

"I think you always play," Rivers said. "We can fight for justice, but we should still do our jobs. I really believe that. By doing our jobs, people are seeing excellence from Americans—Black Americans and white Americans. I would still do my job."

I wasn't surprised that Rivers landed where he did. An NBA lifer, he began his playing career in 1984 and had coached for the last twenty-one seasons in a row. He was fiercely competitive and totally invested in the Clippers' title push. What's more, he had just demonstrated that he was capable of balancing his work and his activism.

But Rivers didn't leave his answer there. As his press conference wrapped, he added what I took to be a crucial footnote. "If my players told me no, it would be no," he said to me. If the games were going to continue without incident, Rivers wouldn't have felt the need to say that. And if there was going to be a stare down between the players and the owners, Rivers was picking his side.

The Raptors, who swept the Nets in the first round, were scheduled to open their second-round series with the Celtics on Thursday. VanVleet and Smart sounded serious, and their feelings were unlikely to ease over the next forty-eight hours. Meanwhile, athletes from across the sporting world were expressing their outrage over Blake's shooting.

Protests were picking up in Kenosha, where a state of emergency was declared and the National Guard was deployed, and in other cities around the country. On Tuesday night, seventeen-year-old Kyle Rittenhouse allegedly shot three protesters with a semiautomatic rifle, killing two, after driving to Kenosha from his home in Illinois. Video of Rittenhouse firing his weapon spread on social media, as did another video of him walking toward police officers without being arrested.

As that chaotic, awful scene was playing out, I stayed up late to write a story on Rivers's comments about the boycott. Then I went to bed, uneasy.

* * *

The NBA scheduled a tripleheader for Wednesday, August 26, and I planned to be at all three games. Despite everything circling in the news, the playoff stories marched on.

Giannis Antetokounmpo and the Bucks had the chance to close out the Orlando Magic in Game 5 of their first-round series. Then, with their series tied 2–2, the Houston Rockets and Oklahoma City Thunder would face off in a pivotal Game 5 between former teammates James Harden and Chris Paul. In the nightcap, LeBron James and the Lakers, holding a 3–1 lead, would seek to eliminate the Blazers.

The NBA's postseason schedule was unrelenting, but a lineup like that made me marvel. On a single day, I would get to see the three finalists for 2020 MVP—Antetokounmpo, Harden, and James—plus future Hall of Famers like Paul, Anthony Davis, and possibly Russell Westbrook, who was due back soon from a leg injury. That same day, two of the top three contenders—the Bucks and Lakers—could advance to the conference semifinals.

There were so much going on within the playoffs, to say nothing of the Blake shooting, that I resolved earlier in the week to break my self-imposed limit of two games in a day. I arrived at AdventHealth Arena shortly before the 4:10 p.m. tip-off to find that most of my media colleagues had skipped the first game of the day. I wasn't surprised.

Despite Antetokounmpo, the small-market Bucks didn't move the needle like the Rockets or the Lakers. Milwaukee had taken total control of its series with three consecutive double-digit wins over Orlando, and Game 5 figured to be a run-of-the-mill victory. The Bucks under coach Mike Budenholzer also kept a low profile, leaning heavily on platitudes during their postgame press conferences. If not for my intense interest in Antetokounmpo's career arc, which had built up over years of tracking his remarkable progress from life as an unknown Greek teenager, I would have waited for the Rockets and Lakers games too.

I took an empty seat in the front row of the media section and went through my typical pregame routine, plugging in my laptop, setting up a bottle of iced tea and a can of sparkling water, and charging my iPhone and Bose noise-canceling headphones. Satisfied that everything was in order, I stashed my backpack under my chair, sat down, and looked up to survey the court with about twenty minutes on the game clock before tip-off. I had developed a habit of milling around before games to capture video of warm-up dunks and photos of star players for Instagram; the demand for this type of content from diehard fans far exceeded the supply offered by the small media contingent.

Before I headed down to the baseline, I noticed something that I had never seen before in my thirteen years of covering NBA games or in my thirty years of attending them: There was only one team on the court. Everything else looked normal. The Magic were going through their typical layup lines to my left. The three referees were standing near center court in their uniforms, and the scorer's table was ready to go inside the plexiglass box. The Bucks' graphics were on the videoboards. The arena lights were on, and the music was thumping.

But the Bucks were nowhere to be found.

Doc Rivers's comments about the boycott popped into my head, but I didn't want to rush to any conclusions. I checked Twitter and didn't see anything out of the ordinary, so I decided to take a lap around the back hallways to see what I might discover.

As I left my seat, I alerted Jason Murray, my editor, that we were possibly looking at a boycott and that we should get to work on a coverage plan. Time was precious this late in the afternoon, as there were only a few hours left before the first deadline to get a story in the paper. Still, I wanted to err on the side of caution. I had seen players wait until the last minute before taking the court, and there was always the possibility—however remote—that the Bucks were having a team meeting in the locker room and that they would rush out just in the nick of time.

The Magic were still the only team on the court when it was time for pregame introductions. The Bucks' ball boy was standing with his arms crossed under the hoop. The referees were jogging and stretching, giving Milwaukee every chance to show up. At 3:54 p.m., I tweeted: "The Orlando Magic have been warming up by themselves for about 10 minutes. No sign yet of the Milwaukee Bucks just minutes before scheduled tip." Not long after that, the Magic left the court and retreated to their locker room.

Before I followed the Magic to the back, I asked Monty McCutchen, the NBA's vice president of referee development, what would happen if the Bucks never showed up. McCutchen had developed a well-earned reputation as one of the league's best officials during a long career before moving into his management role. An affable guy and the rules czar, he loved to talk hoops and explain the intricacies of officiating.

If anyone knew and could explain how and when the league would determine a forfeit or a postponement, it was McCutchen. The NBA occasionally postponed or canceled games due to inclement weather, and the league delayed a Lakers game in January following Kobe Bryant's death. There were established procedures. But McCutchen looked back at me, shrugged, and reluctantly offered, "We've never been here before." I deduced quickly that the man who had spent so much of his life making calls wouldn't be making the call on this one.

"Both teams have cleared the court," I tweeted at 4:01 p.m., alongside a photo of the lonely referees and empty hardwood. "Protocol for how or when to declare a forfeit or postponement remains unclear. Bucks have expressed outrage over Jacob Blake police shooting in recent days."

NBA Twitter loved to connect the dots, and word of a possible boycott spread instantly. After all, Hill had questioned whether games should go on that week, the Bucks were Wisconsin's only NBA team, and they played their home games less than one hour from Kenosha.

I left the gym and walked through the hallway toward the Magic locker room. In pre-pandemic times, there was always a buzz in an arena before a game, especially during the postseason. Players jumped up and down and shouted encouragements to one another. Fans clutched food and drinks while heading to their seats. Mascots and dance team members made their final preparations. It was a time for anticipation, nervous energy, and noise.

The hallways in the bubble were always much quieter, with no fans and far fewer arena staffers, but now they were a ghost town. All I saw were bags of workout equipment, exercise bikes, hand sanitizer stations, and piles of cords used for the television broadcasts. No players. No coaches. No people. No noise.

I kept walking slowly so that I could take a long look at the Magic's locker room, and I caught a glimpse of Nikola Vucevic's face through the partially closed door. The All-Star center, still wearing his full uniform and warm-ups, looked back at the entryway with his hands on his hips. His quizzical expression matched my internal monologue: *What the heck is going on?*

I kept walking through the concourse toward the Bucks' locker room. Before I got there, I encountered a few league officials taking phone calls and typing out text messages as well as a few security guards. One official told me, "You can't be here." I wasn't fazed. As a reporter, "You can't be here" was an occupational hazard. That wasn't the first time I would be ejected for no good reason, and it certainly wouldn't be the last.

A guard directed me farther down the hallway to a makeshift holding area. The locker room was closed as I walked past, and I couldn't make out any voices clearly. Two other reporters were already standing vigil, and quiet still reigned.

Gradually, the pieces started coming together. The Bucks hadn't left the AdventHealth Arena, because their bus was still waiting for them. The players were still in their locker room, because voices occasionally traveled through the walls. The coaches were nowhere to be found, so they were likely in there too. League staffers and Bucks employees looked like they had been caught off guard, but no one was panicking.

The locker room had only one way in and one way out, so the players couldn't leave the arena without walking past reporters. The Bucks were inside a converted equipment storage room that had a maximum COVID-era capacity of forty-nine people and lacked a private bathroom. While the players might remain out of sight for a few hours, they wouldn't be able to hide forever. This was a good old-fashioned standoff. The Bucks had to know that the media wouldn't leave without hearing from them. If they tried to make a run for the bus, reporters would shout questions and cameras would film their exit.

By 4:18 p.m., a young staffer started packing up the rack of basketballs in a green travel bag. Game 5 wasn't going to take place. By 4:25 p.m., my first-run story, which I had written on my iPhone from the holding pen and sent via Slack to my editor, went live: "The Orlando Magic showed up for their NBA playoff game. The Milwaukee Bucks didn't, days after the police shooting of Jacob Blake in Wisconsin. A history-making boycott is underway in the Bubble." One tweet from the *Washington Post*'s official account that linked to the story drew more than 10,000 retweets and 26,000 likes, exceeding the interest in a typical NBA bubble story by a factor of 100.

The wait was on. Within the hour, top editors at the *Washington Post* were clearing room for the Bucks on A1, the front page of the paper. This was a relatively rare move for sports stories. Typically, A1 was reserved for the hardest of hard news, with a heavy emphasis at that point on the Trump administration, the presidential election, congressional politics, and the coronavirus. Big basketball stories—like the Toronto Raptors winning the 2019 title or the bubble opening during the pandemic—generally landed on D1, the front of the Sports section. NBA players boycotting a game to protest a police shooting during a summer defined by social justice activism was an A1 story.

This wasn't just a newspaper thing. While the Bucks would lead ESPN's *SportsCenter*, they would also be a top story on the major networks' nightly news shows. This was a "stop the presses" moment unfolding in real time, and Milwaukee's collective action was the type of attention-grabbing statement that Kyrie Irving and others had sought when they advocated for not playing in the bubble.

As I waited in the hallway, I thought back to perhaps the most famous sports protest of all time: Tommie Smith and John Carlos, two Black runners competing for the United States, raised their black-gloved fists during the national anthem while on the medal stand at the 1968 Olympics. They faced immense backlash from the International Olympic Committee, the media, and viewers.

That protest was more than fifty years ago, but the same national racial tension was present after George Floyd's death. In fact, President Trump had tweeted, "When the looting starts, the shooting starts," on May 29 in response to the initial Floyd protests. That phrase was used by Miami police chief Walter Headley in 1967. It had become popular among writers and commentators to compare the unrest of the late 1960s to 2020, and Trump responded to the protests by preaching a "law and order" message, just as Richard Nixon had in 1968.

It was too early to know how the Bucks' actions would be received by their fellow players, their teams, the NBA, politicians, and the outside world. But most NBA players were Black, most were millionaires, and many had expressed support for racial justice protests and opposition to Trump. That combination of factors made them big and easy targets for detractors, especially those seeking to politicize their action.

As I waited for the Bucks to come out and explain their stand, there were two competing thoughts in my head. First, I wanted them to appear quickly because I was worried about my deadline. Second, I hoped that they understood the enormity of the situation. If they came out unprepared or if they refused to answer questions, the criticism from bad-faith actors was bound to be swift. Months of thoughtful protests by dozens of players were suddenly at risk of being minimized, and I could already imagine talking heads warming up condescending and race-baiting takes.

I spent nearly an hour chewing on those thoughts before two Bucks players finally emerged from the locker room. Khris Middleton, a low-key All-Star forward, was wearing his full sweatsuit as if he had arrived at the gym ready to play. George Hill, who had spoken out about Blake's shooting earlier in the week, was wearing a black T-shirt. They both shuffled by with bowed heads as they went to use the bathroom. Neither said a word; given the circumstances, no writers sought to engage with them. This was an awkward intrusion on their privacy.

Even so, their dress and need to use the restroom signaled that the Bucks' action might not have been fully choreographed. A few players went through their standard individual warm-up routines well before

I arrived at the gym. Why dress for a game if you didn't intend to play? Why huddle up for so long that you needed a bathroom break if you knew exactly what you wanted to say?

Still, there was no answer. I could hear faint conversations going on in the locker room, and at multiple points it sounded like the Bucks were making telephone calls on a speakerphone. Jon Horst, Milwaukee's general manager, was the first authority figure to address the media, telling reporters at 4:40 p.m. that his team was "not coming out for a while" and that the organization would be issuing a statement. An NBA public relations official came by fifteen minutes later, letting us know that the Magic had left the arena and that he didn't expect the Bucks to address the media.

At 5:04 p.m., the NBA issued a press release saying that the Bucks-Magic game was "postponed" and that it would be "rescheduled." There was no mention of a forfeit or punishment, and the NBA was careful not to use the word "boycott." The Bucks, in the eyes of the league office, had decided "to not take the floor." Additionally, Wednesday's two other games were postponed and would be rescheduled.

This statement, which referenced conversations with the National Basketball Players Association, comprised two sentences and sixty-three words. While it provided the answers to the mechanical questions that I had asked McCutchen about an hour earlier, that wasn't going to be enough. Not by a long shot.

The NBA's shuttle bus system ran like clockwork, taking media members from the Casitas to the arenas every thirty minutes. And, like clockwork, a new group of reporters kept showing up for the stakeout every thirty minutes that afternoon. After a few hours, the Bucks had drawn a bigger media crowd than an average Lakers game for the first time all summer.

Antetokounmpo, who was wearing a Black Lives Matter shirt and his game shorts, exited the locker room to use the bathroom. The same scene from earlier repeated: Antetokounmpo walked silently to and from the lavatory, and the anxious reporters left him in peace.

Another hour passed, and I was starting to fray. My iPhone was running low on battery, my laptop was still back at my seat in the arena, and my legs were so tired from standing that I plopped down on the concrete concourse. I was starting to sweat my 8:00 p.m. deadline. Just after 6:00 p.m., my phone lit up.

Alexandria Ocasio-Cortez, a Democratic U.S. representative from New York, had tweeted a link to my story, casting the players' protest as labor activism. "NBA players are courageously on strike (withholding labor), NOT boycotting (withholding their money)," she wrote on Twitter. "The difference is important because it shows their power as workers. The courage this takes is profound. WNBA organizing in this moment MUST be recognized too. #StrikeForBlackLives."

Ocasio-Cortez wasn't the only voice weighing in on the "boycott" versus "strike" debate. Some labor experts preferred "wildcat strike," because the Bucks' action wasn't sanctioned in advance by the National Basketball Players Association.

At 6:15 p.m., the NBA's public relations official brought welcome news: The Bucks planned not only to issue a statement, but also to address the media in person. This was a much better idea than not talking.

The security staffers on hand set up a light barricade in the hallway to physically separate the media from the front of the locker room, where the Bucks planned to issue their statement. There were twenty or so reporters there by that point—all the print writers plus various employees of the television networks—and we lined up like we were covering a Hollywood red carpet. Still, the Bucks didn't emerge. TNT aired a live shot from the tunnel, and their cameras caught me holding my head with both of my hands as the deadline stress mounted.

At 6:45 p.m., Bucks owners Marc Lasry, Wes Edens, and Jamie Dinan issued a joint statement by email: "We fully support our players and the decision they made. Although we did not know beforehand, we would have wholeheartedly agreed with them. The only way to bring about change is to shine a light on the racial injustices that are happening in front of us. Our players have done that and we will continue to stand alongside them and demand accountability and change."

This jibed with some of what I put together while waiting, and it certainly took the edge off the possibility of a protracted labor battle. This wasn't exactly a premeditated action by employees against their employers like many on social media were opining.

Instead, it was shaping up to be an impromptu demonstration against systemic racism by employees who had the backing of their sympathetic bosses. There was no telling how this situation might play out, but any talk of substantial punishment from the Bucks or the NBA office already seemed highly unlikely. Doling out fines, suspensions, or forfeits would have been out of step with the expression of support from Bucks ownership.

A league staffer, who looked tense when the wait began, came over and indirectly confirmed my read of the situation. "You're getting a great chapter for your book," he quipped. That wasn't the first or last time I heard those words that afternoon, but I took it as a sign that a compromise was in the works. If the Bucks or other NBA teams were planning a broader labor stoppage, there wouldn't have been any jokes. Not even gallows humor.

The Bucks emerged from their locker room around 7:15 p.m., more than three hours after the scheduled tip-off time. They had changed into casual clothing, and most sported T-shirts with messages like "Change the narrative" and "Black all the time." More than a few looked nervous, probably because their action had already created a national storm. Antetokounmpo stood with his hands in his pockets. A few of his teammates kept their gazes fixed toward the ground. Most wore masks, conscious of the fact that they would be filmed while standing in a non-socially distant manner.

Hill and Sterling Brown moved to the front of the group. Antetokounmpo was easily the Bucks' best and most famous player, and he would have been their natural spokesman on basketball matters. Instead, Hill emerged as a leading voice for the group. The veteran point guard wore a black T-shirt that bore a long quote from President Barack

Obama: "Change will not come if we wait for some other person, or if we wait for some other time. We are the ones we've been waiting for. We create the change that we seek."

While the thirty-four-year-old Hill was a journeyman who had played for five teams in the previous five seasons, he was one of Milwaukee's most experienced and respected players. He had lobbied for his teammates not to take the court, and he later told Taylor Rooks in a GQ magazine story that his protest was motivated by Blake's shooting and the authorities' treatment of Kyle Rittenhouse.

Brown, twenty-five, was a bit player for Milwaukee, but it made sense when he stepped forward next to Hill. In January 2018, Brown was tasered and arrested by Milwaukee police for a minor parking offense. He sued the city and eventually received a $750,000 settlement, in November 2020. Brown had spoken openly about police misconduct since the incident, and his presence added a personal element to the Bucks' action. He couldn't be written off by critics as a grandstanding millionaire. He had been on the wrong side of police officers who abused their authority in the same state where Blake was shot.

Hill spoke first, apologizing to the reporters for the delay. "We thought it would be best for us as a team to brainstorm a little bit and educate ourselves and not rush into having raw emotion and giving you guys things like that," he said, adding that the Bucks would not take questions. "On behalf of our team, we're going to place a statement as a team today and go back to continue to educate ourselves and get better awareness of what's going on."

In the statement, which was emailed out by Bucks public relations at 7:31 p.m., the organization announced that the team had "boycotted" Game 5.

"The past four months have shed a light on the ongoing racial injustices facing our African American communities," Brown said, reading from a printed copy. "Citizens around the country have used their voices and platforms to speak out against these wrongdoings. Over the last few days in our home state of Wisconsin, we've seen the horrendous video of Jacob Blake being shot in the back seven times by a police officer in

Kenosha, and the additional shooting of protesters. Despite the overwhelming plea for change, there has been no action, so our focus today cannot be on basketball."

Hill picked up from there. "When we take the court and represent Milwaukee and Wisconsin, we are expected to play at a high level, give maximum effort and hold each other accountable," he said. "We hold ourselves to that standard, and in this moment, we are demanding the same from our lawmakers and law enforcement. We are calling for justice for Jacob Blake and demand the officers be held accountable.

"For this to occur, it is imperative for the Wisconsin State Legislature to reconvene after months of inaction and take up meaningful measures to address issues of police accountability, brutality and criminal justice reform. We encourage all citizens to educate themselves, take peaceful and responsible action, and remember to vote on November 3."

With that, the Bucks departed AdventHealth Arena. Reporters rushed to upload videos of the statement and scurried to the nearest keyboards. I had only twenty-six minutes, but I made my deadline.

I packed up my computer and headed for the shuttle bus, snapping one final photograph of the arena at 7:59 p.m. just in case the owners and players couldn't reach a resolution. The hardwood was entirely empty, and the bright lights still illuminated the Black Lives Matter decal and the NBA logo at center court. Towels, intended for use that night, remained untouched in stacks by each bench. The hoops stood tall, waiting. I tweeted out the photo with the caption: "How long will the NBA Bubble's AdventHealth Arena remain empty?"

At that moment, no one knew the answer. NBA commissioner Adam Silver and the owners, NBPA executive director Michele Roberts and her union leaders, the television networks, and the players all had to wait to see how the situation would shake out.

The statement from the Bucks' players made clear their reasoning and included a specific request for action from state officials in Wisconsin, but crucial pieces of the puzzle were still missing. The statement hadn't asked for anything directly from the NBA or its owners. It hadn't provided a timeline for the stoppage, other than to say that "our focus

1. Casitas 4 at Walt Disney World's Coronado Springs Resort was home to media members for more than three months during the NBA bubble in 2020.

2. The author dressed up in a basketball-themed, COVID-friendly outfit before flying to Orlando for the NBA bubble in July.

1. The NBA set up makeshift stations at the arenas to conduct virtual postgame interviews involving players and media members from across the world.

2. Veteran referee Scott Foster (right) helped turned pickleball into one of the most popular activities inside the bubble.

3. Following "Mikey" the egret around the Coronado Springs Resort was the author's favorite pastime during the long summer months inside the bubble.

4. After Rudy Gobert's positive test for COVID-19 shut down the NBA season on March 11, 2020, the Utah Jazz center returned to score the first official points of the bubble.

1. NBA teams practiced inside ballrooms at the Coronado Springs Resort's Convention Center.
2. Members of the Milwaukee Bucks and Houston Rockets kneel during the national anthem as part of a coordinated demonstration against police brutality.

3. Due to space constraints, the media seating at the Visa Center was as close to the action as modern NBA reporters will ever get.

4. Los Angeles Lakers star Anthony Davis peeks in during LeBron James's postgame interview with media members.

1. Sterling Brown (front left) and George Hill (front right) address the media after the Milwaukee Bucks decided not to take the court, to protest the police shooting of Jacob Blake in Kenosha, Wisconsin.

2. During a late-night protest, dozens of activists seeking the arrests of officers involved in the shooting of Salaythis Melvin stopped a charter bus that was transporting media from the ESPN Wide World of Sports Complex to the Coronado Springs Resort.

3. Jamal Murray splashes Coach Michael Malone as the Denver Nuggets celebrate their comeback from a 3–1 deficit to eliminate the Utah Jazz in the first round.

4. Philadelphia 76er Joel Embiid reacts after a painful playoff loss to the Boston Celtics.

5. The AdventHealth Arena at ESPN's Wide World of Sports Complex near Disney World played host to the 2020 NBA Finals.

1. During the NBA Finals, Los Angeles Lakers star LeBron James and other players conducted socially distanced virtual interviews from simple podiums.

2. James celebrates his fourth championship by spraying media members with champagne.

3. The author drenched in champagne courtesy of LeBron James during the Los Angeles Lakers' title celebration.

today cannot be on basketball." Were the Bucks planning to resume the following day, or were they going to wait for the Wisconsin legislature to pass a bill? Those were two different alternatives.

The statement also hadn't included word from the five other teams affected by the shutdown on Wednesday or any of the other teams still residing in the bubble. Later that night, Roberts issued a statement on behalf of the union that said its members "stand with the decision of the players of the Milwaukee Bucks to protest this injustice and support the collective decision to postpone all of today's games." Wildcat strike or not, the players seemed to be unified, although the next steps weren't clear.

The Bucks succeeded in shutting down the bubble, but how and when play resumed would need to be a collective decision. Had the Bucks' stand shifted player sentiment enough that they would pack it up and go home? Had the players simply had enough of living in isolation? Were all these sacrifices still worth it? The best teams were six or seven weeks away from finishing the NBA Finals. After an emotional week and a fraught day, mid-October never seemed further away.

When I got back to my room that night, I messaged a friend who was planning to send me a care package by FedEx. "Wait a few days," I suggested. "Just in case."

12

The Aftermath

On August 27, the *Washington Post*'s A1 headline blared: "Sports halted as players protest Blake shooting." The story landed alongside two dispatches from the Republican National Convention and an update on Kyle Rittenhouse's arrest for allegedly shooting three people at protests of Jacob Blake's shooting by police. The Bucks' statement had broken through and reverberated in many directions.

The WNBA canceled its games on Wednesday. Major League Baseball, already dealing with schedule disruptions due to the pandemic, saw three games called off, including one involving the Milwaukee Brewers. The National Football League's Detroit Lions canceled practice, and five Major League Soccer games were not held. Tennis star Naomi Osaka issued a statement saying that "the continued genocide of Black people at the hand of the police is honestly making me sick to my stomach."

TNT commentator Kenny Smith walked off the *Inside the NBA* set in solidarity. Basketball legend Bill Russell, who once left a 1961 preseason game due to racist behavior from fans in Kentucky, proclaimed that mistreatment of Blacks by police "has to stop" and, quoting civil rights icon John Lewis, that protesters should "keep getting in good trouble."

President Barack Obama, who gave Russell the Presidential Medal of Freedom in 2011, was one of numerous political figures to weigh in. "I commend the players on the Bucks for standing up for what they believe in," he wrote on Twitter. "It's going to take all our institutions to stand up for our values."

Meanwhile, Jared Kushner, a senior White House adviser and the son-in-law of President Trump, trotted out some of the critiques that I had anticipated as Wednesday afternoon unfolded. "NBA players are very fortunate that they have the financial position where they're able to take a night off from work without having to have the consequences to themselves financially," Kushner said dismissively in a CNBC interview. "They have that luxury, which is great. With the NBA, there's a lot of activism. I think that they've put a lot of slogans out. But I think what we need to do is turn that from slogans and signals to actual action."

Whether Kushner knew or cared, the players were already one step ahead of him. After the games were postponed, the National Basketball Players Association called a meeting on Wednesday night. Even in good times, unanimity among hundreds of professional athletes was impossible due to stubbornness, ego, and conflicting interests. These weren't good times: Emotions were raw from the Blake shooting, players were exhausted from a heavy schedule, the playoff pressure was turned up, and not everyone agreed with what the Bucks had done.

The dissenting voices questioned why the decision to protest had been made unilaterally and without notice to the union or to players on the other teams. There were practical consequences to the timing of the protest. If the Bucks had simply played their game and won, the Magic would have been free to leave the bubble the next morning. If the Lakers had won their game on Wednesday night, the Blazers would have been headed home too. NBA players stick to maniacal routines during the playoffs, and the Bucks had thrown off their colleagues without warning. Multiple Lakers described waking up from their customary afternoon naps to discover that their game was postponed and that a firestorm was brewing on social media.

The fact that the Bucks hadn't given the union or the other teams any advance warning was no small matter. Other teams could have decided on their own whether they wanted to follow the Bucks' lead. Some games could have theoretically gone on without interruption. The union could have organized a mass protest and prepared its members for possible backlash.

Practically speaking, the Bucks' impromptu protest had forced the players from every other team to adopt their position. If any teams wanted to play on Thursday, they would be open to accusations that they didn't support the Bucks. If any players disagreed with the nature of the Bucks' protest or feared reprisals for shutting down the sport, they had no choice but to swallow those feelings. If any union members in the meeting didn't trust the others to act in a united fashion, the future of the bubble would be even more precarious. What would happen if another high-profile police shooting took place? Would a team take the next logical step by suspending its season and going home?

Indeed, some players were so frustrated by the situation that they threatened to leave the bubble on Wednesday night. Shams Charania of *The Athletic* reported late Wednesday that the Lakers and the Los Angeles Clippers, perhaps the two highest-profile teams in the bubble, were ready to call off the experiment entirely, and they abruptly left the meeting.

"I was ready to walk away," LeBron James later confirmed in an interview with the *Road Trippin'* podcast. "I called my wife and my mom and told them that I was probably headed home. We sat there and talked for two, three, or four hours and there was still no plan. I walked out because my time is very valuable. When you're dealing with a lot of emotions, a lot of ego, a lot of guys that are passionate about themselves and what they believe in, then it's hard to figure out a plan."

Boston's Jaylen Brown stood up for the Bucks in the meetings, explaining later that he thought the world "will appreciate what Milwaukee did" on behalf of players who felt "helpless and tired" after Blake's shooting. Meanwhile, Chris Haynes of Yahoo reported that Clippers guard Patrick Beverley erupted at the NBPA's Michele Roberts during the meeting, although multiple players later downplayed the exchange.

Putting aside the arguments, the players were in a bind: Returning to play would undercut the Bucks' action, but refusing to play would carry drastic financial consequences. "There was no way that any of us could go on the floor," James said on *The Shop*, his HBO show. "We were trying to figure out: If we leave or if we stay, what is our plan? What is our call for action?"

Trying to process the players' unhappiness in that moment was unnerving, as they seemed both emotionally exhausted by the Blake news and physically exhausted by the relentless playoff schedule.

Earlier in the summer, it was Beverley who declared that if James was going to play in the bubble, then everyone was going to play. Now the reverse was true. If James and the Lakers were out, then everyone was going home.

For all its faults, the bubble was producing better basketball than I had imagined, and the most anticipated matchups were only a few weeks away. The players had come so far and sacrificed so much that I wouldn't have faulted them for pulling the plug. But I would have been crushed all the same, like a child watching a wave wipe out his ornate sandcastle.

Despite the players' evident frustration and the dire late-night reports, I remained cognizant of the immense forces that would compel the players to stay. This wasn't just a matter of optics but of money. The union's leadership had agreed to participate in the bubble concept because the alternative would have been financially devastating. No games meant no revenue. No revenue meant pay cuts and a possible termination of the Collective Bargaining Agreement.

The same calculations applied now. If most of the playoffs were canceled, a labor war would be inevitable. NBA commissioner Adam Silver and the owners would have to draw a line. A one-day protest or a short schedule delay was a much different business proposition than losing hundreds of millions in revenue with a burst bubble.

The players understood this too. Some NBPA members could afford to never work another day in their lives, but many others could not. Rookies, minimum-salary players, and journeymen would be hit hard by a lost postseason and a protracted labor battle. A major function of any union is to protect its members from unexpected financial calamities, requiring Roberts to stand behind the Bucks while also laying out the significant consequences of a longer shutdown.

While Silver took stock of the situation from outside the bubble, Roberts had been living at Disney World alongside the players for months. After a lengthy legal career and a successful run as the head of the NBPA, the sixty-three-year-old Roberts had purchased a new home in Harlem and announced her plans to retire shortly before the pandemic hit. Once it became clear that the NBA was headed for major financial difficulties, the longtime lawyer agreed to stay on in her role.

"I don't regret that I didn't get out in time," Roberts told me in August. "If this all happened right after I left and I was not able to play a part in shepherding the players through this, I would have been miserable. I care about these men. If this is the way my career ends, that's far better than watching from the outside."

Roberts's time in the bubble was spent attending games, interfacing with union leadership, and having as many personal interactions as possible with the players. Her favorite routine was sitting by the pool at night as players came by to solicit career advice, talk about their families, or ask questions about the coronavirus. "You have conversations that you're not going to have by phone or text," she said. "I don't want to go home because I'm going to miss the intimacy. It's once in a lifetime."

The great joy of Roberts's job was standing up for her players in public. She was their advocate, especially when it came to their right to protest. "I would fight tooth and nail if there were any effort to suppress the expression," she said. "If a fan genuinely finds the idea of Black Lives Matter so offensive that they don't want to watch basketball, I'm not losing sleep over it. I don't understand how you could be so filled with venom over an expression of humanity that you would turn your back on something you otherwise enjoy. If someone thinks it's disrespectful to the flag, then they're just wrong."

Yet Roberts was pragmatic too. A burst bubble could trigger a battle with owners who were already losing huge chunks of their revenue during the pandemic. This was a particularly bad time for millionaires to go to war with billionaires. Silver had famously said that any player would be "free to leave" the bubble at any time, but as a collective they were clearly stuck. The players had to find a way to make things work.

Danny Green, the first member of the Lakers to speak with the media after the boycott, confirmed that his teammates "considered all options" about whether to leave or to stay. "You want to do what's right and what's best for the majority," he said. "If we leave, that wouldn't have benefited everybody. There's guys on rookie deals, free agents, and guys who haven't made any money."

The players also weighed what would happen to the momentum of their activism if they left the bubble and its nationally televised stage. "Staying is probably the better way to do it," Green reasoned. "To keep our platform for everyone. When we're dispersed and divided, we're not as strong."

Cooler heads prevailed by Thursday morning, with Adrian Wojnarowski of ESPN.com reporting that the players were still committing to finishing out the postseason. Getting back on the court remained a delicate process, as the NBA, members of the Board of Governors, union leaders, and high-profile stars sought a compromise.

Timing remained a question. If games simply picked up like normal on Thursday or Friday, the players would face accusations that the shutdown was a meaningless publicity stunt. They would also be headed right back into the emotional grinder with high-stakes playoff games. Players on the Toronto Raptors and Boston Celtics had discussed boycotting their Thursday game before the Bucks' protest. There was no way they would want to play on Thursday now.

However, if the players dragged their feet or pushed too hard in their conversations with the league office and owners, they might extend their stay in the bubble or do damage to key business relationships. A week off in August would need to be made up on the back end in October, something no one wanted.

Thursday morning saw an emergency meeting of the NBA's Board of Governors and extended conversations with the players that were brokered by Charlotte Hornets owner Michael Jordan, the only Black majority owner in the NBA. While Thursday's slate of games was pushed off, the fear factor from the night before eased as the two sides met Thursday afternoon to iron out an agreement.

Clippers coach Doc Rivers, who had addressed the players at the heated Wednesday night meeting, noticed an "amazing difference" in tone during Thursday's focused dialogue. "The progression of that was absolutely perfect," he said. "It didn't have to be a contentious meeting, and it wasn't. It was a discussion about what they needed and wanted. Adam Silver and the owners were on board. We all needed a moment to breathe. It's not lost on me that George Floyd didn't get that moment. We did, and we took it."

On campus, I was relieved to have an evening off and used the afternoon to get in some extra miles. As I did laps around the Coronado Springs Resort, I saw players out and about for the first time in weeks. They had no games, no practices, and no media commitments, so Clippers superstar Kawhi Leonard took an oversized golf cart out for a spin and Lakers center Dwight Howard found an empty bus bench for a lengthy phone call. Even in this moment of peak tension, the bubble humanized the players. Leonard, who traveled by helicopter to games in Los Angeles, was stuck puttering around an empty parking lot like a septuagenarian.

The talks between the owners and players benefited from groundwork laid before the bubble. After all, the owners had already placed the Black Lives Matter decals on the courts, approved the racial justice jersey slogans, and agreed to fund a ten-year, $300 million foundation. The two sides weren't starting from square one. As James noted, they needed to come up with new proposals that were meaningful and easy to implement in a timely manner.

The solution couldn't just be a matter of money, like expanding the scope of the new foundation. The owners couldn't be seen trying to buy their way out of an entrenched problem, and the players couldn't put a price tag on their principles. Such a proposal might slow down the process too, if any owners believed that the league's existing commitment was sufficient.

NBPA president Chris Paul and James reached out to President Obama late Wednesday, seeking his advice for crafting their platform. According to his retelling on HBO, Obama counseled the players that the broader societal issues were "not going to be solved overnight" and that they needed to view their activism from a long-term perspective. Obama's chief suggestion was to set up a social justice counsel within the league that would pursue "best practices that are going to start making incidents like that less likely."

That became the first pillar of the players' requests. From there, they turned their attention to the presidential election, which was now less than three months away. The Black vote would be critical in swing states from the Midwest to the Southeast. James and other professional athletes had successfully launched the "More Than a Vote" campaign to increase registration and fight suppression in Black communities. Empty basketball stadiums happened to make great polling locations in city centers, and several teams and cities had already committed to opening their arena doors for such purposes. Why not try to compel every owner to join that cause?

By Friday morning, the NBA and NBPA issued a joint statement, announcing that the players had received three "commitments" from the owners following "candid, impassioned, and productive" talks. First: the formation of a social justice coalition—comprising players, coaches, and owners—to advocate for "meaningful police and justice reform." Second: The owners agreed to "continue to work with local elections officials" to use team-owned arenas as polling locations. Third: The two sides would create a new round of television ads and signs for the arena that encouraged voter participation.

All things considered, this struck me as an elegant solution. The players got something to show for their efforts. Obama's idea for a social justice coalition was a no-brainer, and it should have already existed. The new polling locations represented a big win. Within a week, the Milwaukee Bucks, Golden State Warriors, Houston Rockets, New York Knicks, Utah Jazz, and Los Angeles Clippers had announced that their arenas or facilities would be utilized. All told, at least twenty-three teams used their arenas or other facilities to facilitate the voting process.

"As Trump and his followers do everything in their power to make it harder for Americans to vote, NBA players are stepping up to protect our democracy," Ron Wyden, a Democratic senator from Oregon, wrote on Twitter.

The owners, whose political leanings didn't exactly match the players' preferences, had avoided a partisan fight. They also hadn't been forced to make major financial concessions, a step that would have established a slippery slope in the event of future protests or flare-ups. "We look forward to the resumption of the playoffs and continuing to work together—in Orlando and in all NBA team markets—to push for meaningful and sustainable change," read the joint statement from the players and owners.

The shutdown was set to end Saturday, with Game 5 between the Bucks and Magic appearing first on the docket. The game that never happened would get a second chance three days later.

"Fifteen years in this league and I've never seen anything like it," Paul said after the bubble was saved. "Guys are really coming together and speaking and seeing real change. Guys are tired. When I say tired, I don't mean physically tired. We're tired of seeing the same thing over and over again. It's emotional, especially when you're a Black man. We're all hurt. Everybody expects us to be okay because we get paid great money. We're humans. We have real feelings."

That bone-deep fatigue was a sensation that everyone seemed to share. One day before the shutdown, Clippers forward Paul George revealed that he met with a psychiatrist because he was experiencing "anxiety and a little bit of depression" during a shooting slump. After living in isolation, George concluded that he had "underestimated mental health" and had briefly "checked out."

Green, who was also enduring inconsistent stretches of play, said that the "bubble is only as good as your play" and told reporters that he missed his dogs. "If you're not playing well, the walls are going to close in," he said. "You have nothing to do but to look at social media all day and all they're doing is bullying you." The Lakers guard then appealed to the league's decision makers, arguing that pets "would definitely lighten the mood."

Rivers acknowledged that he had missed the bubble's effect on his players. "That's nothing to do with politics or anything else," he said. "That's to do with real life. I knew it was hard, but I didn't see the impact."

In the day-to-day rush, it was easy to lose track of everything. During the shutdown, I decided to take stock of myself. I had gained some weight at Disney World thanks to late-night room service and an abundance of free snacks. I was still walking every day, but not as far as I had during the hiatus. I was sleeping way less than normal, rushing from deadline to deadline without planning anything more than a day in advance. My iPhone screen time had spiked to record highs, and I had tripled my daily meditation routine to compensate. I had also taken to shopping online when I couldn't sleep. I now owned the same polo shirt in seven different colors. Since when did I even wear polo shirts?

None of these developments individually was a major cause for concern. I rationalized that the playoffs always led to an increase in my workload and stress, and that things would eventually go back to normal. Taken together, though, I had to admit that the bubble had made me less happy, healthy, and balanced, no matter how much I was enjoying the games.

In his first interview after the shutdown, James defused questions about the stormy Wednesday meeting and the Lakers' desire to leave early by appealing directly to the reporters in the room. "I've had numerous nights and days thinking about leaving the bubble," said James, who was still separated from his wife, Savannah, and three children. "I think everyone has, including you guys. I don't think there's one person that hasn't had a mind to say, 'Oh, I've got to get the hell out of here.' It probably crosses my mind once a day."

The Blake shooting was the last straw, but the players had been pushed to their limits by nearly two months in isolation. Mark Tatum, the NBA's deputy commissioner, said in a late-September interview that he remembered the shutdown as "a well-needed break for everyone to take a breath and refocus" that was caused by "a combination of frustration, a lack of progress, and being here in this campus environment."

Hearing Tatum talk through the period, it struck me that the league's decision makers felt responsible, at least in part, for the conditions that led to the Bucks' action. The league office had a major hand in setting the nonstop schedule, crafting the health protocol, keeping family members out of the bubble at the start, banning dogs, and all the rest of it.

Silver and the owners weren't living in the bubble they had helped create, and thus couldn't dismiss concerns raised by Roberts and the players. They sent the players down to Central Florida to save the season, and they shared responsibility during the toughest moments. "The key was the continued commitment of the league and the NBPA to keep doing what we could to combat systemic racism and deal with the social and racial inequities in this country," Tatum said. "That ongoing dialogue allowed us to move forward."

I was thrilled that games were set to resume because I still wanted to see a champion crowned and I didn't want outsiders to label the players as quitters. The last thing I wanted to see was a labor war, and I agreed with Green that the players' voices would get lost if they went home. In hindsight, the shutdown wound up feeling like the bubble's halftime break.

At the same time, I knew that the NBA couldn't just pick up where it had left off. The Bucks would need to go back to the same locker room, process the same frustrations over Blake's shooting, face the same postseason pressure, and take questions about the entire ordeal from reporters. The three-day stoppage had restored order and sanity, but there were still six more weeks of Groundhog Days to come.

Milwaukee closed out Orlando with a blowout win in Game 5 to advance to the second round. The Lakers eliminated the Blazers later that night in comfortable fashion, as James and Anthony Davis combined for 79 points. The one-sided results felt inevitable. The favorites had some time to rest, and the underdogs had three days to think about how close they were to the comforts of home.

Portland star Damian Lillard, who had injured his knee earlier against Los Angeles, left the bubble early rather than wait around to watch the closeout loss. While his teammates prepared for their season finale, Lillard posted a photo to Instagram with his son in his arms. "Dislocated finger . . . Lateral knee sprain . . . but this is good for the soul . . . missed my baby boy," he wrote. Father and son both grinned from ear to ear.

The teams still in the bubble, even the victorious ones, remained a long way from joy. A backbreaking week added one final, incomprehensible blow when actor Chadwick Boseman died at age forty-three after a publicly unknown four-year battle with colon cancer. James, Antetokounmpo, and countless other players paid tribute to the *Black Panther* star.

Milwaukee had little to say on Saturday about beating Orlando or about its upcoming matchup with the Miami Heat. The game was a formality, with Antetokounmpo overwhelming the Magic, and their Blake protest was still on their mind. "Walking into that space, remembering what our players did, the phrase being on the right side of history applies," said coach Mike Budenholzer. "You felt something going back in there. Trying to end racial injustice and end racism and make this world a better place is still more important than us winning."

Khris Middleton said that playing Game 5 was "very difficult" after "an extremely long couple of days emotionally." There were no regrets, even though interest in the protest took off far beyond their expectations. "We stuck together just like a brotherhood should," he said. "I didn't think it would become as big as it became, the history. We were proud of that decision. We truly felt it wasn't the right day to play the game."

The Bucks confirmed that Hill and Brown decided not to play shortly before tip-off, and that the rest of the team had rallied around them. "I decided, as a leader, I'm not playing this game," Antetokounmpo said. "I can't leave my teammates behind. They felt some type of way about the situation that was going on. They weren't in the right space to play the game, and I 100 percent fully supported them. We decided later as a team to not go out there."

The protest, Antetokounmpo added, had brought back memories from his rookie year. As a nineteen-year-old from Greece, Antetokounmpo was naive about many aspects of American life. He famously had never tried a smoothie before arriving in the NBA, tweeting "MAN GOD BLESS AMERICA" after his first taste in 2014. That same season, veteran forward Caron Butler, a Wisconsin native who was arrested more than a dozen times during his childhood, advised Antetokounmpo to take steps to avoid appearing threatening in public because of his skin color.

"Over here is different," Antetokounmpo said, recalling Butler's words of wisdom. "You've got to be careful. He told me when you walk down the street, take off your hoodie. I was like, 'Why?' I didn't understand it then. I understand it now."

During the three hours that they spent in the locker room, the Bucks made two important phone calls back to Wisconsin. They dialed Josh Kaul, the state's attorney general, to get an update on Blake's case and the investigation that followed. Kaul later commended the Bucks at a press briefing for "stepping up and participating in the dialogue about these issues and making their voices known."

The Bucks players also held an emotional call with Blake's father, Jacob Blake Sr. The elder Blake later told Dave McMenamin of ESPN. com that the call took place "five minutes after they walked off the court," and that their action "touched me so deeply." Blake Sr. thanked the Bucks on behalf of his son's children for the "pick-me-ups," and he urged protesters to remain nonviolent.

"His dad was tearing up and telling us how powerful what we did that day was for him and his family," Antetokounmpo said. "That's bigger than basketball. You're going to remember the way we felt for the rest of our lives."

That would be the closest that the Bucks got to closure. State legislators in Wisconsin, who were singled out by the Bucks in their statement, held a special session on August 31 to address police conduct. Democratic governor Tony Evers called the session to pursue legislation that would ban chokeholds, establish uniform standards for use of force, and enact other regulations. Yet the Republican-controlled Assembly, which was required by law to meet, adjourned after less than a minute.

Budenholzer and his players could only express dismay at the political inaction. "It doesn't matter whether you're a Republican or Democrat," the coach said, "it seems like you should be in the chambers having conversations and debating."

13

Ousted

Most everyone in the bubble spent the first week following the shutdown in a blurry fog, that out-of-body detachment that unfolds when someone dies or a long relationship ends.

The Magic and Blazers were sent packing on Saturday. That same day, the Oklahoma City Thunder were run off the court in Game 5 by the Houston Rockets after Chris Paul had spent the previous seventy-two hours scrambling to save the bubble. Sunday's three games were all decided by double digits, including Boston's Game 1 trouncing of Toronto in the second round. On Monday, the Heat soundly beat the Bucks in their second-round Game 1. The first seven games played after the shutdown were all lopsided, and the bubble desperately needed a spark.

Raptors coach Nick Nurse, a basketball lifer who occasionally pushed his players' buttons in the media, was plainspoken after the series-opening loss to the Celtics. "We didn't play nearly well enough, hard enough, good enough, fast enough, or tough enough to win today," he said. "We got our butts kicked. Nothing was much fun out there today." Other than that, Mrs. Lincoln, how was the play?

The Raptors' minds remained elsewhere. Serge Ibaka, a native of the Republic of the Congo, had little to say about the loss, instead declaring that "the same system killing Black people in the U.S. is killing my people back in Africa." Kyle Lowry, one of the toughest competitors in the league, noted that "basketball always matters, but in this situation and at this time, it's taking a backseat." The Raptors were a gritty and proud team that shocked the basketball world by gutting out the 2019 championship, and they were clearly struggling to balance their title defense and pain.

In theory, help was on the way. The NBA's health and safety protocols allowed the eight teams that reached the second round to bring authorized guests to the bubble. There were plenty of available hotel rooms now that fourteen of the twenty-two original teams were back at home. All six teams in the Yacht Club had been eliminated once the Lakers knocked out the Blazers, and the Houston Rockets were the sole survivors in the Grand Floridian.

Each player was offered a room for up to four guests, including parents, significant others, and children. The language of the guest policy barred "any individual the player has not previously met in person or with whom the player has limited in-person interactions," which was jokingly referred to as "the groupie rule." All guests had to go through a quarantine period upon arrival, remain on campus, undergo testing, agree to wear masks, and travel only by official methods.

The families—mostly wives, girlfriends, and young children—tended to travel in large groups, and they drastically increased the number of Louis Vuitton bags, Gucci sunglasses, and Versace blouses at the Coronado Springs Resort. I had forgotten what perfume smelled like after two months in the bubble, until three members of the Raptors' family section rode bikes past me one afternoon. I walked head-first into their aromatic wall and immediately started coughing inside my mask.

While family members were required to watch the games respectfully and avoid heckling, they were given excellent seats near the court. I was convinced that their arrival had the potential to influence the results, especially given the emotional intensity following the Jacob Blake shooting. Giannis Antetokounmpo and his girlfriend, Mariah Riddlesprigger, had announced the birth of his first son, Liam, in February. Just five months later, father and son were separated. Was there a better good-luck charm than a cute newborn son wearing his father's jersey while sitting in a courtside seat?

But even baby Liam's arrival wasn't enough to shake Antetokounmpo and the Bucks out of their funk. The MVP made just six shots and missed eight free throws in the Game 1 loss to the Heat, and he looked out of sorts while Miami's Jimmy Butler dominated down the stretch. Afterward, Antetokounmpo took exception when asked whether he had approached coach Mike Budenholzer about switching onto Butler late in the game. "To guard him? No, I didn't," Antetokounmpo said, with an edge to his voice. "Why would you ask that? I'll do whatever Coach wants me to do."

This was a telling exchange, and a sign that cracks were beginning to show for the Bucks. Antetokounmpo was the Defensive Player of the Year and Butler was Miami's best perimeter player. Conventional wisdom dictated that Milwaukee should counter might with might in the playoffs, especially if Butler, who scored 40 points in Game 1, had it rolling.

The matchup decision wasn't cut-and-dried. Antetokounmpo had struggled with foul trouble throughout the bubble, and he was more effective as a help defender near the basket area than as an on-ball stopper on the perimeter. For critics, Antetokounmpo's response showed a lack of competitive zeal and a programmed approach to the game, and it confirmed fears that Budenholzer was reluctant to adjust in the playoffs. To Antetokounmpo's defenders, his explanation reflected a loyalty to his coach and a commitment to the Bucks' scheme.

Either way, the Bucks, like the Raptors, were off on the wrong foot. No one wanted to cite the Blake shooting as an excuse, but there was a lingering sense that this was still the wrong time to play. That feeling came through in small ways, like how Antetokounmpo, who was inseparable from his two NBA-playing brothers in the bubble—Thanasis, with him on the Bucks, and Kostas on the Lakers—didn't light up when asked about his family's arrival after nearly two months apart. "Having my son and my girlfriend, it's nice to see some familiar faces," he said, flatly. "We've still got a job to do."

Living up to expectations was a new concern for Antetokounmpo, who had overperformed at every step of his career. When he entered the 2013 draft at age eighteen, some teams wanted him to remain overseas for seasoning. Instead, he came to the NBA immediately and started twenty-three games as a nineteen-year-old rookie. By age twenty, he was a full-time starter for a playoff team. By age twenty-one, he was Milwaukee's second-leading scorer. By age twenty-two, he was an All-Star, an all-NBA selection, and the NBA's Most Improved Player. By age twenty-three, he ranked in the top five in scoring. By age twenty-four, he was MVP, an All-Star captain, and the face of a Bucks team that reached the Eastern Conference finals.

By age twenty-five, Antetokounmpo was battling LeBron James and Kawhi Leonard to be viewed as basketball's best player. I respected Antetokounmpo as much as any player in the sport. He had risen from serious financial hardship and beaten extraordinary odds to reach the NBA, then responded to his new life as a millionaire by committing himself fully to self-improvement. He transformed from a shy beanpole to a snarling hulk, rarely missing games due to injury. He learned how to run an offense, read a defense, and maximize his physical gifts. He worked tirelessly on his outside shooting, trying to conjure passable results from his mechanical form.

My favorite Antetokounmpo note: He increased his scoring, rebounding, and Player Efficiency Rating every year during his first seven seasons. My grandfather worked in automotive factories in Michigan for his entire adult life, and I pictured Antetokounmpo as a living, breathing assembly line. His stats were his widgets. As he learned the NBA game and adapted to American life, Antetokounmpo managed to find new ways to improve his output year after year. And he never settled, even when he reached league-leading heights.

Despite his superhuman size and strength, Antetokounmpo reminded me of one of my all-time favorite players, John Stockton. They had entirely different body types, hailed from entirely different backgrounds, played entirely different styles, and possessed entirely different skill sets. But Antetokounmpo, like Utah's great point guard, will retire knowing that he fulfilled every bit of his potential.

However, Antetokounmpo was learning that even more was needed to beat the Heat. After leading the Bucks to a 56-17 record in the regular season, he was tiring early, making mental mistakes, and struggling to pierce Miami's "wall" defense, which sought to keep him away from the basket. Budenholzer was stubbornly limiting Antetokounmpo to no more than thirty-six minutes per game, far below the forty-plus minutes that superstars in their primes often logged in crucial playoff contests. Milwaukee regularly floundered when Antetokounmpo left the court.

If Antetokounmpo and the Bucks were starting to look uncomfortable in their role as favorites, Butler and the Heat relished being the underdogs. The Heat swept the injury-ravaged Indiana Pacers in the first round, and they didn't fear Antetokounmpo because they had Bam Adebayo, a versatile All-Star center, to counter the MVP's physical gifts. With Adebayo protecting the hoop and a deep cast of wings that played disciplined team defense, Miami matched up well with the East's top team despite finishing the season with a 44-29 record and the East's No. 5 seed.

I thought Milwaukee would and should win the series, but I knew from personal experience that Butler wouldn't let the Heat go quietly. In 2015, when I was writing at *Sports Illustrated*, I penned Butler's first magazine cover story. Tracing his life story, I found a relentless competitor whose all-gas, no-brakes philosophical approach to basketball and life traced back to his days as a homeless teenager in small-town Tomball, Texas. Maybe Butler was the type of player to deliver the spark that the bubble needed.

As a youth, Butler was estranged from his father and kicked out of the house by his biological mother at age thirteen. He couch-surfed for two years until Michelle Lambert, the mother of one of Butler's friends, agreed to take him in. Lambert, who is white, told me that the Butler she first met was a "damaged little bird" who didn't trust anyone. Butler, the high school player, was a raw and egotistical loudmouth who didn't receive a Division I offer. "It was always me against the world," Butler said in 2015. "I thought like that for so long."

Butler's unconventional path to the NBA carried him from junior college in Texas to three years at Marquette, where coach Buzz Williams broke him down with tough love and encouraged him to embrace the dirty work of defense and rebounding. "He told me that I fucking sucked," Butler said, chuckling as he thought back on the conversation. He knew that was the message that he had needed to hear.

Williams saw a young man who possessed a great motor, a complete game, and a high basketball IQ, but who needed an authority figure. When Butler conceded a game winner in the 2010 NCAA tournament, he was so upset that he posted a picture of the play in his bedroom as a constant reminder of his shortcoming. "He realized that lives change on a single possession," Williams said.

I quickly learned that Butler, who hadn't known a comfort zone as a child, was willing to push himself and others in ways most people wouldn't. He favored sunrise workouts and bonding with workaholics, and he clashed with costars if he didn't believe they were sufficiently devoted to the game. He confronted his coaches and teammates face-to-face and in media interviews, leaving a trail of hard feelings as he departed the Chicago Bulls, the Minnesota Timberwolves, and Philadelphia 76ers in a span of two years.

As I put the finishing touches on his profile for *Sports Illustrated*, Butler cursed me out at length over the telephone. I did my best to keep my cool, but the profanities kept flying. I understood his frustration; the fact-checking process was a hassle for everyone. Butler showed no signs of slowing down, so I finally raised my voice in response. His demeanor changed instantly, and we worked through the outstanding issues. I hung up the phone thinking that he had been testing me.

To me, it was a procedural phone call. To Butler, it was an opportunity to compete. I have collected hundreds of refrigerator magnets from my travels as an NBA writer, and I filed my story feeling like I had just collected my Jimmy Butler magnet. I got my own taste of Butler's fierce, incessant desire to prove his worth and independence. He wasn't afraid to burn bridges, deviate from workplace norms, or even damage professional relationships because he had lost almost everything during his turbulent adolescence. "Going fast is instilled in Jimmy," Lambert explained. "If you're moving and producing, you stay in the plans. If you stop or slow down for a second, it all might disappear."

The Heat were a perfect fit for Butler, and he realized it immediately when he visited as a free agent in 2019. Miami, the city, was synonymous with palm trees, sunshine, and nightlife. The Heat's 2012 and 2013 titles were so glitzy and glamorous that those teams were nicknamed the "Heatles." LeBron James had "taken his talents to South Beach" to join Dwyane Wade and Chris Bosh on a star-studded super-team that basketball fans either loved or hated.

Once James returned to Cleveland in 2014 and the Heatles disbanded, the organization's dominant personalities were team president Pat Riley and coach Erik Spoelstra. Both shared a single-minded focus on winning and hard work. Riley was in his mid-seventies and had spent more than half of his life as an NBA player, coach, and executive. He won his first title as a hard-nosed guard on the 1972 Lakers and went on to win seven more as a head coach and lead executive. Still not satisfied, Riley attended the Heat's games in person despite the bubble's inconveniences. He enthusiastically cheered wins from a 200-level box with second-tier access that allowed him into the gyms but prevented him from accessing the court, contacting the players, or living at the team hotel.

Spoelstra, a former player at the University of Portland and the son of a longtime NBA executive, had worked himself up through the ranks. He started as a video coordinator and assistant coach before eventually guiding the Heatles to four straight Finals in his early forties. Known for answering questions with as few words as possible, Spoelstra—"Spo" to his players—lorded over what became known as "Heat Culture" and held his players to high standards of fitness and accountability.

Heat Culture was defined by a total commitment to the team concept and self-improvement. The Heat were famous for grueling training camps and measuring their players' body fat percentages. Riley was always pitching stars in free agency, but their approach was designed to squeeze the most out of everyone who came through the door. Rookies would develop under watchful eyes. Veterans would be encouraged to get into the best shape of their lives. Role players would be asked to do what they did well and not much else. Everyone would be expected to grind.

Butler, who was close friends with Wade, knew what to expect and ate it up during his first free agency meeting in 2019. "It was so conversational," Spoelstra said. "You just felt after 20 minutes that we were so aligned on how we viewed competition and work and culture. We really just had dinner. We were talking shop. He interrupted Pat and I, probably five minutes into the conversation, and said, 'Hey, I'm in.' We were like, 'What? We haven't even given you our pitch yet.' "

I hadn't known what to make of Spoelstra when I covered the Heatles' four Finals. He treated his postgame interviews like dental surgery, gritting his teeth through most questions and rushing out the door as quickly as possible. He guarded injury updates and possible strategic adjustments like state secrets. At the time, I wondered whether he was striking a dour pose to compensate for his relative youth and inexperience.

In the bubble, I realized that Spoelstra was fully comfortable in his own skin. Like many workaholics, including Butler, he was impatient and hated wasting time. The media sessions were a hurdle between Spoelstra and whatever was next on his to-do list. Only rarely did he offer extended thoughts, and those riffs invariably stressed the value of hard work and usually sought to praise players for their commitment behind closed doors.

During the dog days of August, afternoon temperatures approached one hundred degrees and my clothes stuck to my body during outdoor walks. I could only make it about three miles before I needed to stop for water. I embraced the conditions as an exercise in masochism and noticed that almost everyone scheduled workouts to avoid the worst part of the day.

Spoelstra didn't care one bit, barely sweating in the miserable heat. He kept his stern face, moved briskly, and offered economical waves as he passed. I never missed a day in August or September, and I doubt he did, logging his daily miles by himself. To complete the caricature, Spoelstra often wore shirts with a simple message across the chest: Heat Culture.

The bubble wasn't built for everyone, but I knew Spoelstra, Butler, and company would hold up better than most. They thrived in the discomfort and inconveniences that were rattling other teams. While the Heat might get outplayed by a more talented opponent, they weren't going to let Disney World's conditions break them.

Game 2 felt like a must-win for the Bucks, and they looked nervous when they fell into a first-quarter hole. Offense came more easily for the Heat, who moved the ball around and saw seven players score in double figures. Antetokounmpo plowed his way to 29 points and 13 free-throw attempts, but the Bucks' vaunted drive-and-kick offense was stalling. Milwaukee's attack was predicated on Antetokounmpo getting to the basket, drawing a crowd, and finding open shooters on the perimeter. The Bucks lacked playmakers, but they made up for it throughout the regular season with role players who were confident sniping away from outside.

Miami stymied the approach by making life difficult for Antetokounmpo inside and rotating diligently to contest shots on the perimeter. In Game 2, Milwaukee's outside shooting dried up. Antetokounmpo didn't trust his shaky jumper, and none of his teammates could get it going. When Antetokounmpo went to the bench midway through the first quarter, the Bucks could barely function, committing turnovers and launching hopeless shots until he returned.

Late in the game, Antetokounmpo resolved to attack the basket time and again, converting enough of his free throws and eking out enough layups and dunks to keep the Bucks within striking distance. Yet Miami still held a 4-point lead and the ball with less than fifteen seconds remaining as Milwaukee's bench looked on in agony.

With its season suddenly on the precipice, Milwaukee trapped Butler, forcing a turnover that Brook Lopez converted for a layup to cut Miami's lead to 113–111. Butler was quickly fouled, and he made one of his free throws to push the lead back to 3 with seven seconds left. Needing to force overtime, the Bucks went to Khris Middleton, who hoisted a shot from a few steps behind the 3-point line. Middleton leaned forward on his follow-through, contacting Heat guard Goran Dragic, who had set his feet and put his arms straight up to contest the shot. Inexplicably, referee Marc Davis called a foul on Dragic as Middleton let his body crash to the court.

This was a gift that might force overtime, rekindle the Bucks' fading hopes, and potentially swing the series. Middleton made all three of his free throws to tie the score at 114, with four seconds left on the clock.

Butler hadn't been able to duplicate his Game 1 magic, and his late turnover and missed free throw contributed directly to Miami's tricky predicament. But there was little doubt where the Heat would go for their final shot. Butler received the ball in the left corner, shadowed by Wesley Matthews. As the clock ticked under two seconds, Antetokounmpo raced over to double-team Butler, certain that he would attempt a game-winning shot rather than pass to the open man.

The instinct was correct, but Antetokounmpo was too eager. As Butler launched a step-back in the corner, Antetokounmpo closed out hard and his momentum carried him into the shooter. This was a bump rather than a body blow, but Antetokounmpo clearly made contact and Butler fell to the court. Davis, who had just called the foul on Dragic on the other end, blew his whistle again. Butler would get two free throws to win the game.

Antetokounmpo glanced at Davis in disbelief, but he didn't stomp, shout, or charge the referee. Instead, he walked to the sideline and sat down on the videoboard that separated the crowd from the court, leaning forward with his elbows resting on his knees. Budenholzer and several Milwaukee players lobbied on Antetokounmpo's behalf, but the MVP didn't move, except to duck his head and rub the top of his hair in frustration. His hopes for a game-saving block had given way to a game-losing blunder. There was no time left on the clock, thus there would be no chance for redemption.

Butler hit both free throws, and the game was over. By barely avoiding a late-game meltdown, Miami had pushed Milwaukee into an 0-2 hole. Instead of resurrecting the Bucks, Davis, the referee, helped kill them.

As I walked to the locker room a few minutes after the buzzer, I overheard a snippet of a phone call between Marc Lasry, one of the Bucks' co-owners, and Kiki VanDeWeghe, the NBA's executive vice president of basketball operations. The Bucks' dream season was falling apart, and Lasry wasn't happy. In a story that ran the next morning, ESPN's Jackie MacMullan quoted a text message from Lasry: "To lose a game like that is just wrong."

Budenholzer, never a fire-and-brimstone guy, objected too. "I'd say we're disappointed with the judgment, the decision, the timing," the coach said. "It's a tough job. I have a lot of respect for the officials. We have our way of seeing things. We're going to disagree."

The one key figure who didn't dispute the call was Antetokounmpo. "I tried to make it tough for Jimmy," he said, slowly, with an even tone and a distant look in his eyes. "The ref said there was contact. Maybe there was. It is what it is. I tried to contest the shot." Antetokounmpo was more interested in explaining why he chose to double-team, defending his decision as "the right play" because Butler was "not going to pass" with so little time left. "I've done this multiple times in my career," he said.

I greatly admired Antetokounmpo's accountability in that moment. He looked and sounded like someone who believed that he had cost his team a game and, possibly, a season. Players threw referees under the bus all the time, and that would have been an easy way out. From his reaction on the court to his postgame comments, it was clear that Antetokounmpo didn't blame anyone but himself.

Fouling Butler was perhaps the biggest mistake of Antetokounmpo's career. Butler had learned the hard way in college that "lives change on a single possession," and here was Antetokounmpo forced to reckon with that same hard truth. The Bucks needed that miracle fourth-quarter comeback. To have it slip away in a momentary lapse by their best player was cruel. They weren't officially eliminated, but they were done.

While Antetokounmpo didn't point the finger at anyone else, the media and Bucks fans were happy to pick up the slack. Arrows flew in every direction, and rightfully so. Budenholzer wasn't playing Anteto-kounmpo nearly enough, as evidenced by Milwaukee's atrocious early play without him. Point guard Eric Bledsoe was adding to his reputation as an erratic postseason performer. Milwaukee's 3-point shooting, chemistry, and off-court vibes were all totally different from the regular season, and general manager Jon Horst's veteran additions weren't bringing much to the table. The Bucks also missed guard Malcolm Brogdon, who was traded away before the season in a cost-cutting move by ownership.

Milwaukee's house came crashing down in Game 3. Anteto-kounmpo tweaked his ankle early and pressed the issue on offense, managing just 21 points on 21 shots and missing all seven of his 3-point attempts. The Heat ripped off a stunning 17–1 closing run to claim a 115–100 win, as the Bucks didn't make a basket in the final 4:40 and now sat one loss from a humiliating sweep.

There was nothing left to say, although Antetokounmpo did softly acknowledge that he "could play more" minutes if needed. It was way too late to have that conversation. Budenholzer defended his careful treatment of Antetokounmpo and Middleton by saying that playing thirty-six minutes was "pushing the ceiling" in a hard-fought playoff game. The comment made little sense, given that rival stars were regularly playing more than forty minutes in the bubble, and plenty of critics pointed out that Budenholzer played Middleton forty-seven minutes in the very next game.

Game 4 added injury to insult for the Bucks, as Antetokounmpo went down in a heap after spraining his ankle for the second time in two games. In one of the bubble's eeriest scenes, Antetokounmpo writhed in pain and shouted a profanity that echoed throughout the gym. He was helped to the sideline by his brother Thanasis and did not return. Yet the Bucks shocked everyone in the building by rallying for an overtime win behind Middleton's 36 points, as the Heat uncharacteristically let up against their undermanned opponent.

But that victory only helped the Bucks save a little face. Milwaukee elected to hold out the injured Antetokounmpo for Game 5, and Miami closed the door with a 103–94 victory to take the series. Butler barely smiled as he walked off the court in victory. Miami was now 8–1 in the playoffs, but his mind was focused on the future, like always. "We got eight more to get," Butler told TNT, as the first Finals appearance of his career suddenly seemed within reach.

All season, the Bucks had been penciled into the Eastern Conference finals, at minimum. They were one of only twelve teams in NBA history to record a +10 point differential, meaning they outscored their opponents on average by more than 10 points per game all season. Of those twelve teams, eight went on to win the title. The Bucks were eliminated from the playoffs more quickly than any of the other eleven.

For the first time in his career, Antetokounmpo was a disappointment. The guy who had made incremental progress for seven straight years had now taken a major step backward from his 2019 Eastern Conference finals appearance. Buzz about Antetokounmpo's 2021 free agency and the possibility that he might leave Milwaukee had been building for some time, and he spoke carefully after the season-ending loss.

"Hopefully we can learn from this and get better as a team and come back," Antetokounmpo said, trying not to make a bad situation worse. "Hopefully we can build a culture in Milwaukee that, for many years, we can come out and compete every single year for a championship."

I left the series convinced that Budenholzer was holding back Antetokounmpo and that Bledsoe could not return if Milwaukee wanted to take the next step as a franchise. The anti-Bucks voices who said that they needed more playmaking and that they had blundered by trading Brogdon were proven correct. Antetokounmpo had a bubble to forget, and he needed more help.

The Blake shooting didn't create these problems, but it contributed to Milwaukee's inability to solve them quickly. In my eyes, the Bucks' exit was the bubble's saddest. This had been a great team before the pandemic, and they were reduced to a shell of themselves at Disney World.

Budenholzer, for his part, choked up at his final press conference when asked how he balanced his disappointment in the Bucks' performance against his pride in how they handled their protest.

"I think what the team stands for, the character, the humanity to stand and be on the right side of history like we did, that was emotional," the coach said. "It's such a great group. Winning is important. We had high expectations starting the season, throughout the season, coming here. You always want to realize those expectations. It would be great if you could have both. If you have to choose one, I'd like to have guys who have high character and stand for something."

Budenholzer jumped up from his chair, thanked the media, and raced for the door. Poof. The Bucks, one of my three favorites to win the title, were gone. They had barely made it to Labor Day.

14

West Threats

The playoffs don't begin until an underdog wins a series. In the first round, all eight favorites had advanced. While Miami finished one game behind Indiana in the regular season standings, the Pacers' extensive health problems set up the Heat to advance easily. Out West, the Houston Rockets needed seven games to survive the Oklahoma City Thunder in the No. 4 versus No. 5 matchup, but they escaped all the same.

The entire season felt like a countdown to the clash between the Lakers and the Clippers in the Western Conference finals. The NBA had scheduled the two teams on opening night and Christmas Day to fuel the rivalry, and then again on the first night of the bubble restart.

There were plenty of reasons for excitement, starting with star power: LeBron James, Anthony Davis, Kawhi Leonard, and Paul George in the same series would be an embarrassment of riches. The franchises were perfect contrasts, too, with the Lakers as glitzy blue bloods and the Clippers as scrappy upstarts.

The Clippers tried to spin their relative lack of postseason success with a marketing campaign focused on authenticity and tenacity. Their messaging, which rolled out on buses and billboards across Los Angeles, was "streetlights over spotlights," "we over me," and "driven over given." The Clippers were willing to concede that Hollywood stars had always preferred the Lakers. They knew they could never out-Showtime the Lakers, so they wanted to be the city's basketball team of substance, not style.

James and Leonard were perfect front men for the rivalry because they had so many organic differences. James was a national phenom as a high schooler and a No. 1 overall pick. Leonard went to San Diego State—not exactly Duke or Kentucky—and wasn't a lottery pick. James won his first title as the superstar face of the riveting Heat.

Leonard won his as a complementary piece on the buttoned-up San Antonio Spurs.

James was one of the most prolific scorers and sharpest passers in league history. Leonard first rose to prominence as a defensive menace who shadowed James throughout the 2013 and 2014 Finals. James was the sport's most famous active player, using Instagram to welcome fans to his workouts and family dinners. Leonard was a recluse who didn't bother to maintain an online presence. James was a master of the media and a constant content creator, capable of shaping entire news cycles with a single quote. Leonard took forever to get ready for postgame interviews and mumbled through clichés once he got in front of the microphone.

For all their personality differences, James and Leonard were both complete players and proven winners. Both were seeking a title with a third separate franchise. James had won in 2012 and 2013 with the Heat and 2016 with the Cavaliers; Leonard had won in 2014 with the Spurs and 2019 with the Raptors. Both men also used their influence to line up their rosters. James and his close friend, agent Rich Paul, had set up the trade for Davis in 2019; Leonard had agreed to sign with the Clippers if they would trade for George that same summer. Lakers versus Clippers promised to be a clash of superstars, styles, and hand-picked sidekicks.

But the Heat's upset of the Bucks was a shock to the system. It was one thing to hear James say that the bubble was a "new season" and that what happened before March was irrelevant. It was quite another to see Giannis Antetokounmpo go home without getting close to taking his shot at James or Leonard. The Bucks were exposed so thoroughly that it was time to reconsider whether the Lakers and Clippers were still locks.

Of the two, the Clippers looked shakier in the first round. The Lakers made quick work of the Blazers in five games. Portland was exhausted from its push into the playoffs, had no one to guard James or Davis, and lost Lillard to a knee injury. Luka Doncic and the Dallas Mavericks, by contrast, pushed the Clippers to six games despite losing Kristaps Porzingis to injury halfway through the series.

The Clippers had many problems, none bigger than Doncic. The twenty-one-year-old Slovenian sensation capped an exquisite second season with a thrilling run through the bubble. Although Doncic was a natural showman who loved playing to the crowd, working the referees, and wearing his heart on his sleeve, he quickly settled into the bubble environment. Doncic was a decorated professional overseas for years before he came to the NBA in the 2018 draft, and he possessed a pure love for the game. If the NBA wanted to hold the Finals outdoors on blacktop or at a space station on the moon, Doncic wouldn't bat an eye.

Doncic arrived with a bang, scoring 42 points in a Game 1 loss to the Clippers, the most ever by an NBA player in his postseason debut. The Clippers' plan all along had been to construct an elite defense around Leonard and George, two of the game's top perimeter stoppers. At a preseason hype event, George said that he bonded with Leonard because they both believed in playing hard on defense, a "lost art" in the high-scoring modern era.

Yet Doncic shredded the Clippers with enough ease that coach Doc Rivers was left to rationalize the situation. "I'll give up the points," Rivers said. "I don't want to give up the points and the assists." No team was better equipped on paper to stop Doncic and limit his supporting cast simultaneously, but the Clippers' defense hadn't looked quite right in the bubble.

George had admitted that he was struggling mentally, backcourt stopper Patrick Beverley was nursing a calf injury, Lou Williams was caught up in the Magic City fiasco, and center Montrezl Harrell missed the first eight games after leaving the bubble to attend his grandmother's funeral. Rivers was plugging holes all over the place and still encountering leaks.

In a wild Game 4 that saw huge momentum swings, Doncic struck again. After blowing an early lead, the Clippers forced overtime by erasing a 4-point deficit in the final minute of regulation. The two sides traded haymakers in overtime, with Marcus Morris, a midseason pickup, draining a clutch 3-pointer with nine seconds left to give the Clippers a 1-point lead.

After a foul, Dallas set up on the left sideline with 3.7 seconds left. Doncic, who was initially guarded by Leonard, used a screen as he received the inbounds pass to get a more favorable matchup with Reggie Jackson. Feeling it, Doncic took a dribble to his left, crossed over to his right, and then crossed over again to set up a step-back jumper leaning to his left.

Jackson, sent back on his heels by the quick series of moves, tried to lunge forward to contest the shot, but Doncic still had a clean look from two steps behind the arc. He released the ball with less than a second to play, and the deep 3-pointer rattled home as time expired. The picture-perfect "Hero Ball" shot prompted pandemonium from Doncic's teammates, who mobbed him at center court. Commentators rushed to compare the shot to early-career playoff buzzer-beaters by James and Michael Jordan.

Doncic finished with 43 points, 17 rebounds, and 13 assists—a stat line that had never been matched in all three categories in playoff history. He did it all on a sprained left ankle that had forced him from the court early in Game 3. "I was just trying to make it," he said. "I can't explain the emotions, not only when the ball goes in but when I see the whole team running toward me. That was something special. One of the best feelings I've ever had."

In hindsight, Doncic's shot was arguably the best basketball moment of the entire bubble. It was so good that I forgot I was sitting in an empty gym. The entire scene felt ripped from a storybook: his youth and fearlessness, his willingness to pull up so far from the hoop, and his ability to will the underdog Mavericks to victory without an injured Porzingis. Dallas coach Rick Carlisle, known for dry wit but not hyperbole, compared Doncic to Hall of Famers Larry Bird and Jason Kidd.

"Those guys are from the same fabric competitively," Carlisle said. "Their will to win and resourcefulness. It's not just about putting the ball in the basket. It's about giving teammates confidence. He sees the game in 6G, not 5G. It's another level beyond what most people see it. That game was from another planet."

The Clippers responded to the heartbreaking defeat by turning to veteran tricks. They had baited Porzingis into a Game 1 ejection, then turned their attention to goading Doncic with trash talk and physical treatment. At one point, Harrell was caught on camera calling Doncic a "bitch ass white boy." Harrell later apologized for crossing the line, and Doncic accepted.

But that was only the beginning of the Clippers' instigation tactics. In Game 5, Morris came across the court to step directly on Doncic's injured ankle as he waited for an inbounds pass. In Game 6, Morris was ejected for delivering a hard foul to Doncic's head. Doncic gave Morris the benefit of the doubt on the first one, but he leaped off the hardwood to protest the second. Dallas's Boban Marjanovic had to yank Doncic by the jersey to keep him away from a fight. This was the most action that the seven-foot-four center had seen since his cameo in *John Wick—Chapter 3*, the Keanu Reeves movie.

Just as Lillard had taken shots at Beverley, George, and the Clippers for their trash talk, Doncic expressed his disgust with Morris. "Terrible foul," he said. "Two games in a row he did something like that. I really hoped the first one wasn't on purpose but looking back at the foul this game, you know what I think. I don't want to deal with that kind of player."

While the Clippers cranked up the antics after Doncic's shot, they also raised their standard of play. In Game 5, the Clippers' final contest before the three-day shutdown, Leonard and George combined for 67 points in a 154–111 rout. The Clippers set franchise records for points scored and margin of victory in a playoff game to take a 3–2 series lead. This was a championship-worthy response from the Clippers, who finished off the war of attrition with a 111–97 victory in Game 6.

The feeling for the Clippers was relief rather than accomplishment. In my eyes, it was a red flag that they needed to engage in so many extracurricular activities. Dallas lost Porzingis, yet the Clippers still struggled to contain Doncic, kept blowing double-digit leads, and had breakdowns in crucial moments. The Clippers were still very impressive on their best days, but their baseline left a lot to be desired. "I thought we joined the series late," Rivers acknowledged after Game 6.

Something felt slightly off. The Clippers hadn't enjoyed much lineup continuity with all their injuries, but they had noticeable gaps in their focus and effort level too. Leonard was solid in clutch situations during the Raptors' 2019 title run, but he was outdueled by Doncic at times and had a few brain farts. George, an up-and-down postseason performer throughout his career, spent much of the first-round series mired in a terrible shooting slump.

I came back to the contrasts between James and Leonard. Almost every day, I saw James palling around with Davis. They laughed together at practice, communicated constantly on the court, talked each other up during interviews, and developed the habit of listening in on each other's postgame press conferences. James even liked to sit off camera and interject with jokes at Davis's expense. The two Lakers stars always headed to the bus together, and they appeared to be inseparable friends despite their age difference and short history as teammates. Their two-man game was cohesive on the court, and it didn't skip a beat in the bubble.

Leonard and George didn't display the same off-court camaraderie or on-court chemistry. During George's two seasons in Oklahoma City, he was open about his friendship with Russell Westbrook. When George re-signed with the Thunder, the two stars partied together and smoked cigars to celebrate. Leonard, though, had a way of keeping everyone at arm's length.

There was a warmth missing between the two Clippers stars that might not have been a problem during a normal season, when players came together for games and practices and then went their separate ways. But a title push in the bubble was a much different proposition. When George was open about his mental health struggles, Rivers and others rallied around him. Even so, the Clippers sometimes played like strangers, and they weren't always on the same page in interviews.

I wasn't ready to abandon the Clippers as my title pick, although I made a mental note that Doncic had provided the blueprint for how to beat them. Ignore their jeering from the bench. Don't be afraid of their defense despite their big names. Show George respect, but be ready to capitalize if he wavered. Most importantly, apply constant pressure because the Clippers were prone to blowing early leads and making late-game mistakes. Unfortunately for the Clippers, their second-round opponent, the Denver Nuggets, could check most of those boxes.

First, though, the Nuggets had to survive a thrilling seven-game series with the Utah Jazz. The Northwest Division rivals were evenly matched: Denver, the West's No. 3 seed, finished the season with a 46-27 record, barely edging out the Jazz, who were 44-28 and the No. 6 seed. Both teams had taken hits to their rotations, with Denver guard Gary Harris dealing with a long-term hip injury and Utah forward Bojan Bogdanovic undergoing wrist surgery during the hiatus. Of course, Jazz stars Rudy Gobert and Donovan Mitchell were the first NBA players to test positive for COVID-19. Nikola Jokic, Denver's All-Star center, was also late arriving to the bubble after catching the virus during an overseas trip.

The matchup was impossible to prognosticate, given all the injuries and health concerns. Game 1 went to Denver in convincing fashion despite Mitchell netting a career-high 57 points. Disney World's small confines were on display the next day, when Nuggets guard Jamal Murray came across Mitchell on campus. "The crazy thing about being here in the bubble is I've got to see this dude right after the game," Murray said, turning his camera to a seated Mitchell. "He just dropped 57!" Their head-to-head showdown was just beginning.

If Mitchell's 57 points weren't enough, surely Utah was done, right? Nope. The Jazz rallied to win three straight, claiming blowouts in Game 2 and Game 3 before eking out a 129–127 shootout in Game 4. Now it was Denver that seemed toast, down 3–1 in the series. Murray had exploded for a career-high 50 points in Game 4, yet Mitchell had bested him ever so slightly with 51 points in the summer's best scoring duel. Without Harris, their top perimeter defender, the Nuggets had no answer for Mitchell. He scored 14 points in the final three minutes to put away Game 4.

Facing elimination, Denver coach Michael Malone and his staff wore all black on the sidelines for Game 5. It was setting up to be a bitter early exit for the Nuggets, who came within one win of the Western Conference finals in 2019. Before the hiatus, Jokic established himself as the best center in basketball and the Nuggets stacked up wins in the shadow of the two Los Angeles powers. Then Jokic, Malone, and other team staff members all contracted COVID-19 during the turbulent four-month layoff. Getting knocked out in five games by a red-hot Mitchell would represent clear regression for a rising young franchise.

Murray, a twenty-three-year-old point guard from Canada, had other plans. I was fascinated by Murray since shortly after he became a 2016 lottery pick. He was a maniacal worker like Jimmy Butler, but for totally different reasons. While basketball filled in the family gaps for Butler, Murray's relationship with the sport was forged by his demanding father, Roger.

As a child and adolescent, Murray was groomed for a future life as a professional athlete. Roger Murray put his son through extensive shooting drills and endless conditioning exercises, taught him how to meditate, and banned his use of a cell phone. A profile by Jackie Mac-Mullan of ESPN.com revealed that Roger Murray even held basketball workouts on hockey rinks so that his son could work on his balance. "We didn't have time for emotions," the younger Murray explained. "Getting it done is what matters."

His father's methods helped Murray land a scholarship to Kentucky and a starting job in the NBA. It struck me that Murray's monastic upbringing, as tough as it was, might have been the perfect preparation for life in the bubble. It was difficult to judge whether Roger Murray had pushed his son too hard, but his focus on mental health training stuck out as a big advantage.

I had first tried meditating about three years before I arrived at Disney World, and I typically topped out at ten minutes per day. In the bubble, I found myself relying on morning sessions that lasted up to thirty minutes and a shorter second round before bed. I noticed LeBron James going through deep breathing exercises before games as the bubble wore on too. If anyone could maintain calm in these uniquely stressful circumstances, I figured it would be Murray.

Watching Murray warm up for games was a treat. A smooth shooter, he always made sure to launch from various angles and different spots on the court. The highlight, though, was his dribbling routine, which took place long before tip-off when he would have the court mostly to himself.

With headphones over his ears so that he could fully zone out, Murray walked from the baseline to midcourt while dribbling multiple basketballs. He varied his pacing, dribbled between his legs and behind his back, and worked on both hands equally. As Murray got going, he moved in a precise full-body rhythm, like a gymnast on a pommel horse. His concentration was impeccable.

Murray showed his competitive fire in Game 5 versus the Jazz, scoring 42 points and dishing 8 assists in a 117–107 Denver win. The score was tied with a little more than three minutes remaining before Murray scored 9 points in sixty-two seconds by hitting four consecutive jump shots. In the final minute, Murray drew extra attention and made an unselfish read to Jokic for a dagger 3-pointer.

The closing effort with Denver's season on the line had it all: shotmaking, poise, and good decisions. "The young man is growing up and turning into a superstar on the biggest stage," Malone said. It was easy to hear the pride in Malone's voice. Murray was prone to wild swings in the 2019 playoffs, but he had just played two sensational games in a row.

As it turned out, Murray had far more up his sleeve. Game 6 was delayed by the Bucks' shutdown, which did nothing to throw off Murray's rhythm. On the contrary, he scored 50 points for the second time in three games to top Mitchell's 44 in a 119–107 victory. Murray, who wore sneakers with airbrushed pictures of George Floyd and Breonna Taylor, hit nine 3-pointers and then held back tears during a postgame interview.

"In life, you find things that hold value," Murray told TNT. "It's not just in America. It happens everywhere. For us to come together in the NBA, it doesn't take one meeting, it takes phone calls and persistence. We've been trying to fight for 400 years. These shoes give me life. Even though these people are gone, they give me life and help me find strength to keep fighting."

The television broadcast followed Murray on his way to the locker room, and he doubled over in the tunnel with his hands resting on his knees. The scene was a reminder of Murray's composure and the bubble's ability to swallow its inhabitants. Even when Murray sought a quiet moment to himself after an exhausting game during a gutting week, he was physically trapped by his surroundings and the cameras kept rolling.

The Nuggets and Jazz were running on empty for Game 7. After six games of effortless scoring explosions, both teams went ice-cold. Mitchell had scored at least 30 points in five of the first six games—topping 50 twice—but Utah managed only 36 points in the first half of Game 7. Murray had tallied an astonishing 142 points in the previous three games combined, but Denver scored only 30 points in the second half. The two heavyweight fighters were falling asleep on their chairs before the start of the 15th round.

If the first 47 minutes and 45 seconds were utterly forgettable, the last 15 seconds constituted the bubble's wildest ending. With Denver leading 80–78, Mitchell drove to his right from the top of the key. Denver's Gary Harris poked the ball free from behind, straight into Murray's hands near the baseline. Rather than wait for a Jazz player to foul him, Murray took off in transition to lead a four-on-one fast break. From the sideline, at least one Nuggets assistant coach and one player motioned for Murray to play it safe by pulling the ball out to avoid a turnover.

Instead, Murray dropped a bounce pass to Torrey Craig on the right wing, hoping that the forward could convert a layup to put the game out of reach. Craig rose over Mike Conley but missed the relatively clean look, and the Jazz regained possession with five seconds left and no timeouts. Utah pushed the ball in the other direction as the Nuggets scrambled to get back into defensive position. Conley got the ball with two seconds left and dribbled to the left angle, where he launched a 3-pointer over Murray, who raced to put a hand in his face.

Conley released his shot from almost the exact same spot as Luka Doncic's stunning game winner against the Clippers. He was a few steps closer, but he was in the same gym and on the same side of the court. Like Doncic's shot, the buzzer sounded before the ball reached the hoop. Unlike Doncic's shot, the ball caught the back iron and ricocheted off, giving Denver the 80–78 victory. The Nuggets completed their 3–1 comeback to win the series in seven, staving off elimination in three straight games.

The next ten seconds would have made a perfect *Wide World of Sports* montage: "The thrill of victory . . . the agony of defeat." Utah's Royce O'Neale walked to the bench holding his head in disbelief, and Joe Ingles doubled over to clutch his shorts and stare at the court. A stunned Mitchell collapsed to the hardwood with his head in his hands, his chest still heaving.

Murray, who raised his two fists after Conley's shot glanced off, offered a conciliatory hug to Mitchell. Denver's guard prevailed in an epic seven-game shootout by a matter of three or four inches, and he knew that he dodged a bullet. The basketball gods could have broken his heart, but they chose Mitchell's instead. My head was spinning from the end-to-end sequence. There were so many layers to process.

Harris, injured for months, had only returned to the series in Game 6, after the three-day shutdown. If the Bucks hadn't protested, would he have even come back? Would any other Nuggets player have been able to poke the ball free in the closing seconds?

Meanwhile, Mitchell had remained on the court in frustration after his turnover rather than hustling to get back into the play. Perhaps he assumed Murray would pull up and take the foul. By the time Utah got the ball back with five seconds left, Mitchell was still out of the play and unable to take the last shot. If he had gotten the ball instead of Conley, would he have hit the potential series-clinching shot?

And what was Murray thinking? After so many composed performances, he played with fire in the closing seconds and barely avoided getting burned. If Conley drilled that shot, Murray's remarkable series would have gone for naught and he would have spent years trying to explain his decision to race up the court. Just like Buzz Williams said, "Lives change on a single possession."

I pondered those alternate histories before realizing that I was about to get an answer to a question that had nagged at me for months: How would players celebrate a dramatic clinching victory in the bubble's empty arenas?

The Nuggets hadn't won the championship, but they were elated. Murray shuttled back and forth between interviews, still in disbelief. "If we had lost the game because of that . . ." he said as he passed by reporters for the third time, leaving the sentence halfway compete. "We are laughing right now but it could be tragic," Jokic said, in a perfect deadpan.

Malone, who had worn black for the third straight game with his season on the line, revealed that his clothing choice was a tribute to Johnny Cash. "I don't know what Jamal was doing on the layup to Torrey Craig, but we'll talk about that a different time," Malone said. Murray tried to pass the buck to Craig for missing the layup; Craig said that he was thrown off because he thought Murray was going to shoot rather than pass.

Game 7's ending had a March Madness feel, and the Nuggets looked and acted like sheepish, giddy teenagers. Murray bided his time during Malone's postgame press conference, and then sprayed his coach with a full bottle of water. As he walked out of the interview room, Murray tossed the empty bottle back and hit his coach. The celebration wasn't exactly a champagne bath, but it was a dash of pure joy.

The Nuggets coaches, who would have been packing up and clearing out if Conley's shot had gone down, now suddenly had to prepare to face the Clippers in the second round. Thoughts of Kawhi Leonard and Paul George could wait until the morning. As Denver headed for the bus, staffers shouted, "Victory!" at the top of their lungs. Without a crowd to make noise for them, they handled it themselves. "Respect to the Utah Jazz and respect to Donovan," Murray said at night's end. "It was a great battle. I don't know what else to say. I'm speechless."

Murray wasn't the MVP of the playoffs, but he, like Butler, had emerged as a much-needed spark following the three-day shutdown. After Game 7, I began viewing Murray as the MBP: Most Bubble Player. His alternating seriousness and exuberance perfectly captured Disney World's contradictions. One day, the bubble brought you to your knees. The next, it made you scream in delight.

15

Humiliated

Over the years, I developed a shorthand term for overachieving teams that fell short of being true title threats: cute stories. Often, cute stories were younger teams with rising stars. They were typically easy to root for and inspired their fan bases and local media to salivate over their future and wonder whether, if things broke exactly right, they might shock the world in the present.

The Nuggets were shaping up as the ultimate cute story. Jamal Murray's scoring heroics radically exceeded his previous standard of play. The unexpected 3–1 comeback came against a good, but not great, Utah team. There was a "nobody believes in us" vibe baked into Michael Malone's all-black outfits. And there was that zany escape in Game 7.

Most importantly, in my view, the Clippers would enjoy major matchup advantages on the wing thanks to Kawhi Leonard and Paul George. Despite the Clippers' vulnerabilities, which had been revealed by Luka Doncic and the Mavericks in the first round, everything pointed to the Nuggets' thrill ride coming to a screeching halt.

Labeling a team as a cute story was dismissive, and fans often took offense. There was no single way to win a championship, but title winners almost always possessed elite superstars who were in their primes. The Clippers had two such candidates in Leonard, who was the reigning Finals MVP, and George, a top three MVP finisher in 2019. The Nuggets had Jokic, the best center in the game, and Murray, who was playing out of his mind but hadn't made an All-Star team yet.

The Clippers opened the series with a 23-point victory in Game 1. Leonard barely missed all night, Marcus Morris hit four 3-pointers, and the contest was over by halftime. This was a classic schedule loss. The Nuggets had only one day off after beating the Jazz, and Murray lacked his usual pop.

In the heat of their famous rap battle, Jay-Z accused Nas of falling "from top ten to not mentioned at all." Denver was staring at a similar predicament after emerging as the bubble's darlings. The other three second-round series had far more intrigue: The Heat were in the process of stunning the Bucks, the Celtics and Raptors were evenly matched, and LeBron James's Lakers, easily the biggest show in town, were facing James Harden's Rockets. If the Nuggets didn't push back quickly and forcefully, most observers were going to write them off and pencil the Clippers into the Western Conference finals.

The Nuggets pulled even with a 110–101 win in Game 2 that left me disgusted with the Clippers. Throughout his career, Kevin Durant had cited a favorite quote: "Hard work beats talent when talent fails to work hard." Few things in the NBA ground my gears like a top team squandering an advantage through complacency, and the Clippers had looked like straight A students who decided that they didn't need to study for their final exam. They fell behind 14–2 in the opening minutes and trailed 44–25 at the end of the first quarter.

The performance didn't raise as many eyebrows as it should have, in part because Leonard shot an uncharacteristic 4-for-17 from the field. It was his worst shooting night of the playoffs, and unlikely to happen again. Given that it was so early in the series, coach Doc Rivers tried not to dwell on the performance, giving credit to the "aggressive" Nuggets.

Just as easily as the Clippers had turned off the switch, they flipped it back on. George scored 32 points and hit five 3-pointers in a 113–107 victory in Game 3, with the Clippers limiting Murray to just 14 points and closing out the fourth quarter in steady fashion. Leonard helped seal the win with a fingertip block of a Murray dunk attempt. Slow-motion replays captured Leonard extending his massive hand just high enough so that his middle finger could bat away Murray's slam at the last possible moment. The highlight play felt like big brother putting little brother back in his place, or like a cute story team running into a wall that it wouldn't be able to climb.

Flush with confidence after the win, Clippers guard Patrick Beverley couldn't help himself. Beverley, who had only been a bit player during the playoffs after missing time with a calf injury, had previously tangled with Damian Lillard. Now he set his sights on Jokic. "He presents the same thing Luka Doncic presents: a lot of flailing," Beverley said. "He puts a lot of pressure on the referees to make the right calls."

As a beefy and skilled center, Jokic represented the toughest matchup for the Clippers' defense. Jokic had scored 26 points in Game 2 and 32 points in Game 3, and Beverley was trying to draw the Serbian big man into a mind game. In my view, Beverley was right on the merits but wrong in his manner. Jokic liked to sell contact, but there was no good reason for Beverley to launch an unnecessary broadside at this point of the series.

Jokic was a seven-footer, and Beverley was a six-foot-one point guard who would never be called upon to stop him. What's more, Jokic had attempted only two free throws in Game 2 and four in Game 3. His trips to the line hadn't impacted the result, even if Clippers center Ivica Zubac had fouled out in twenty-one minutes. Coaches and players tended to save their complaints about flopping and the officiating until after losses. And usually it was stars, not role players, who voiced the concerns.

In any case, Beverley's line produced genuine confusion from the Nuggets. Jokic was twenty-five years old, and this wasn't his first post-season rodeo. He had never shown much interest in trash talking, and he maintained a cool, almost bored, demeanor with reporters. "What's flailing mean?" Jokic asked. "They had twenty-six free throws and we had ten. I'm just showing the ref it's a foul." Malone dismissed the jab and got in one of his own: "I don't listen to Patrick Beverley a whole lot. If Kawhi Leonard was talking, I might listen."

Beverley's commentary seemed less important than Denver's inability to stop Leonard. In a Game 4 victory, he tallied 30 points, 11 rebounds, 9 assists, and 4 steals, taking full control of the game and giving the Clippers a commanding 3–1 series lead. Plenty of Twitter quipsters joked that the Nuggets weren't comfortable in a series until they were trailing 3–1. Others noted that the Clippers had blown a 3–1 lead to the Rockets in the second round of the 2015 playoffs.

This felt like a different series. The Clippers weren't the Jazz, and they were a deeper group than the squad that had collapsed against the Rockets. Leonard was posing problems that the Nuggets couldn't answer, and Murray had topped 20 points just once in the first four games. Rivers, who had coached the 2015 Clippers, made sure to strike a measured tone after reaching the cusp of the franchise's first-ever conference finals. "No one cares," the coach said, describing a muted locker room after the Game 4 win. "It was a zero reaction. We haven't done anything yet."

Rivers's wariness proved well-founded. The Clippers built a 16-point lead in Game 5 before the wheels fell off on the defensive end. Malone was back in his all-black attire, and Murray and Jokic were back gunning freely with nothing to lose in another elimination game. Denver opened the fourth on a 21–8 run, scoring virtually every time it came down the court. The Clippers' bench, which had been the NBA's best during the regular season, combined for just 16 points on 20 shots.

The concerns raised by the Clippers' Game 2 showing were back, albeit now with more rubberneckers watching and wondering whether they would actually blow a 3–1 lead again. Rivers bemoaned his team's lack of defensive discipline, Leonard acknowledged the season-long struggle to hold leads, and George tried to look ahead to Game 6. "We had them on the line, and we gave a game up," he said. "We have to come in and put them away."

Writing the prescription proved to be much easier than filling it. Game 6 was practically a duplicate of Game 5: The Clippers built a 19-point lead shortly after halftime before the Nuggets came storming back again. Jokic, prodded days earlier by Beverley, was sensational, turning in a 34-point, 14-rebound, 7-assist night that was his best of the playoff run to date. The Nuggets ran off a 30–11 run in the second half to tie the score, and then pushed it to a 51–20 run as the shell-shocked Clippers failed to stop the bleeding.

In the near-empty building, the confidence disparity between the teams was conspicuous. Had Game 6 taken place in a non-pandemic year, the Nuggets' crowd would have gone crazy over the Clippers' latest collapse. But the bubble's conditions made it worse. The Clippers were living out a recurring nightmare—their worst nightmare—onstage with no distractions or even background noise. All eyes were focused on the missed shots, turnovers, and blown defensive assignments.

From my media seat directly across from the Clippers' bench, I could feel the coaches slumping into their chairs every time Jokic hit a clutch jumper. I could also hear how quiet the Clippers were on the court. The press conference yapping had given way to no chatter at all. They looked tired and overwhelmed. Rivers had noted how his team had "no reaction" after its Game 4 win, and they were flat in a different way during this baffling Game 6 loss. When the dust settled, Denver had erased a 19-point second-half deficit to win 111–98, turning the tables so decisively that both teams emptied their benches in the final minute.

The Clippers' postgame reaction was as disconcerting as their second-half play. Their main voices were all singing different tunes, setting off my alarm bells. Rivers pointed to the fact that his overhauled roster, in its first season together, hadn't shared the court much during the bubble because of injuries and personal matters. "This is a veteran team as far as where they're from, but they're not a veteran team together," he said.

If that assessment sounded strange from a coach who had spent the previous twelve months ramping up for a title push, George's attempt to project confidence didn't convince anyone. "Positive," he said of the team's mood. "This group is staying together. We're still in the driver's seat. It's not a panic mode." George doubled down on the idea that the Clippers were in command, adding that "the Nuggets are fighting and keeping their season alive, and I think to this point we've allowed them to do that."

Technically, neither team was in the driver's seat with the series tied 3–3. And Los Angeles didn't have much say over whether Denver's season was staying alive. The Nuggets had all the momentum, while the Clippers faced all the pressure. If given the opportunity to trade rosters for Game 7, Malone would have said "no" immediately. I bet Rivers would have thought hard about it, with so many of his role players coming up empty and his team's defense breaking down left and right in fourth quarters.

The harshest exchange of the entire bubble came during Leonard's postgame interview. A reporter in Los Angeles went straight for the throat on the Zoom call: "Did you guys just choke today?" I racked my brain to remember whether I had ever heard the "C-word" directed at any player, let alone a superstar like Leonard, during an NBA press conference. Nothing came to mind. During the 2011 Finals, a reporter set off a three-day news cycle by asking LeBron James if he was "shrinking" during big moments. "Shrinking" wasn't nearly as bad as "choking."

Saying that a player or team "choked" was provocative because it implied a character flaw, and there were plenty of available euphemisms to get the same point across. In this case, it accurately described what was happening. If writers and social media users were going to use the term in stories and tweets, maybe it was only fair to put the notion directly to Leonard.

Leonard was a two-time champion who had delivered during the Raptors' 2019 title push, including a series-winning buzzer-beater against the Philadelphia 76ers in the second round. He would have been well within his right to get up and leave on the spot or call out the question for being out of bounds. Instead, he appeared to half-flinch. "We just went cold," he said. "We went cold in that third quarter. That's it. We got into the paint and were passing the ball, but we got a little stagnant and just couldn't make shots."

Game 7 came down to Leonard, who was supposed to be the best player in the series and, perhaps, the entire sport. What more motivation did he need? His season was on the line, his team was embarrassed in back-to-back games, and he had been disrespected by a reporter. If Leonard handled his business in Game 7, the Clippers would do their part to set up the long-anticipated date with the Lakers.

Instead, the Clippers lived down to every mocking stereotype that haunted them for years. Fragile. Splintered. Cursed. Chokers. Los Angeles led by 12 points late in the second quarter, the third straight game it had staked a commanding first-half lead. And for the third straight game, Denver erased it in a flash. Murray scored 11 points in the final four minutes before halftime, and the Nuggets went on a 16–5 run to open the second half.

Déjà vu didn't begin to describe the feeling in the building. With the wind at their backs, the Nuggets unleashed a balanced scoring barrage by moving the ball ahead of the Clippers' demoralized defense. Seven different Nuggets players scored in the third period, setting up Murray and Jokic to bring home the win in the fourth.

Much like in Game 6, the Clippers' collapse was so complete that they couldn't even keep it close enough for a tense endgame. Los Angeles went the first seven minutes of the fourth quarter without making a shot, and Denver somehow built a 20-point lead. After one especially bad turnover, Rivers clutched his head with both hands as Denver's Gary Harris raced ahead for a transition layup. The season was falling apart before the coach's eyes, and he was powerless to stop it.

Leonard and George were too. Hopes for a takeover performance from Leonard quickly faded, as he scored just 14 points and shot an abysmal 6-for-22 from the field. George was arguably worse, finishing with 10 points on 4-for-16 shooting while missing nine of his eleven 3-point attempts. The Clippers' superstars combined for just one free-throw attempt, and their second-half play was troubling in its lack of urgency. When Giannis Antetokounmpo felt the Bucks' season slipping, at least he put his head down and repeatedly attacked the hoop. Leonard and George settled for jumper after jumper, never altering their ineffective approach.

Even if one or both had stepped up, it still might not have been enough. Murray went off for 40 points—his fourth time reaching that mark in the playoffs—and looked fearless the whole way. Jokic put up a 16-point, 22-rebound, 13-assist triple-double, doing all the walking after Beverley's misguided talking earlier in the series.

The Nuggets had done the unthinkable, winning six straight elimination games in a span of three weeks. What's more, they had sent the Clippers packing with such force in Game 7 that they barely celebrated on the court afterward. Malone, still in his Johnny Cash getup, accepted a handshake from Rivers. Murray got pats of appreciation from Beverley and Lou Williams. Jokic didn't even crack a smile. The Clippers headed to their locker room in a daze.

There was no doubt in my mind that this collapse was worse than 2015 for the Clippers because they had much higher internal and external expectations. They had blown leads of 16 points, 19 points, and 12 points in consecutive games. They had been outscored by a combined 94–59 in the fourth quarters of their last three losses, and they had gotten next to nothing from Leonard and George in Game 7.

After spending all year circling the Lakers, the Clippers hadn't held up their end of the bargain. They went out of their way to talk trash and play rough in the playoffs, and they fell on their faces. They were, in the end, all bark and no bite. Worst of all, they quit on one another during the toughest moments.

I wondered whether they would have blown the series if they had played Game 5 and Game 7 at home in Staples Center. It was a tempting, but meaningless, hypothetical. I also wondered how owner Steve Ballmer would react. The Clippers spent a year preparing to chase Leonard in free agency, and they parted with promising guard Shai Gilgeous-Alexander, five first-round picks, and two pick swaps to acquire George.

On top of that, the Clippers bankrolled a giveaway of one million backpacks to Southern California students on behalf of Leonard. The unprecedented act of generosity was a clever method of catering to their new franchise player.

As I waited for the Clippers to give their final press conferences of the year, I wondered how Ballmer, the sport's richest owner, would process this brutal humiliation. Would he question the entire plan? Would he look for a fall guy? He had to make this terrible feeling go away and change the perception of his franchise for good. How would he deploy his unlimited financial resources in search of a new competitive advantage? Two million backpacks? Three million? Magic Johnson gleefully twisted the knife. "The Lakers will always own Los Angeles," he wrote on Twitter. "It will never change."

The explanations and excuses were flying after Game 7. Rivers said that he would "take any blame" for the loss as coach, then added that his rotation included players "that just couldn't play minutes" because they weren't in top shape. His anxiety had shown through during games as he exhorted his team and worked the referees from the sidelines, and he acknowledged that he was "never comfortable" when the Clippers claimed early leads because of the "conditioning" issue.

Leonard didn't reveal much, other than to say that the Clippers needed to "build some chemistry and get smarter" to finish out games. "We shot ourselves in the foot in the last three games," he said. "The last three games mirrored each other."

After scoring 18.2 points per game in the regular season, Williams averaged 12.8 points per game and shot just 24 percent on 3-pointers in the playoffs. The sixth man, who said the Clippers were "pissed off," acknowledged that his team had "the talent to win but I don't think we had the chemistry to do it, and it showed."

The thirty-four-year-old Williams, who was put through the extra hotel isolation period because of his side trip to Magic City, admitted that the bubble wore on him. "I haven't seen my two daughters in sixty-eight days," he said. "I know the exact amount of time I hadn't seen them. When you deal with that type of stuff and you're in a controlled environment, you're thankful that you're safe. But it can be taxing."

George's interview was the most baffling of all. The Clippers had embraced, and even fueled, talk of a championship push since the previous summer. Rivers said explicitly that the franchise had fallen short of expectations. Williams said the same thing. Yet George, who shot below 40 percent in the playoffs, was reading from a different page.

"The fact of the matter is we didn't live up to that expectation," he said. "But I think internally we've always felt this isn't a championship or bust year for us. We can only get better the longer we stay together and the more we're around each other. The more chemistry for this group, the better. I think that's really the tale of the tape of the season. We didn't have enough time together."

The Clippers faced some major roster decisions, but George stuck to his long-term message. "That hurts," he said, when asked about all the blown leads to the Nuggets. "That hurts. It hurts. It hurts. But you move on. Year one together. First run together."

I thought George sounded confused, and I wasn't alone. The reporters in the room exchanged raised eyebrows and judgmental glances after he left. Again, I wondered what Ballmer would think when he heard those comments. Move on? Just like that?

Leonard, George, and Williams had all agreed on one thing: The chemistry was off. That seemed to signal that major changes were coming. Harrell, Marcus Morris, JaMychal Green, Patrick Patterson, Reggie Jackson, and Joakim Noah were all upcoming free agents. Beverley and Williams hadn't made much impact in the playoffs. All told, everyone outside of Leonard and George looked expendable. George's "first run together" was shaping up to be a "first and last run together" for much of the group.

And then there was Rivers. The longtime coach built the Clippers into a winner after his 2014 arrival, survived the Donald Sterling scandal, oversaw the winningest stretch in franchise history, and delivered six playoff trips in seven seasons. He received contract extensions in 2018 and 2019, he was a central figure in the free agency recruitment of Leonard, and he served as a major voice in the bubble's social justice campaigns. Rivers, in short, was a savior for the Clippers.

But Ballmer had loaded Rivers's coaching staff with multiple head coaching candidates and invested heavily in his medical staff. Rivers made questionable lineup decisions against the Nuggets, and his team never lived up to its full potential on offense or defense. Ballmer was a results-oriented tech titan who had no interest in excuses and little patience. In addition to the investments in the roster and the charitable efforts, he was in the process of building a billion-dollar arena complex in Inglewood. He had even paid $400 million in cash to New

York Knicks owner James Dolan to buy the Forum, an arena near his proposed site, to end a legal battle and ensure that he could go forward with his proposed development.

As I pondered the Clippers' next steps, I thought back to the defining move of Ballmer's tenure prior to Leonard's signing: the 2018 trade of Blake Griffin. It was a cutthroat deal. Months after pitching Griffin on his future as a franchise icon and inking him to a long-term extension, the Clippers shipped him to the Detroit Pistons with little warning. It was the right trade for the franchise, but it was unbelievably cold, bordering on betrayal.

Ballmer made his priorities clear with that trade: He wanted to win championships, not friends. All was fair in love and war, and basketball was both to Ballmer. Bubble or no bubble, I suspected that a big head needed to roll after the Denver series. Leonard and George were the franchise cornerstones, and they had just arrived. The front office was an excellent, collaborative group without a glaring weak link. By process of elimination, that left Rivers. Sure enough, the press release hit the in-box thirteen days after Game 7: "Doc Rivers departs L.A. Clippers."

"I am extremely confident in our front office and our players," Ballmer said in a statement, which deemed Rivers's exit to be a "mutual decision" between owner and coach. "We will find the right coach to lead us forward and help us reach our ultimate goals."

Even with the benefit of a prepared statement directed to Clippers fans, Rivers sounded pained by the parting. "When I took this job, my goals were to make this a winning basketball program, a free agent destination, and bring a championship to this organization," he said. "I won't be able to see them all through. Though it was a disappointing ending to our season, you are right there, and I know what this team is capable of accomplishing."

The bubble opened in July with three title favorites, and now only one remained. While the Clippers had outlasted the Bucks, their demise was even more spectacular. Leonard was at home. Antetokounmpo was at home. Suddenly, the path was wide open for LeBron James and the Lakers.

16

Balls of Steel

"The Happiest Place on Earth" was doing a remarkable job of bringing a team's vulnerabilities into the light. For the Sixers, it was their lineup problems and stylistic approach. For the Bucks, it was late-game offensive execution and the emotional weight of Jacob Blake's shooting by police. For the Clippers, it was chemistry, chemistry, chemistry. All three teams should have fared better than they did, and I was certain that all three would have gone further in an alternate world without a pandemic.

I was worried that the same fate would befall the Toronto Raptors, who claimed the East's No. 2 seed with a 53-19 record. The defending champions arrived in Florida before the other twenty-one teams due to their need for international travel, and their core players made it clear that the Blake shooting had left a mark on their collective psyche. Before the three-day shutdown, Toronto easily swept the injury-ravaged Brooklyn Nets in the first round, putting up a whopping 150 points in the closeout win.

The Raptors were a different team in the initial aftermath of the shutdown, opening their second-round series against the Boston Celtics with two straight losses. Nick Nurse knew the Raptors were in trouble after they got their "butts kicked" in a 112–94 loss in Game 1. The attentive second-year coach was used to his team exerting maximum effort and making life miserable for opponents. Instead, the Raptors were flat and admitted that their minds were still on Blake after the loss.

Boston, the East's No. 3 seed after going 48-24 in the regular season, then took Game 2 by a 102–99 count. This was a fluky and maddening loss from the Raptors' perspective. Celtics guard Marcus Smart, a career 32 percent 3-point shooter, hit six 3-pointers, including five in the fourth quarter. If nothing else, Smart's barrage snapped the Raptors out of their funk.

"We're pretty pissed right now," said Kyle Lowry, a hard-nosed point guard who helped lead the 2019 title team. "This is not a situation we'd like to be in, but this is not a normal situation in the playoffs where we lost two home games. We've just lost two games."

There would be little chance of coming back from an 0–3 hole, bubble or no bubble, so Nurse sought to manufacture any advantage that he could during his postgame comments. That meant working the referees with colorful language and passive-aggressive digs. "I think Smart fouled the shit out of Pascal Siakam," Nurse declared when asked about a late drive to the hoop by his forward. Meanwhile, Boston's Jayson Tatum led all scorers with 34 points in another strong performance. Nurse called it "frustrating" that the All-Star forward attempted fourteen free throws, adding that the referees "took very good care of him tonight."

The Raptors knew that their season was reaching a breaking point. They were already playing with house money: Kawhi Leonard's departure in free agency removed any pressure or expectations from their title defense. During the regular season, they played fun, exhilarating basketball. Siakam made a nice fourth-year leap to earn his first All-Star nod, and guard Fred VanVleet was having a breakout season in a contract year. This was a proud team with numerous high-IQ players, including Lowry and center Marc Gasol.

Without Leonard, it mattered more how the Raptors played than how deep they went in the playoffs. A second-round loss wouldn't be the end of the world. However, rolling over would be out of character and a letdown for Toronto's rabid fan base.

Boston did its best to send Toronto packing early. Kemba Walker scored 29 points in Game 3, and the quick point guard capped one of his best games of the playoffs with a brilliant sequence on Boston's final possession. With the score tied at 101 and five seconds left, Walker dodged a double-team, drove into the paint, and slipped a no-look pass through two defenders to center Daniel Theis on the baseline. Theis caught the pass and rose quickly for a dunk, finishing the play with 0.5 seconds on the clock.

Nurse kicked the court and immediately called timeout. Lowry reacted with dismay, raising both of his hands with his palms up to ask Siakam why he hadn't rotated to guard Theis. Siakam seemed confused as to whether it was really his responsibility. Gasol looked annoyed. On the other side, Tatum triumphantly raised both of his fists in the air as Walker accepted chest pounds from the bench.

But Toronto still had a half second to save its season. Lowry, who had collapsed to the court after taking a flying knee to the groin in the third quarter, lined up to inbound the ball from the right sideline. Every option was available to him with Boston leading by 2 points: The Raptors could try a lob pass to the hoop, they could run to the ball for a quick catch-and-shoot 3-pointer, or they could aim for a stop-and-pop jumper to force overtime.

Celtics coach Brad Stevens added a layer of intrigue to the tense proceedings by inserting Tacko Fall, his seven-foot-five rookie center, to guard Lowry. Fall's claim to fame before this moment was that he had been a prop during the 2020 Slam Dunk Contest, with Orlando's Aaron Gordon vaulting over him on his final attempt. Fall played just thirty-three minutes in the regular season and three garbage-time minutes in the playoffs. Before the pandemic, the home crowd at Boston's TD Garden would chant "We want Tacko!" late in blowout wins and erupt in cheers when Stevens obliged.

Now, the six-foot Lowry had to contend with the NBA's tallest player as he set up the most important sequence of Toronto's season. VanVleet cut toward the ball angling for the right corner, but two Celtics defenders anticipated that he would be the first option and were waiting for him. Siakam then curled to center court near the 3-point line, but Marcus Smart switched to protect against a game winner from the top of the key. The play seemed bottled up: Gasol jockeyed for position with Jaylen Brown in the paint for a possible lob, and VanVleet frantically tried to create space near Lowry to receive a pass.

Amid all the confusion, OG Anunoby drifted to the far-left corner. It was fitting that the twenty-three-year-old forward was left wide open, with the nearest Boston defender some fifteen feet away. Anunoby was an unheralded defensive specialist, a valuable but easy-to-overlook cog in Toronto's success who never called attention to himself. He was known for being quiet on the court and unforthcoming in interviews. As Lowry surveyed his dwindling options, Anunoby didn't even raise his hands to call for the ball.

Nevertheless, Lowry launched one of the best and most audacious passes I had ever seen in my life. With both hands on the ball, he flicked his wrists and snapped a high-arching pass that cleared Fall, whose arms were raised above his head. Lowry sailed the ball some fifty feet, but his pass was so accurate that Anunoby only had to take a half step to his right to prepare for a quick catch-and-shoot attempt from just behind the 3-point line. Sensing the looming threat in the left corner, Brown sprinted from the center of the court and launched himself at Anunoby to block his shot or obscure his sight line.

Anunoby's 3-point attempt left his hands with 0.1 seconds remaining, cleared Brown's fingertips, and nestled into the hoop for a 104–103 victory as the buzzer sounded. Gasol and Siakam raised their arms, Lowry broke into a wide smile, and VanVleet jumped on Anunoby to begin a dogpile. Anunoby walked calmly toward the bench as his teammates engulfed him. He hit the bubble's best shot, and he didn't so much as blink in celebration. "I expected to make it," he explained. "I don't shoot trying to miss."

VanVleet said that Anunoby's non-reaction to "the biggest shot of his life" was "true OG form," and Nurse told reporters that he had ripped off the game-winning play design from an old instructional video starring Hubie Brown, the longtime coach and radio broadcaster. Lowry couldn't stop grinning or deferring credit. "The pass was nothing," he said, after posting 31 points and 8 assists. "All the credit goes to the shot. That's a great moment for that kid. That's the type of moment that his even-keel attitude helps him stay calm. He's built for that."

This was just the latest example of Lowry delighting in his younger teammates' successes, a pattern that picked up after the Raptors won the 2019 title. The thirty-four-year-old point guard had endured plenty of criticism during a fourteen-year career that saw him move from Memphis to Houston before finally breaking through in Toronto once he reached his late twenties. After years of playoff shortcomings, Lowry savored the championship validation and often looked to pay it forward, whether by angling for VanVleet to get a new contract, counseling Siakam through playoff struggles, or hyping up Anunoby's unbelievable 3.

But Lowry turned self-aggrandizing while delivering a line that best captured the Raptors on their exuberant night. Asked how he had delivered in the clutch after taking the below-the-belt shot that doubled him over in pain, a deadpan Lowry said, "Obviously, I've got balls of steel." A crude and macho reference, yes, but also a fitting label for his fourth-quarter play, his gutsy pass over Fall, Anunoby's cold-blooded winner, and the Raptors' resolve after Theis's dunk.

Toronto was far from done, scoring a 100–93 win in Game 4 with hot outside shooting to even the series. While Bucks coach Mike Budenholzer had refused to extend his stars' minutes, Nurse was taking the opposite approach. Lowry, VanVleet, and Siakam each played at least forty-three minutes in Game 4, and Nurse relied on a seven-man rotation.

Boston counterpunched with a strong 111–89 win in Game 5, putting together a balanced performance that left me thinking they should be viewed as the East's favorite. All five Celtics starters scored in double figures, and they jumped on the Raptors early to take a 3–2 series lead. "You can't go through a playoffs without having heartbreakers," Stevens said, referring to Anunoby's momentum-swinging 3-pointer. "You can't go through a playoffs without something bad happening. You just have to be able to respond. I knew we had good competitive character. You really saw that on display."

I respected how even-tempered Stevens was after every game, win or loss. Like Heat coach Erik Spoelstra, he enjoyed afternoon walks by himself in the heat, multitasking by taking phone calls along the way. I grew up in Oregon, where hikers almost always say "hello" when they pass on the trail. Stevens's unfailing politeness—he nodded, waved, and smiled, no matter what—reminded me of home.

Stevens struck me as someone who lived his values, treating others how he wanted to be treated and never skipping steps. He preferred to praise or critique his team rather than singling out individual players, and he had no interest in mind games. His leadership style was about composure and putting his players before himself. If Stevens was on an airplane when the oxygen masks deployed, I imagined him walking from seat by seat with a reassuring smile to make sure all the passengers were breathing properly into their bags. These qualities, frankly, tended to make him a terrible quote.

I liked watching Stevens manage games with his arms crossed like a chess player, but I was really taken by Nurse and the Raptors, particularly when they reached crisis moments. I loved watching the Raptors lose because of how much they hated losing.

Lowry was seething during Game 5, as Toronto never found a way to dig out of a large first-quarter hole. With the Celtics keeping the Raptors at bay as the fourth quarter approached, Lowry couldn't control his frustration any longer and let loose on an official. Serge Ibaka wasn't pleased at the game situation or at Lowry's outburst, and he let his teammate know about it. "Come on, we're losing, man!" he shouted. VanVleet walked over to play peacemaker before Lowry talked himself down.

This was the feistiness that the Sixers, Bucks, and Clippers lacked. Even better, the mischievous Nurse could be counted on to push buttons with his team now facing elimination. Siakam was ineffective throughout the series: He wasn't getting to the free-throw line, he wasn't shooting with confidence, and he wasn't getting to the rim as often as he should.

The Cameroonian forward bottomed out with just 10 points, 4 rebounds, and 2 assists in Game 5, and Nurse wasn't afraid to prod him. "I'm not sure why he's been so out of rhythm since the restart in the bubble," the coach said of Siakam. "He hasn't had a lot of great games. It's too bad because he was spectacular in last year's playoffs and spectacular all year long. We still have some games to play. Hopefully he can get his rhythm."

Nurse was gentle with his bedside manner, but he was still going further than most modern coaches when it came to publicly critiquing a franchise centerpiece. Siakam had signed a four-year, $130 million maximum contract the previous fall and blossomed into a perennial All-Star type during the regular season. Players in that situation often assumed they would never hear a negative word from their coaches, who usually lacked leverage and job security. Nurse, the reigning Coach of the Year, was on solid footing, and he was savvy enough to phrase his commentary as a lament so that he could call out Siakam without embarrassing him. Trying to spark Siakam felt like a healthier approach than denial.

What really set Nurse apart was his resourcefulness, honed during his nearly thirty years coaching in the American minor leagues and overseas before he took over the Raptors in 2018. He emptied the toolbox in Game 6 by unveiling a lineup that featured Anunoby, a six-foot-seven forward, at the center position. Boston's quickness and versatility had posed matchup problems for Gasol and Ibaka, Toronto's two most accomplished big men, so Nurse turned to his center-less lineup for the final eight minutes of regulation.

The trade-offs were clear as day: Boston kept feeding Theis for dunks and layups around the basket, while Toronto countered with an offensive boost courtesy of Norman Powell, a veteran wing who joined Lowry, VanVleet, Siakam, and Anunoby in the potent new look. The two sides kept exchanging punches in the fourth quarter until the defensive intensity picked up over the final two minutes. With neither team able to score, the game went to overtime tied at 98.

In overtime, Nurse stuck with his new group, which had taken the court only a few times together during the regular season. Powell rewarded his coach's faith with a clutch 3-pointer and two late free throws, but he missed a potential game winner with the score tied. A second overtime was needed.

There, Powell came through with 10 more points to seal a 125–122 victory. After barely making an impact in the first five games of the series, Powell finished with 23 points to save the season and make Nurse's lineup gamble look like a genius maneuver. "Fuck, that was great," Lowry said, ecstatic and relieved. "Thank you, Norm. That was fucking unbelievable. Shit. That was cool. We needed that."

Siakam wasn't the hero of the night: He finished with 12 points, 8 rebounds, 6 assists, and several late miscues. Still, he hit a key jumper midway through the second overtime and logged a game-high fifty-four minutes. Nurse needed every one of those minutes to keep his versatile, center-less lineup on the court throughout the extended crunch time. "We're at a stage where the stakes are super high," the coach said. "Only good teams can win at this stage. For us to be good, we've got to have those little contributions from all over the place."

Again, I marveled at the Raptors' pluck. For years, they had been the lowest-hanging fruit in the playoffs. They blew a Game 7 at home in 2014. They were swept out of the first round by the Washington Wizards in 2015. They were knocked out in the 2016 Eastern Conference finals in six, with LeBron James making it clear he didn't fear them while delivering blowout wins in the final two games. Then the Raptors were swept out by James's Cavaliers in 2017 and 2018.

Nurse's ascension, Leonard's arrival, and the 2019 title forged a tough-minded identity, one that stood up well even after Leonard's abrupt exit. Lowry set the tone for the group, and he was such a gamer that he showed off a picture of his bloodied chin, which required three stitches, during his press conference after Game 6. He tilted his camera around the room so that everyone could see his badge of honor.

The series with Boston was tied 3–3, even though Toronto easily could have lost five of the six games. The Raptors would have been done if Lowry's pass didn't connect, if Anunoby missed his miracle shot, if Nurse didn't go small, or if Powell didn't come through. But they somehow lived to fight another day.

I wasn't sure who would win Game 7, but I was convinced that Boston was the better team. The Celtics had been more consistent from game to game, they had forced the Raptors to adjust to their preferred style, and Tatum had badly outplayed Siakam. On the bus ride to the arena, two reporters were doing radio interviews simultaneously. Both picked the Raptors, citing their experience and grit. Their "balls of steel," to borrow Lowry's phrase.

Toronto, though, had run itself ragged in the two-overtime thriller. Nobody, aside from VanVleet, could hit a shot for the Raptors in Game 7. Gasol was too slow to stay on the court for long. Lowry fought gamely but looked gassed. Anunoby was a nonfactor on offense. And Siakam, who logged more than forty minutes for the fourth time in the series, still couldn't get on track.

The deciding contest belonged to Tatum, who led all scorers with 29 points in a 92–87 victory. Boston closed out the win by beating Toronto at its own game: Smart rushed back in transition for a sensational block on Powell, and Tatum outhustled everyone to an offensive rebound on a missed free throw. At the buzzer, Tatum raised his arms high to celebrate. "He's a superstar," Walker said. "He showed it tonight. Anybody who had any questions or doubts about that, he showed it. Game 7. He's a special kid."

Lowry tipped his cap. If he had to go down, he wanted it to be like this. "It was an unbelievable battle," he said. "Those guys beat us fair and square. It's sad. We had more to give. The bubble was challenging. It was well put together. We used our platform for our voices to be heard on social injustices. The bubble was a success. Time to leave this motherfucker."

Siakam was his own worst critic. Throughout the postseason, he shot poorly, lost trust in his perimeter jumper, and forced the issue off the dribble. In the seven-game series, he shot 4-for-32 on 3s and committed fifteen turnovers. The loose, athletic forward was tied up in knots during his first postseason as a featured offensive option. "I wasn't really able to help my teammates," he said. "I take a lot of the blame."

During the series, Nurse was cheeky, confrontational, pointed, and innovative. He was so invested in the competition that he occasionally resorted to breathing exercises during his postgame interviews to level off his emotions. The Raptors—especially Nurse and Lowry—were built for the bubble. I often saw Nurse racing a bicycle around the staid Disney World campus, searching for whatever adrenaline he could find.

Toronto's season was over, and Nurse knew changes were coming. He was wistful in defeat, laying out his plan to regroup with Siakam during the off-season, while acknowledging that VanVleet, Gasol, and Ibaka were all headed for free agency. Raptors president Masai Ujiri would likely prioritize youth and financial flexibility until he could find another superstar to replace Leonard. Some of the key pieces from the title team were bound to head their separate ways. "I already miss this team," Nurse said.

He wasn't the only one.

17

Unauthorized Guest

By September, the coronavirus was an afterthought in the bubble. No players, coaches, media members, or other inhabitants of the Coronado Springs Resort had tested positive. More than half the teams had been eliminated, leaving the campus emptier and feeling safer. Families had arrived without incident, as did a second wave of reporters who relieved their colleagues and planned to cover the final few rounds of the play-offs. Social justice issues had also taken precedent over health concerns, particularly during the three-day shutdown in late August.

The health rules were clear. The routines were internalized. The mandatory daily testing was second nature, and I got my test first thing every morning to ensure that I didn't land myself in another quarantine. After long nights of writing, the prospect of trudging down to the testing room made it harder to get out of bed. Still, it was a minor inconvenience that was clearly worth it from a health perspective. In the bubble, getting a test was as easy as wearing a mask, so I did both gladly and was thankful for a privilege that still wasn't available to many Americans.

I consider myself a law-abiding citizen in general, but I took no chances in the bubble. I steered clear of gray areas. When I realized that I had forgotten to wear a mask while using the shared laundry room once, I raced up four flights of stairs with my shirt over my mouth to find a face covering. Only then did I run back to move my clothes to the dryer. There was no one else around.

Throughout my stay, I never stepped foot in another person's hotel room, not even when a friend asked for urgent editing help late one night. I was convinced that the NBA's security system—with its proximity alarms to track close contact between guests, electronic room keys, video surveillance, and tip hotline to report violations—would be able to detect that I was in someone else's room. Other than fist bumps and elbow taps, I didn't touch anyone until Ruth Bader Ginsburg's death on September 18. That night, I hugged a distraught colleague at the arena and worried that the quick embrace would somehow irk the authorities.

I still don't know whether I was being overly paranoid. In the early days, multiple players were sent back into isolation for rules violations, like leaving their room during the initial quarantine or straying off campus to pick up a food delivery. One writer, who arrived halfway through, had his isolation period extended because he sat in front of his hotel room door to get fresh air during quarantine. The NBA held random spot checks to make sure our proximity alarms were charged up, issued rules clarifications and updates by text message, and carefully policed mask-wearing at the arenas. As I walked the loop one night, a security guard in an SUV pulled up next to me and demanded to see my credential before letting me go on my way.

Compliance with the rules was excellent, especially when compared with the outside world. There was no debate over masks in the bubble. Everyone wore masks. Social distancing was maintained at almost all times, especially indoors and at meals. The postgame interviews presented some early challenges because the rooms were small, leading reporters to cluster together and drift closer to the players. Still, it was nothing compared with Los Angeles, where I regularly squeezed into scrums with dozens of reporters and cameramen jockeying for position in cramped locker rooms. By the end of the playoffs in the bubble, interviews shifted to larger rooms, reporters sat in spaced-out chairs, and the players spoke from a small stage that ensured significant distancing. There were typically only about a dozen reporters on hand, making the press conferences feel like a sparsely attended school board meeting.

The virus didn't feel like a constant threat, not like it did in the outside world. At home, I had eliminated all trips to the grocery store and had cut down on my runs to the bank. In the bubble, I got my meals from servers who wore masks and gloves and stood behind a glass barrier. There was nowhere to spend cash on campus besides the barbershop, so I didn't even need an ATM. I arrived with $400 in cash, and it easily lasted for my entire stay.

There were hand sanitizer stations and disinfecting wipes everywhere on campus, yet I rarely saw anyone feel the need to use them. A few reporters had arrived wearing surgical gloves, but those disappeared within a few days. Players often lingered in hallways to chat with reporters and staffers after games, which was officially discouraged, but there was far less mingling than in pre-pandemic times. The NBA tightened policies that limited social interactions between players and reporters almost as soon as the media arrived, and the rules were followed, albeit with a lot of grumbling.

This was a strict existence, and I felt an obligation to the community to not screw it up for everybody. I was wary of the Big Brother security presence, but I was genuinely afraid of being the weakest link. The last story I ever wanted to file to my editors was "Playoffs postponed after Ben Golliver tests positive and exposes Lakers to coronavirus."

The more days that passed without any positive tests or health protocol violations, the more certain I became that there wouldn't be any major incidents. While anxiety, boredom, and loneliness were all serious issues, this was a three-month experiment, not a yearlong ordeal. There were some coping mechanisms available. The NBA had ceased its drug-testing program, and alcohol was served to players at on-campus restaurants and could be ordered by delivery. Poolside cigars were popular, especially among a handful of referees. There was also peer pressure among the players. A championship was at stake, and adhering to the coronavirus regulations was as important as making the extra pass or getting back on defense.

While Stephen A. Smith of ESPN pointed out the limited sexual opportunities for players before the bubble opened, the topic was taboo during interviews at Disney World. The on-site reporters assumed that there were unseen rule benders and rule breakers in the bubble, but what happened in the players' hotels largely stayed in the players' hotels because of the health protocols and strict access issues. Once wives and girlfriends arrived after the first round, I assumed that the players had survived the most challenging portion of their bubble experience on this front.

The Rockets found out the hard way that it wasn't quite that simple. Houston was talented but inconsistent, and general manager Daryl Morey had pinned his team's hopes on an unconventional devotion to small ball. Houston almost exclusively played lineups without centers, sacrificing size and toughness inside to create more space for its star guards to operate.

To upset the top-seeded Lakers in the second round, the undersized Rockets would need all hands on deck. That included twenty-seven-year-old forward Danuel House, whose athleticism and outside shooting made him a good fit alongside James Harden and Russell Westbrook. While House had to work his way up through the G-League after going undrafted, the four-year pro was an integral piece of the puzzle, averaging 11.4 points while attempting almost six 3-pointers per game in the playoffs.

To counter the Lakers' Goliath frontcourt of LeBron James, Anthony Davis, and Dwight Howard, the Rockets deployed P. J. Tucker, a sturdy six-foot-five forward, to bother Davis on defense while loading the court with shooters to launch 3-pointers on offense. The plan worked reasonably well in Houston's 112–97 victory in Game 1: Harden and Westbrook outscored James and Davis, and the Rockets outshot the Lakers from the perimeter and used their small lineups to push the tempo.

In defeat, James referred to the Rockets as a "100-meter dash team" and compared them to the NFL's St. Louis Rams of the early 2000s, who were dubbed "The Greatest Show on Turf" for their electric offense. "There's no way you can simulate that speed," James said. "You can watch it on film, but we got a feel for their speed tonight."

Houston came back to earth with a 117–109 loss in Game 2, with Westbrook shouldering much of the blame. The 2017 MVP had tested positive for COVID-19 before he arrived at the bubble and then suffered a quad injury that sidelined him for a portion of the first round. Westbrook made his name on relentless energy and physicality; when he was on, he bullied his way to the hoop, drained midrange jumpers, and pushed the pace in transition.

But Westbrook had long possessed erratic tendencies, and his play was beyond volatile in the bubble. Game 2 was perhaps his most damaging performance. Westbrook committed seven turnovers and five fouls, and he made only four of his fifteen shots. The Lakers were giving him ten feet of space and daring him to shoot, but he couldn't resist and missed six of his seven 3-point attempts. Many of the misses were pure bricks. This was hardly Westbrook's first bout with playoff struggles. His teams were eliminated in the first round for the last three years as he struggled to shoot efficiently and take care of the ball.

Years earlier, Westbrook's frantic performances in high-pressure moments led me to coin a favorite phrase: He played with purpose, but he didn't play with a purpose. While no one could question his determination or effort, he lacked feel and a wider vision of the game and all ten players. As a series unfolded, he didn't orchestrate the action to set up his teammates for success or probe his opponents for unexpected vulnerabilities. By contrast, Chris Paul, the player Houston traded to acquire Westbrook in 2019, played with a purpose. He knew how to deploy a scalpel, rather than relying solely on a blowtorch. James, the Lakers' superstar, always played with a purpose in the playoffs.

"Right now, I'm just running around," Westbrook said after the Game 2 loss. "I've got to look at film and figure out how to be effective." I took his admission as validation for my long-held theory, and I wondered whether it represented good news or bad news for the Rockets. Self-awareness wasn't always Westbrook's specialty. At the same time, Houston needed a confident, effective Westbrook to overcome the Lakers' size advantage. A wobbly Westbrook would doom the Rockets.

Before Westbrook got his shot at redemption, the Rockets received news that blossomed into a scandal that broke their spirits. On the morning of September 8, a Tuesday, Houston was informed by the NBA that House and veteran center Tyson Chandler were being investigated for a suspected violation of the bubble's health and safety protocols.

A woman, later identified as a contract employee working for the company that provided COVID-19 tests on campus, had made an unauthorized late-night visit to the Rockets' hotel. The woman managed to pass through security checkpoints and enter an area of the Grand Floridian hotel that was accessible only to NBA teams.

Houston was the only remaining team at that hotel after seven other teams had been eliminated. "I like it," Westbrook had said after Houston's first-round series victory over Oklahoma City. "We get to go back to a campus where it's just us. No other teams. Just us at the Grand Floridian."

The Rockets might have enjoyed the extra privacy, but they were still being monitored by security guards and watched by surveillance cameras. The NBA's security team, armed with evidence of the unauthorized visitor and fearing a possible health and safety breach, held out both House and Chandler from Game 3 as it pursued an investigation.

This was a nightmare scenario on multiple levels. For the Rockets, who didn't find out about the investigation until hours before Game 3 tipped off, House's unexpected absence represented a massive competitive disadvantage. He had scored 13 points in twenty-seven minutes in Game 2, and Houston's options to replace him in the rotation weren't great. The real killer was the timing, as previous protocol violators like Richaun Holmes and Lou Williams had received ten-day quarantines as punishment. If the NBA gave House a similar sentence, he would miss the rest of the series even if it went seven games.

Under normal circumstances, the NBA would announce any suspensions for a playoff game before tip-off. Here, House and Chandler sat out Game 3 in a tied series for "personal reasons" while the league's investigation continued. This was a potentially explosive situation, as the NBA was opening itself to charges of favoritism and a lack of transparency by holding out players without providing a public explanation.

To make matters worse, the Lakers were the team benefiting from the decision. In one of the worst public relations scandals in league history, disgraced former referee Tim Donaghy had alleged that the Lakers had benefited from rigged officiating during a 2002 playoff series against the Sacramento Kings. Former commissioner David Stern once said that his dream NBA Finals matchup was "the Lakers versus the Lakers" due to their immense television appeal, and some fans and conspiracy theorists have long felt that the glitzy, big-market franchise was the darling of the league office.

The NBA didn't have a choice when it came to House. If any player had unauthorized contact with someone who wasn't living inside the bubble, he risked exposure to the coronavirus. He also risked exposing his teammates, coaches, opposing players, referees, and media members if he played in a game. Per the NBA's rules, unauthorized guests from outside the bubble were forbidden, and the only option for rule-breakers was total isolation.

Los Angeles took Game 3 by a 112–102 count, as James finished with 36 points and set the NBA's record for career playoff wins. The contest was competitive until the Lakers made a push early in the fourth quarter. Houston was dangling, both in the series and in anticipation of a ruling on House's status.

When the Rockets took the court for Game 4 on Thursday, September 10, the NBA still hadn't made up its mind. Although House maintained his innocence, the NBA hadn't cleared him, officially suspended him, or issued a detailed explanation of its investigation. House remained confined to his hotel room. Chandler, a veteran center who wasn't in the playoff rotation, was cleared of any wrongdoing and allowed to return.

The Rockets, people with direct knowledge of the investigation told me, felt "blindsided" by the NBA's treatment of House. The NBA and the NBPA had exchanged communications in between Game 3 and Game 4, but Houston had largely been kept out of the loop and hadn't been presented with evidence of House's alleged wrongdoings. The Rockets' frustration was palpable. Their season was on the line, as were the futures of coach Mike D'Antoni and numerous players.

"The NBA is treating House as guilty until proven innocent," one person with direct knowledge of the investigation told me. "They're prioritizing their perception of safety over everything else. The NBPA feels its hands are tied. Anytime the union talks about due process or presumption of guilt, the NBA immediately says, 'Safety, safety, safety.' There has to be some limit or balance."

Houston had a reputation for responding poorly to playoff adversity. Harden played badly in a season-ending loss to the Spurs in 2017. The Rockets missed twenty-seven consecutive 3-pointers in a Game 7 loss to the Warriors in 2018. Harden and Paul butted heads during a second-half collapse against the Warriors in a 2019 second-round exit. Houston even audited the officiating during its 2018 loss, arguing to the league office that the referees tilted the series in Golden State's favor. That unsuccessful effort led to accusations of poor sportsmanship and a persecution complex.

True to form, the Rockets, still in limbo, crumbled in Game 4. The Lakers won 110–100, but the game was all but over at halftime. Harden shot just 2-for-11 from the field and committed five turnovers in a listless performance. D'Antoni bemoaned his team's "lack of spirit" during a flat and ugly first half. There was precious little effort on defense. Standing in the hallway after the game, reporters could hear angry shouting through the walls of the Rockets' locker room.

Harden, at his best, dominated the basketball, controlled the action, and devastated opponents with precise footwork, well-honed moves, and powerful finishes. Harden, at his worst, detached from the action and his surroundings. After Game 4, sensing that momentum was gone for good, he avoided eye contact, barely engaged with questions, and fiddled with his ice packs during a postgame interview. He was over it. Westbrook offered no explanation for the poor showing either.

D'Antoni refused to blame House's situation, dismissing it as a "great excuse to trot out." Away from the cameras, the Rockets' frustration with the league boiled over. They lost both games without House and still didn't know exactly what he had done or whether he would be available for Game 5. The Lakers ran them out of the gym and could eject them from the bubble with a win on Saturday.

"If it was a star player, there's no way the NBA would handle it this way," one person close to House with direct knowledge of the investigation told me after the Game 4 loss. "They want to make an example out of somebody."

I didn't buy that argument. It was easy to cast House as a sacrificial lamb, but the stakes were huge. A coronavirus outbreak could require a multi-week delay and ruin the carefully scripted playoff schedule. Other teams would need to idle in the bubble, and the integrity of the playoffs would be thrown into question. The NBA had explained the rules before everyone arrived, and it spent incredible amounts of money to put on the games, create the health protocols, and enforce the safety standards. If the league didn't throw the book at House, it would be betraying the bubble's ideals.

Even so, I empathized with House and the Rockets because they deserved a clear presentation of the evidence and a swift judgment. On September 11, the day before Game 5, it finally came. "The NBA has concluded its investigation of a recent violation of campus health and safety protocols," a league press release read. "Danuel House had a guest in his hotel room over multiple hours on September 8 who was not authorized to be on campus. Mr. House is leaving the NBA campus and will not participate with the Rockets team in additional games this season." The investigation fully cleared Chandler and Houston's other players, coaches, and staff members.

House, who was married with three children, never stated his innocence publicly or addressed reporters before leaving the bubble. The Rockets never disputed the NBA's ruling. The NBA, which dumped the news on a Friday afternoon, never offered additional details about how it caught House, or why Chandler had been suspended and then cleared. The House investigation wrapped three days after it began, and it was swept under the rug. Months later, when the Rockets returned for a new season in December, House issued a public apology "to my team and the organization and the owner for the mishap that happened in the bubble." He offered no further details.

Smelling blood in Game 5, the Lakers eliminated the Rockets with an easy 119–96 victory. Harden scored 30 points, but he committed six turnovers in another uneven performance. Westbrook was bad and inefficient again, adding just 10 points while shooting 4-for-13 from the field. The contest was all but over within three minutes, when a James dunk gave the Lakers a 13–2 lead.

Houston just couldn't bring itself to make extra-effort plays, and it had no answers for Los Angeles's size and physicality. James knew it. "Y'all grabbing the whole fucking game," James yelled at Robert Covington, when the Rockets forward appealed to an official for assistance. "As soon as someone touches you, y'all got something to say. Y'all grabbing the whole game. Play ball."

Late in the contest, Westbrook lost his composure when William Rondo, the brother of Lakers guard Rajon Rondo, began heckling him and calling him "trash" from his courtside seat. William Rondo, a manager of the barbers in the bubble, was escorted out of the arena by security for violating the NBA's arena conduct policy for family members. "You're supposed to shut your mouth and watch the game," Westbrook said. "Those are the rules, especially when you have families and people here. It's all good. I get it. He wanted to take up for his brother. But those rules stand for everybody."

With the season over, there was no levity in defeat. Westbrook wore a cutoff T-shirt that read, "The sky is falling." He acknowledged that his positive COVID-19 test, which cost him three weeks of training time, and his subsequent leg injury had left him "trying to catch a rhythm" in the playoffs. D'Antoni sounded like a man who knew he had coached his last game in Houston after four winning seasons, saying meekly that he "couldn't ask for a better situation" and "hopefully it keeps going."

Harden admitted what was obvious to observers all week: The House investigation stopped the Rockets in their tracks. "It affected us because obviously it's a distraction and he's a huge part of our rotation," Harden said. "You still have to go out there and try to compete and try to win games. It's very, very frustrating. I'm going to keep chipping away. We're a piece away. We're going to keep trying to grow and put the right pieces around me and Russell."

I couldn't tell if Harden was just saying the right thing or if he truly believed it. The Rockets weren't "a piece away," not when they had been easily ousted in the second round. They weren't likely to "keep trying to grow," not if D'Antoni, their trusted coach, was going on move on. And they weren't guaranteed to build around Harden and Westbrook. The pair didn't show much playoff chemistry, and Westbrook played so poorly that he looked like an obvious trade candidate.

Morey, meanwhile, still hadn't escaped the shadow of his tweet in support of Hong Kong protesters. I thought back to my early summer view of Philadelphia and Houston as the league's top two boom-or-bust teams. The Sixers went bust in the first round. Now it was the Rockets' turn. House's rule violation was the straw that broke the camel's back, but this camel needed a chiropractor and some bed rest well before NBA security got involved.

Even if the NBA hadn't investigated and kicked out House, the Rockets weren't going to beat the Lakers. After the feel-out loss in Game 1, James ruthlessly picked apart a defense that didn't have the right pieces to stop him. The gap between James and Harden in the series was vast, especially when it came to composure, orchestrating the offense, and manipulating matchups. Both players were perennial MVP candidates, but only one played like it.

I knew the Rockets were toast before the NBA's ruling on House came down. James took the court for Game 4 with an exuberance that he hadn't displayed previously in the bubble. The four-time MVP sat down on a barrier that ran along the sideline and promptly swished a 3-pointer while seated. Then he put on an extensive Dunk Contest–like show during warmups, throwing alley-oops to himself and finishing them in jackhammer fashion.

Usually, James managed his energy before games. But there he was, sending ball boys running for cover with his dunks, bouncing giddily off his teammates, and high-fiving Dwight Howard when Anthony Davis drilled a half-court shot.

This joy didn't seem coincidental. The Lakers had the Rockets on the ropes. Giannis Antetokounmpo and the Bucks had been eliminated earlier in the week. Kawhi Leonard and the Clippers were up 3–1 on the Nuggets, but they hadn't looked like world-beaters. James, who finished with 29 points, 11 rebounds, and 7 assists in Game 5, sensed that his path to the title was clearing by the day.

By the time the Lakers eliminated the Rockets to reach their first Western Conference finals since 2010, James was being trailed after games by a camera crew. Sure enough, Andy Thompson, who shot much of the footage for *The Last Dance*, was on-site leading another behind-the-scenes project. James turned into a Pied Piper with his new followers in tow, cracking jokes with Davis in the arena hallways and interacting with reporters and other onlookers.

The previous summer, James woke up early and endured long days filming *Space Jam: A New Legacy*. Now the NBA's content king had another Michael Jordan sequel in the works. While James was always calculated with his postgame comments, he was taking care to craft his own story as he approached his fourth title.

"Some people are built for this moment and some people aren't," James declared after Game 3, neatly summarizing both sides of the Rockets series in one sentence.

18

Home Stretch

If the Bucks' protest marked the halfway point of the bubble, the end of the second round felt like the last lap of a mile around a high school track. I was never much of a runner, so approaching those last 400 meters always brought a mixture of relief and agony. The finish line was theoretically in sight, but heavy legs and burning lungs guaranteed that the fourth lap would be the longest.

The entire vibe of the bubble changed as the conference finals approached in mid-September. The bubble started with three hotels for the players but was now down to just the Gran Destino Tower. The Rockets, thanks in part to Danuel House, were the last to vacate the Grand Floridian. The frenetic daily doubleheaders and tripleheaders that defined the bubble were no more. From here on out, there was only one game a night at most.

Months after my July arrival, I finally found myself with time to kill. Rather than racing to get my step counts, I slowed my walks around the 1.5-mile oval loop and kept a closer eye on nature. The season had turned ever so slightly, and the worst of the heat and humidity had passed. Taylor Swift's moody new *Folklore* album was the perfect autumn soundtrack for a deserted amusement park where animals were reclaiming their swampy territory from invasive tourists.

I followed an armadillo through a grassy patch one night, ogled an alligator spotted by Nuggets general manager Tim Connelly, and got down on my knees to photograph a red-shouldered hawk. I spied a deer running through the trees and spent about fifteen minutes every day following around the same egret.

The beautiful white birds were a regular site at a wetland near my apartment in Los Angeles, and the egret's presence in the bubble was a comforting reminder of home. As time passed, he let me get within about five feet before he fled. I named the bird "Mikey," after Michael Jordan, and photographed him at least a hundred times as he treated me to gorgeous launches over small lakes. Look, there wasn't much else going on.

Among the media and league staffers, the countdown had started. Even if every series went seven games, there was only one month left. On late-night bus rides home from the arena, the topic often turned to life after the bubble: the first meal, the first time back behind the wheel of the car, the closest coronavirus-friendly vacation destinations. I tried my best not to go there. I had terrible bouts with senioritis in high school and college, and I wanted to give my full attention to the remaining games. I wasn't sure when the NBA would return the following season, and the Finals were fast approaching. I didn't want to check out mentally before my favorite two weeks of the year.

I could tell that the intense early interest in the bubble was fading. The Major League Baseball playoffs were beginning, the NFL season was about to start, and college football was trying to get off the ground. In some ways, the NBA was a victim of its own health success. With no positive tests and no delayed games, the novelty had worn off and the rubberneckers tuned out. I was still hearing from hard-core basketball fans around the clock, but there were fewer interview requests from outside the sports world. I had several friends in September inquire by text message: "Wait, you're still at Disney World?"

With fewer players on campus, the NBA opened select areas to media members that had been off-limits, including the Disney Store and a small shipping office where I could send outbound mail and packages. I made liberal use of both, buying bubble souvenirs for my friends, family, and coworkers. Mailing overpriced T-shirts with Mickey Mouse ears and the NBA logo became my new hobby. Gradually, I started sending stuff back home too: clothes, shoes, and the Lego Lamborghini, bubble wrapped with care after hours of painstaking assembly. While I wasn't in a hurry to leave, I wanted to make a smooth and swift exit when it was time.

The Disney World campus was a ghost town. Only four of the twenty-two teams were still around, and the Lakers were the only one of the three original favorites left standing. Their grip on the title chase felt as strong as ever because they had the two best players remaining in the field: LeBron James and Anthony Davis.

Denver, Miami, and Boston all played impressive and tough-minded basketball to reach the final four, but their best players—Nikola Jokic, Jamal Murray, Jimmy Butler, Bam Adebayo, Jayson Tatum, and Jaylen Brown—were all seeking their first Finals appearances. James was eyeing his tenth, and Los Angeles hadn't yet extended his minutes and upped his workload. "Playoff LeBron" was more lethal than "Regular Season LeBron," and a rested "Playoff LeBron" seemed like an unsolvable problem for the remaining challengers.

Still, nothing was guaranteed. The second round proved that the bubble was an unpredictable and unforgiving place. The Bucks, Clippers, and Rockets all collapsed, while the Raptors were knocked out by the lower-seeded Celtics in a thrilling series. Given how fraught the bubble felt after the Bucks' protest, the second round went as well as anyone could have hoped. There were breakout performances from Murray, Tatum, and Adebayo, plus a dominant display from James and Davis. Once the dust settled on the upsets, the field amounted to the Lakers and the three spoilers.

Before the conference finals commenced, the bubble was briefly halted by another protest. In the hours after the Lakers eliminated the Rockets on September 12, more than two dozen Black Lives Matter protesters staged a demonstration at Disney World. Salaythis Melvin, a twenty-two-year-old Black man, had been shot and killed by an Orange County sheriff's deputy outside an Orlando mall in August. The protesters, seeking justice for Melvin's family and the arrest of the officer involved in the shooting, assembled just before midnight on Buena Vista Drive, near the Gran Destino Tower's front entrance.

The Saturday night protest, which caught everyone inside the bubble by surprise, was planned brilliantly for maximum impact. Although security stations prevented them from getting inside the Coronado Springs Resort, the protesters set up on the main road between the arenas and the players' hotel. They timed the protest after the Lakers game, knowing that James and company would need to pass by while they were in the streets. Finally, they did their homework and knew how to identify the charter buses used by the teams and media members. That task was made easier by the fact that the area near the campus received little traffic, especially at night.

Shortly after I stepped onto the bus back to the hotel, a garbled warning came through to the driver from one of his colleagues. "Be advised that there are protesters by the Coronado Springs entrance." The bus took off like normal and progressed through most of the twelve-minute ride without incident, until we approached the resort. Suddenly, the streets were full of protesters who blocked multiple lanes and swarmed the media bus.

The group was mostly young people, many of whom wore black T-shirts that read, "Arrest the deputy that killed Salaythis Melvin." Signs with direct appeals to players—"LeBron, stand with us" and "Orlando needs you: #23"—were visible on all sides of the bus. They chanted, "No justice, no peace," and "We are here!" as they raised their fists in the Black Power salute. There was no confusion about what compelled them to disrupt traffic. Their message was clearly printed on a banner so big that it required three people to hold it up: "We are here because Orange County Sheriff's Deputy James Montiel shot and killed an innocent black man at the Florida Mall on August 7, 2020."

As the protesters advanced purposefully, I realized we were sitting ducks. The bus was surrounded on three sides, and we weren't going anywhere. I saw a visceral anger in a few of the protesters' faces, which prompted some confusion and a twinge of fear. One minute, I was minding my own business, transcribing quotes, uploading interview clips to Twitter, and chatting about the games that had just taken place. The next, I was imagining different scenarios that could see this protest spiral out of control. Instinctively, I whipped out my iPhone to record the scene.

One man stood directly in front of the bus, shouting profanities and flipping off the driver. "Idiots," the driver replied in disgust. I knew there were police officers staking out the main entry at all hours, but I wasn't sure there was a large enough contingent on hand in the middle of the night to disperse a crowd of protesters.

My mind raced. Would security's priority be to protect the property boundary and the players inside the hotel or to rescue a few dozen writers and staffers? Then I wondered: If even one of the protesters somehow made it onto the bus, would everyone on board be sent back to a weeklong quarantine? The bubble had a way of prompting the strangest questions.

Those anxious thoughts quickly passed once it became clear the protesters were nonviolent. They made no attempt to board the stopped bus or even to throw things at the windows. They wanted to make a scene, and they correctly assumed that we would help get their message out. Video clips shot by multiple reporters went viral, and many major outlets ran stories on the protest.

This was not a terrifying standoff like the ones in Minneapolis after George Floyd's death that played out on television. Still, I worried about what would happen if police officers showed up and the crowd stood its ground. This was my first direct taste of the protests besides a tame walk for justice that passed in front of my Los Angeles apartment. I steered clear of the protests and violence while on lockdown in California, and the bubble always felt separated from the street protests that continued throughout the summer.

The Melvin protest stopped the bus for only six minutes, but it felt longer in the moment. After the traffic lights went through a few cycles, a law enforcement official arrived to wave the protesters onto the median. They obliged, and the bus driver inched forward through the intersection.

I felt relieved but also terribly sad. I knew that the players couldn't have joined the protests without compromising their ability to appear in upcoming playoff games. That felt like a dreadful predicament, especially for the players who wanted to be in the streets protesting and worried that their games were distracting from the movement.

What's more, Melvin had been killed fifteen miles away from the bubble just a few days before the playoffs began, but I had never heard his name before that night. When the Floyd video first circulated, many people asked, "How many George Floyds were out there?" The Melvin protest brought me back to that same mental place. How many people were dying unnecessarily without the public's knowledge or any media coverage?

This brush with the protesters remained one of my clearest memories of the bubble. I could easily make out the anguish on their faces, as they were pressed up on the front of the bus and I stood right behind the driver. Yet the bus's glass windshield—the physical embodiment of the restricted bubble in that moment—made it feel like we were on two orbiting planets. Our arcs came together for a split second and then swung apart for the rest of time. I couldn't interview them, shake their hands, or invite them to have snacks by the pool that was a half mile away. They were on normal earth; I wasn't.

I had spent a lot of time thinking about the bubble's tiny size, but the physical separation was more difficult for my mind to process. Compartmentalizing was a valuable skill, and I had worked hard to focus on my work and to craft routines to avoid thoughts of the outside. The protesters pierced through all of that, and I was grateful for it. I now feared losing touch in an irreversible way.

Coincidentally, I felt the pull from outside the bubble especially hard that week. My parents back in Oregon were keeping me updated on wildfires that raged across the state. They were safe in Beaverton, but the devastation was unimaginable. My younger brother and his wife invited a displaced mother and her three young children to live in a tent in their Portland backyard. Thick ash covered the Portland metro area for days, making pandemic life even more unbearable. After nearly forty happy years in Oregon, my mother was so frustrated that she threatened to move back to Michigan for the first time that I could remember.

A few days after the bus protest, I read an article about Detroit, Oregon. When I was in middle school, one of my teachers organized a fundraiser to help Detroit, a small logging town with a population of 200 people, after a massive flood. We loaded up on yellow school buses, made the one-hundred-mile drive southeast into the woods, and delivered canned goods and used clothing to families whose homes had been decimated. I remembered it as an uncomfortable experience for all parties. We arrived as total strangers at the worst moment of their lives, made small talk for a few hours, and left later that afternoon.

Twenty-five years later, Detroit was leveled again. Wildfires destroyed many of the town's buildings, including City Hall, and the *New York Times* published a frightening account of residents who nearly died after an unsuccessful attempt to flee. There was a good chance that some of those kids I met all those years ago were now parents in the same community, living a nightmare for a second time.

Why did that long-buried memory of Detroit resurface so vividly? No idea. I had only been back to Detroit a few times, and I hadn't done more than stop for gas or take pictures of Detroit Lake. Even so, Detroit was a tipping point. Maybe I felt compelled to act because the protesters shook me up. Maybe I just missed my family, which hadn't been together in full since Christmas. Maybe I felt helpless in the face of an extraordinarily difficult year. If I couldn't walk a mile down the road with protesters in Orlando, I certainly couldn't fly 3,000 miles to give my parents a hug.

I decided to launch a fundraiser in Detroit's name. This was out of character. I hated splitting a dinner bill, much less publicly asking for money. But it felt like the right thing to do for those in need. I realized soon enough that I was one of those in need.

Within a week, listeners to my podcast, the *Greatest Of All Talk*, raised $15,000 for Oregon wildfire relief efforts. My cohost, Andrew Sharp, and I were floored. A few thoughtful people even asked that I pass their donations directly to the mother and children living in my brother's backyard. My parents hand-delivered the money. For the first time during the pandemic, we felt like a family again.

I knew it would take a lot more than $15,000 to save Detroit and the dozens of Oregon communities wrecked by wildfires. If 2020 taught us anything, it was that our new problems were always too big to solve easily. Even so, nothing in the bubble made me happier than the outpouring of support for Detroit, a place that most of the people who donated would never visit.

In my empty hotel room, the immediacy of the giving rocked me. Within one hour of my fundraising appeal hitting the Internet, Venmo and PayPal donations were pouring in. I kept hitting refresh, trying to keep up as the figures accumulated. For days, people left digital notes and sent love from Europe and Asia. The bus's glass windshield made me feel like I was on another planet, but my iPhone's glass screen carried me home.

* * *

Handicapping the Eastern Conference finals was no easy task: The Celtics and Heat weren't quite mirror images, but they shared so many qualities. Executives Danny Ainge and Pat Riley were both former players and coaches, NBA lifers who had been in their jobs forever and cultivated a healthy rivalry. "Danny Ainge needs to shut the fuck up and manage his own team," Riley famously wrote in a 2013 press release following an officiating dispute. "He was the biggest whiner going when he was playing and I know that because I coached against him."

Brad Stevens and Erik Spoelstra were both elite, serious-minded coaches who ascended to their jobs at young ages and preferred to keep the media at arm's length. Jayson Tatum and Jimmy Butler were two of the East's best wings, capable of scoring in bunches and defending multiple positions. Kemba Walker and Goran Dragic were tough covers at point guard, slippery with the ball in their hands and capable of shooting from outside.

Both franchises had reached the 2012 East finals, only to spend the latter portions of the 2010s in rebuilding cycles. Both were unexpected entrants this year: Boston arrived ahead of schedule thanks to Tatum's rise, while Miami's off-season bet on Butler paid immediate dividends. Most importantly, both teams were in the bubble for the long haul. Day after day in September, I kept passing Stevens and Spoelstra on my afternoon walks. They were locked in and ready for what promised to be a hard-fought series.

Although Miami made quick work of Milwaukee, I leaned Boston with my series prediction. Tatum projected as the most talented player, the Celtics showed real resolve in holding off the Raptors, and I thought Daniel Theis could hold up well enough against Bam Adebayo in the middle. If Butler tired or if forward Jae Crowder cooled off after a red-hot showing against the Bucks, I questioned whether the Heat had enough firepower and perimeter shooting to keep up.

A tense Game 1, filled with sharp swings of momentum, lived up to the hype. Boston staked a first-quarter lead, only to allow Miami to storm back before halftime. That script repeated in the second half: Boston retook control in the third quarter, but Miami launched a fourth-quarter comeback to force overtime.

The Celtics had every reason to believe they should have won in regulation. Holding a 105–100 lead with just over a minute remaining, Boston conceded 3-pointers to Tyler Herro, a twenty-year-old rookie, and Butler, a below-average outside shooter, on consecutive possessions. Tatum scored a game-high 30 points, but he didn't make a shot in the final seven minutes of regulation and settled for a step-back 3 that missed at the buzzer.

In overtime, Boston's struggles continued against Miami's fierce and disciplined defense. Nothing was available going to the basket. The Heat were protecting the paint and turning the Celtics into a jump-shooting team, although a Walker pull-up from midrange gave Boston a 114–113 lead with twenty-three seconds left.

The next two plays decided Game 1 and set the terms for the series. Down 1 with the game on the line, Butler barreled to his right past Tatum. He couldn't quite turn the corner, so he used two long steps to adjust his course to the basket and powered through Tatum's body to toss up a double-clutch layup as he drew a foul. Tatum had shadowed Butler carefully, beaten him to the spot, and contested the shot with both arms. The thirty-year-old Butler simply had eight years on Tatum, not to mention a distinct advantage in upper-body strength. Tatum was more polished; Butler was more imposing. Imposing won.

After Butler hit his free throw to give Miami a 116–114 lead, Tatum had his chance for revenge. He drove hard from the top of the key to his right, using his ballhandling and quickness to find a seam to the basket. Butler was an excellent defender—he first made his name defending LeBron James in the playoffs all those years ago—but Tatum was by him and home free for a dunk.

In the second that it took Butler to realize he was beaten, Adebayo came across the paint from his position on the left block. Adebayo's assignment was Marcus Smart, who cleared out to the left corner and stood wide open with both hands in the air calling for the ball. For Adebayo, it was an easy decision: A Tatum dunk was a bigger threat than a Smart 3, especially with just five seconds left on the clock. If Tatum found the open man and Smart somehow launched a shot before a defender could rotate, the Heat would have to live with that.

But Tatum wasn't thinking pass, he was thinking poster dunk. He leaped off one leg and cocked back for a right-handed slam, drifting toward the right baseline in hopes of gliding past Adebayo for a clean finishing window. Adebayo, in midair by now, tracked Tatum brilliantly, using his left hand to cut off Tatum's flight path. Tatum went for it anyway, with such force that the ball bent Adebayo's left wrist back nearly into the rim. Somehow, Adebayo withstood the attack and swatted the ball. The impact of the block sent Tatum crashing to the baseline.

"I had to make a play," Adebayo explained later. "It's the playoffs, and I made a great play. It's hard to explain because it happened so fast for me. Y'all want answers from me? Instincts, I guess."

I was seated along the baseline in the right corner with a direct line of sight to Adebayo's block. To the naked eye, it was the best block that I had seen since James's iconic chase-down of Andre Iguodala in the 2016 Finals. Bang-bang plays at the rim often spark officiating debates, so I rewatched a video clip to see if there had been a foul. I saw Adebayo's wrist bend, I saw Tatum falling out of the frame in slow motion, and I saw Smart in the far corner pleading for the ball. I didn't see any contact. The block was completely clean.

"That can be a poster dunk, and a lot of people aren't willing to make that play and put themselves out there," Spoelstra said. "Jayson Tatum got into the launching pad, and [Adebayo] just made a big-time save for us."

The high-definition television replays were mesmerizing. Tatum had full control of the ball until the very last moment, and he arrived at full speed. Adebayo's hand was fully horizontal, parallel with the rim and just a few inches above the net. To top it off, Adebayo claimed the carom to prevent a second chance for Boston and hit a free throw to seal a 117–114 win.

Butler oozed gratitude afterwards, saying that the block "was a winning play" that "sealed the game for us." He hailed Adebayo for "putting [his] body on the line," adding that the center had "been our savior on that so many different times throughout the year."

Adebayo's block was going to be remembered as the bubble's best defensive play no matter what happened the rest of the way. It was an instant classic. Magic Johnson, prone to Twitter hyperbole, declared it "the best defensive play I've seen ever in the playoffs!!!!" This twenty-three-year-old center, who entered the season with fewer than fifty career starts, had just made a name for himself during the biggest game of his young career. "My emotions were everywhere, but everybody else around me was happy," Adebayo said. "This is one of those things, it doesn't hit you until the game's over."

After fifty-three minutes, the only difference between the Celtics and Heat was Adebayo's wrist ligaments. Tatum, never one to show much frustration to the media, called the block a "good play" and said that the Game 1 loss was "not the end of the world."

Boston, so poised throughout the postseason, didn't remain level-headed much longer. A disastrous third quarter set up Miami for a 106–101 victory in Game 2. The Celtics built a 13-point halftime lead, but they were outscored 37–17 in the third, making just four baskets and committing seven turnovers. They were flustered by the Heat's energy and physicality, and their second-half offense was largely confined to the perimeter. Tatum attempted just one shot in the fourth quarter, his second straight quiet late-game performance. Boston coughed up a 5-point lead in the game's closing stretch.

This was an unfamiliar position for the Celtics, as they had swept the 76ers and taken a 2–0 lead against the Raptors. Going down 0–2 in the bubble sparked a special type of panic. There were rarely two consecutive off days between playoff games, so a series could quickly slip away if a team failed to make timely adjustments. There also wasn't any change of scenery between cities like in a normal year, upping the mental weight of each loss. Even for writers, an 0–2 series always felt like a trap, beckoning observers to jump to conclusions. Boston's dreadful third quarter, which was totally out of character, challenged the assumption that this was going to be a long series. Were the Heat going to dismantle the Celtics just like they dismantled the Bucks?

Months of steadiness on the court and in interviews from the Celtics gave way after Game 2. I walked to the back hallway like usual, expecting Stevens to praise the Heat, stress the importance of limiting turnovers, and get off the stage as quickly as possible. Before that could happen, I heard loud shouting and indistinguishable clattering noises from the Celtics' locker room. They weren't happy.

In many NBA arenas, the locker room entrances were set back from the arena concourse for privacy reasons. That's especially true for home locker rooms, which were often decorated with inspirational murals and cloaked by sets of double doors. I had eavesdropped on locker room arguments in a few arenas, but in some it was impossible. Security guards might hold reporters at a checkpoint outside of earshot while the players cooled off, or the locker rooms might be so secluded that noise didn't escape.

Boston, as it happened, was in the same makeshift locker room in the same arena that Milwaukee had occupied during its protest. Just as I could hear the Bucks making telephone calls on speakerphone, I could make out the Celtics letting off steam after the deflating loss. Reporters tried to identify the loudest voice through the wall, but then Marcus Smart identified himself by storming out of the locker room toward the bathroom. Smart let off a profanity and looked deeply pissed off, wearing the same expression that came across my face any time my mother beat me at Scrabble. In a normal arena, reporters likely never would have seen or heard him.

It wasn't surprising that Smart snapped first. Stevens's default setting was steady, Tatum's was composed, and Jaylen Brown's was thoughtful. Smart had brilliant basketball instincts, but he wore his heart on his sleeve. He was a menace on defense, a wizard at tracking down loose balls, an instigator, and the NBA's best flopper. At six feet, three inches tall, he occasionally held his own as a comically under-sized center. Smart was the most qualified Celtics player to deliver a wake-up call, but he had no intention of meeting the media that night. He ducked out before any reporters could stop him, leaving Stevens, Tatum, and Brown to answer for him.

This type of moment—a heated exchange after a backbreaking loss—was bound to bring out a coach's true nature. I imagined Phil Jackson motivating his players with well-placed jabs, Gregg Popovich going on a rant to deflect attention, or Doc Rivers defusing the tension with a one-liner. Stevens, with his green polo shirt buttoned all the way up, sat tall in his seat, folded his hands in his lap, and removed any trace of anger from his voice. He comported himself like an A student who got caught up in a high school prank and had to explain himself to the principal. "Guys were emotional after a hard game, hard loss," he said, pacing out his words.

I had to hand it to Stevens. At this critical leadership moment, he had no interest in mind games, motivational tactics, distraction techniques, the projection of good humor, or even denial. His only goal was self-control, making sure not to inflame the situation before he doubled back with his players in advance of Game 3. It would be so easy to say something regrettable after a charged altercation, intentionally or unintentionally. Stevens was statuesque. He knew that his team needed time, and that's what he gave them.

The Celtics were upset but not broken. "In families, there's ups and downs, fights and emotions," Brown said, downplaying Smart's outburst. "But that's exactly what we are: a family. We're going to hold each other accountable. He plays with passion. He's full of fire. That's what I love about him most."

Tatum, for his part, was annoyed that the media had witnessed the scene and unconcerned about the Celtics fracturing. "We're frustrated, but that's team sports," he said. "We're not supposed to be happy we're down 0–2. Nothing going on there. Just talking about the game. It's cool. What happens in a locker room has got to stay in the locker room. We're not supposed to come out here and talk about what we talk about as a team after a win or a loss."

The Celtics responded with a 117–106 win in Game 3, with Gordon Hayward returning after missing twelve games with an ankle injury. Tatum, Brown, and Smart all played well. The victory helped put to bed the Game 2 drama, and Stevens praised his team's "character" while making it clear he hadn't given any "rah-rah speeches" to rally the troops. "The first time we were pushed to more emotions that challenged us, we got better," he said. "That's encouraging."

Brown said the altercation was "probably blown out of proportion," adding that the bubble environment had contributed to the outbursts. To Tatum, the fight revealed Boston's competitive desire. "We care about this," he said. "Basketball is a game of emotions. You want guys to be frustrated, upset, to care. It's nothing personal."

Order was restored, but Boston wasn't all the way back in the series. In Game 3, the Celtics survived a strong night from Adebayo and a first-half flurry from Herro, Miami's promising rookie. Herro's 22 points in defeat were an afterthought, but his confidence was striking given his lack of NBA experience.

Herro, a white guard raised outside Milwaukee, emerged as a fan favorite early in his rookie season. That status carried over into the bubble, where the Heat's traveling party seemed to cheer him more enthusiastically than anyone else on the roster.

In the predominantly Black NBA, white players were sometimes treated as novelties or pet projects by predominantly white fan bases. That wasn't the case with Herro, who was a flashy gunner with a smooth handle and complete self-confidence. Herro was his own man:

He appeared in rap videos, favored trendy clothing and sweatsuits, and dated an Instagram model, but he was soft-spoken, deferential to his teammates, and always the first person to acknowledge his whiteness. Butler adored Herro and respected his work ethic, adopting him as a younger brother early during his rookie year.

Herro knew questions about his race would follow him, but he never seemed bothered in the slightest. He wore "Black Lives Matter" as his jersey slogan and shrugged off a question about why he chose the message. "Because Black Lives Matter," he said. "It's something that means something to me. My teammates are predominantly Black, and the league is predominantly Black. There's obviously a problem going on in the world."

So far in the series, Miami had found ways to piece together enough offense against Boston. In a choppy Game 4, Spoelstra was searching for help. Crowder's shooting had regressed against the Celtics, and Miami's best shooter, Duncan Robinson, was cold too. Boston had ratcheted up its defense after the locker room altercation, and Hayward's return had given its depth a boost.

Herro's timing was perfect. Evidently still hot from his Game 3 performance, he entered midway through the first quarter and hit a pair of quick jumpers. At the start of the second quarter, he hit three more in a row. With the game still tight at the end of the third, he hit two more to help give Miami a 1-point lead heading into the fourth. Every time the Heat needed a bucket, Herro was ready, willing, and able.

The fourth quarter was a Herro takeover: a 3-pointer to open the period, another jumper, another 3-pointer, and then a rare layup going to the hoop. He was playing Pop-A-Shot in the Eastern Conference finals, and virtually everything he threw up was going in. Boston never tried to force the ball out of his hands or take other drastic actions to throw off his rhythm. Stevens was daring a twenty-year-old rookie—rather than Butler, Adebayo, or Dragic—to beat his team. It was a reasonable bet.

But Herro was unreasonably hot. With a little over four minutes remaining, he drained a big 3-pointer to push Miami's lead to 8 points. Then, in the game's final minute, he hit a deep dagger and sealed the

112–109 win with a pair of free throws. The box score didn't make sense: Herro had a career-high 37 points on 14-for-21 shooting and five 3-pointers. He tallied 17 points in the fourth quarter and single-handedly outscored Boston's bench 37–22. The only player to score more points than Herro in a playoff game before his twenty-first birthday was Magic Johnson, who tallied 42 points in an epic performance in the 1980 Finals.

"I went from a small town in Milwaukee to Kentucky," Herro said, tracing his journey to the NCAA powerhouse and the pre-draft doubts that followed him. "Nobody thought I would survive there, and nobody thought I would survive here. At the end of the day, I'm just going to bet on myself. That's what I do, bet on myself. I think someone said my wingspan was too short. They say everything, but it's whatever. All you can do is work at it, perfect your craft, come in with a great attitude, and just respect everybody in the building. Good things will happen from there."

Herro put on an iconic bubble display, stepping into tough leaners off the dribble and cashing deep 3s over taller defenders. He read the defense, unleashed hesitation dribbles, improvised with Euro-steps, went under the rim for reverse layups, found tiny crevices to shoot in the half-court, and caught friendly rolls. There was a full mixtape's worth of material baked into his Game 4 performance. "Herro was ridiculously good tonight," Stevens said, with a hint of wonder in his tone. "The rim must have looked like the ocean."

While stars tend to enjoy the spotlight and sometimes resist sharing it, Butler was simply proud. "I've been on teams where I put up a lot of shots and I haven't won anything," he joked. "So obviously that's not the formula."

Butler didn't treat Herro's outburst like a surprise, and he resisted going overboard with praise. Instead, he stressed Herro's preparedness and commitment, and made it clear that Herro had done his job as a trusted part of the team where "we all get a piece of the pie" on offense. At Miami's next practice, Butler showed up wearing Herro's jersey from his Whitnall High School days in Wisconsin.

"[Herro] is a rookie, but whenever he's out there on the floor, the swag that he plays with, the moves that he makes, you'd think he's been in the league for ten-plus years," Butler said. "He's worked at it. He's studied the film. He's the one that's in the gym. He's the one that's communicating like a vet to the vets. He did that. I didn't do it. Nobody else did it. Spo didn't do it. We just pump him with a lot of confidence, and I think he pumped himself with twice as much confidence. He goes out there and he performs. That's on him. That's on nobody else."

Spoelstra was more open and earnest after Game 4 than at any other bubble press conference that I could remember. To him, Herro's big game was a validation of Miami's way. Herro was thrust into a starting role because of injuries to his teammates early in his rookie year, and he struggled at times to defend at an NBA level. But he kept the faith, transforming from a baby-faced teenager into a stone-faced assassin through daily work.

"Everybody is looking for that signature moment," Spoelstra said. "That would be such a great story, right? 'I knew that day he would be this guy.' I think everybody overestimates what you can do in a day and underestimates what you can do in months of work and sweat and grind when nobody is watching. He is relentless with his work ethic. It's that daily grind when nobody is watching and doing it when most people don't."

The answer was vintage Spoelstra. I couldn't help but think about all the miles he walked around the campus when almost no one else was watching. A daily grind, indeed.

But this did feel like the signature moment of the Heat's season. A well-balanced offense received a monster night from an unlikely source, and their focus afterward was on the value of work and unselfishness. Miami was in full control with a 3–1 series lead. Heat Culture was peaking.

Facing elimination, Boston counterpunched to take Game 5, capitalizing on a huge third-quarter run and off nights from Adebayo and Butler to win 121–108. The series was wearing on everyone: Tatum said he was "really anxious" before the game, with the season on the line, and a distraught Adebayo blamed himself in defeat. "This game is on me," he said. "I played terrible. That can't happen. I know that. I feel like I let my teammates down."

Adebayo's block on Tatum opened the series with a bang, and the All-Star center finished off the Celtics with a sensational Game 6. Just as Herro played a half step faster than the Celtics in Game 4, Adebayo was flying around, past, and through defenders in the close-out win. He set a new playoff career-high with 32 points, adding 14 rebounds and 5 assists. In the fourth quarter, Adebayo, not Tatum or Butler, was the best player on the court.

"My family knows how I get when I play bad and especially when we lose," Adebayo said. "I put that on my shoulders because I feel I could have done something different. Tonight, I did something different. I came out being extra aggressive and locked in."

At times during the playoffs, Adebayo was prone to turnovers when he spent too much time weighing his options. Everything in Game 6 was grab and go. His fourth-quarter play was powerful, fast, graceful, and decisive. Adebayo converted a baseline slam set up by Butler, then drove hard to his left to catch Theis by surprise with a two-handed poster dunk. On the next possession, he attacked Theis from the perimeter and uncorked a stutter-step before rising into a tough fall-away jumper in the paint.

For a few minutes, Adebayo was overtaken by the spirit of Anthony Davis or Kevin Durant. He just kept coming at Theis, forcing Boston to send extra help. At one point, Adebayo spun directly into a trap on the right block but managed to find an escape hatch with a quick pass to Butler for a layup. It was pure instinct at full speed, and Boston couldn't keep up. Miami won 125–113 to claim the series in six games.

Spoelstra saluted Adebayo as "one of the great competitors already in this association" and predicted that he would "become one of the great winners," no small praise from a coach who generally avoided hyperbole. Stevens, with his season over, raved too. "Adebayo deciding that he was just going to drive the ball put us in a real bind with the shooters around him," Boston's coach said. "He dominated that fourth quarter. Even the plays where he didn't score, his presence was so impactful."

Boston departed the playoffs with regrets here and there, but no existential crises like the Sixers, Bucks, or Clippers. Tatum was their headliner and top organizational priority, and they were surely pleased with his bubble showing. At twenty-two, he reached the conference finals for the second time in his three-year career and averaged 25.7 points, 10 rebounds, and 5 assists per game in the playoffs. He shot efficiently and often scored effortlessly.

Yet Tatum faded in late-game scenarios against the Heat. While his future as an elite wing seemed virtually guaranteed, he went cold and spent too much time out of the action in the biggest moments of the East finals. This was valuable experience for a young star, not a moral failing. If Boston wanted to take the next step as a franchise, though, Tatum needed to leave a bigger mark.

Elsewhere, Hayward's injury issues and Walker's lack of size were problematic. If Hayward was healthy for the full series, the Celtics probably wouldn't have fallen into the 0–2 hole. Walker was potent at times in the playoffs, but his small stature kept him from attacking the basket against elite defenses and made him an easy target for opposing offenses. Theis held up in the middle well enough, but limited frontcourt depth was Boston's biggest weakness all year. Ainge would need to tinker with his rotation in the off-season.

Brown, at twenty-three, surpassed expectations on the court and emerged as a key voice in the NBPA's social justice initiatives. Boston's young wing duo was right on track, and Tatum and Brown were steadier under the postseason lights than most players their age. I left the bubble penciling in Boston as my favorite to win the East in 2021, assuming Ainge could bring back Hayward and upgrade the frontcourt. Tatum, long discussed through the prism of his potential, had blossomed into a top fifteen player in the bubble. There was still plenty of room for him to keep growing.

The Heat prevailed with better late-game execution and timely individual performances from Butler, Adebayo, and Herro. They clinched their first Finals trip since 2014, completing a tough six-year journey. They had missed the playoffs in three of the previous five years, won just one playoff series since LeBron James returned to the Cleveland Cavaliers, and entered the season as a third-tier contender in the East.

Riley had made some expensive mistakes in free agency, yet he scored big by trading for Dragic, luring Butler in free agency, and plucking both Adebayo and Herro in the draft. Now those four central players were set to make their Finals debuts. Spoelstra was headed to his fifth Finals, a reputation-enhancing accomplishment because it was his first conference title without James, Dwyane Wade, and Chris Bosh. "A lot of guys in our locker room have been told that they are less than," Spoelstra, who could have included himself with that description. "They are the anti-AAU or new-age analytics where you're trying to figure out what a player can do statistically. They just want to roll the ball out and play and compete and fight for it."

Spoelstra and company earned their deep satisfaction. For three rounds, Spoelstra called out defensive coverages play after play, deploying zones when necessary to throw off the opposition. Miami was the lower seed against Indiana, Milwaukee, and Boston, yet it had emerged with a sparkling 12-3 postseason record. There were crucial performances from Butler, Adebayo, Dragic, and Herro along the way, with Crowder and Robinson chipping in too.

I had covered every Finals since 2011, and Miami was the least talented team, on paper, that I had seen capture a conference title during that time. They lacked a first-ballot Hall of Famer like James, Durant, Stephen Curry, Tim Duncan, or Dirk Nowitzki. Some of their key players were extraordinarily young. And the Heat had been blessed with tremendous fortune at key turning points: Giannis Antetokounmpo's ill-advised foul on Butler, Antetokounmpo's ankle injury, Adebayo's block on Tatum, and Herro's remarkable scoring explosion.

Even so, I expected the Heat to be a tough out in the Finals. They wouldn't beat themselves, and they had nothing to lose. "Pat Riley didn't assemble this team for us to play eighty-two games and go home," Adebayo said. "This is all in preparation for how we can win a championship. I love this team that he brought together. We're the underdogs. We're not backing down from anybody."

19

Mamba Shot

The pandemic had a way of playing with the perception of time. March 2020 seemed like it lasted a full year, with each day bringing fresh horrors, new terminology, and changing health guidelines. By the start of the Western Conference finals between the Lakers and Nuggets in mid-September, everything that happened before the shutdown felt like it had taken place five years ago. And no team had been through more before the hiatus than the Lakers.

With a narrow, bubble-centric view, LeBron James and the Lakers reaching the Western Conference finals felt like an inevitability. They entered as the No. 1 seed, beat the Clippers on the bubble's opening night, and cruised through the Blazers and Rockets with an 8–2 record. Zooming out and rewinding the tape told a much different story.

The 2019–20 Lakers engineered one of the most impressive turnarounds in league history, and their sharp change of fortune was easy to overlook with the pandemic wreaking havoc on our collective memory. In the five years before James's 2018 arrival to Los Angeles, the Lakers won a total of 126 games—the fewest of any team in the league. The glamorous franchise of Jerry West, Magic Johnson, Kareem Abdul-Jabbar, Shaquille O'Neal, and Kobe Bryant, which had missed the playoffs just twice between 1977 and 2013, went six straight years without a postseason appearance.

When I moved to Los Angeles in 2015, the Lakers were an utter mess. They went from Mike Brown to Bernie Bickerstaff to Mike D'Antoni to Byron Scott to Luke Walton as coach during a five-year stretch, and top-shelf free agents barely gave them the time of day.

The best reason to go to Lakers games during my first two years in Los Angeles had nothing to do with the basketball product. After each game, Bryant, who was in the twilight of his twenty-year Hall of Fame career, treated the media to brilliant riffs on competition, fatherhood, aging, and anything else that came to his mind. Bryant answered questions in English, Spanish, and Italian, and his lengthy postgame press conferences were so captivating that they distracted from his complicated presence on the court.

Bryant always relished putting the "shooting" in shooting guard, and he retired as the NBA's third-leading scorer, one spot above his childhood hero, Michael Jordan. He had little interest in adjusting his style of play or his ball-dominant role for young and unproven teammates, so he kept shooting even as his efficiency dropped and the losses piled up. This went on for years after Bryant tore his Achilles tendon in 2013, but Lakers fans didn't care in the slightest. Bryant was a Los Angeles icon. The Staples Center crowd would rather watch Bryant miss shots than watch any of his teammates make shots. Lakers fans loved his killer instinct, embraced his "Black Mamba" nickname, and swore by his "Mamba Mentality" approach, which boiled down to ruthless competitiveness and complete self-confidence.

Outsiders could easily argue that Bryant's presence was doing more harm than good in his final years. Top draft picks like D'Angelo Russell had no chance of developing properly in his presence, and his massive contract and huge personality kept the Lakers from enjoying their typical success as a free agency destination. But Bryant's two decades of loyalty to the franchise and his five championship rings had earned him the right to go out on his terms, even if it sometimes came at the franchise's expense.

The final game of Bryant's career, in 2016, perfectly encapsulated his hold on the city, the Lakers franchise, and the NBA community at large. Entering the night, Bryant, thirty-seven, and the Lakers had lost ten of their previous eleven games. Determined to go out with a bang, he attempted fifty shots, the most by any NBA player since the 1960s. When the dust settled, he had scored 60 points for the sixth time in his career in an improbable win and said goodbye to the Lakers faithful with a simple declaration: "Mamba Out!"

It was a perfect ending to Bryant's reign over the Lakers, but the franchise was stuck without a succession plan. They stumbled around for two years until James swooped into town, seeking a new home and a large market to expand his business pursuits after his second tenure with the Cavaliers ran its course.

The Lakers were in such a bad spot that not even James could immediately turn them into a playoff team. After James suffered a groin injury on Christmas, Los Angeles lost all momentum and sputtered to another lottery trip in 2018–19. For James, it was a humbling setback: He had made the playoffs every year since 2006 and reached the Finals every year since 2011.

At that moment, it was fair to wonder whether James's game might start to fade like Bryant's had a few years earlier. James was thirty-four years old, there wasn't much help on the Lakers' roster, and Kyrie Irving had sought a trade from Cleveland in 2017 to step out from James's shadow. James had won his titles with superteams, and he would need a top-tier costar to reclaim the throne from Stephen Curry, Kevin Durant, and the Warriors' dynasty.

Even worse, the Lakers appeared to be crumbling around him. Team president Magic Johnson, a key voice in recruiting James to Los Angeles, abruptly resigned in April 2019, informing reporters of his decision before telling owner Jeanie Buss or James. Shortly thereafter, Luke Walton was sacked as coach. Rob Pelinka, Bryant's former agent and the Lakers' GM under Johnson, stepped in to run the front office. The changing power dynamics prompted questions about Pelinka's limited front office experience, and Johnson even publicly accused his former deputy of "backstabbing" him.

It was all one giant mess of egos, fractured relationships, and unfulfilled expectations. The Lakers were a soap opera, not a basketball team. After watching their machinations up close for four years, I was growing more convinced that James made a mistake by joining the Lakers and that his grasp on the league might be loosening for good. Before Bryant's spectacular finale, his last few years featured plenty of sad and pointless games. I worried that James's illustrious career was headed in a similar direction.

I remember precisely where I was when the tide turned: halfway up a steep hike at Big Sur State Park in Northern California. The Raptors had finished off the Warriors in the 2019 Finals after devastating injuries to Durant and Klay Thompson. Golden State's five-year run was suddenly over, and I was doing my best to get some fresh air after months on the road covering the playoffs. Big Sur was on my bucket list for years, and I was three miles up a tree-lined trail eyeing a Pacific Ocean view when I finally caught a phone signal. My text messages list, Twitter notifications, and phone call log were all blinking with the same urgent news: The New Orleans Pelicans have agreed to trade Anthony Davis to the Lakers.

Down the steep hill I went, as fast as my knees could manage. I raced to find an establishment with Wi-Fi, which was no easy task that far off the grid. When I settled in to write after an hourlong search, I realized that the West's power balance for the upcoming season had shifted in a major way. James had his superstar partner. The Lakers paid a heavy price for Davis, but they were finally back in business.

That summer saw the Lakers hire Frank Vogel during a meandering coaching search that nearly landed on Tyronn Lue, James's former Cavaliers boss. Pelinka tried to lure Kawhi Leonard in free agency, but he was forced to settle for an unglamorous collection of veterans that included Danny Green, JaVale McGee, Dwight Howard, and Jared Dudley. Los Angeles did sign DeMarcus Cousins, but he promptly suffered a season-ending injury.

Between James's lack of a relationship with Vogel and the loss of Cousins, there were still good reasons to doubt the Lakers. Leonard had teamed up with Paul George on the Clippers, who were deeper on paper. While James and Davis were the best superstar duo in the league, the rest of the roster was an open question. I left the Lakers' media day amazed by the rush of interest from local, national, and international outlets, but their first training camp practice was unimpressive.

Did they have enough shooting? What would happen if James or Davis missed time with injury?

It was also hard to shake doubts about the franchise's recent history and internal shake-ups. James was coming off an injury at age thirty-five, and Davis hadn't had much success in the playoffs. I thought the Lakers would be successful but ultimately fall short of the burgeoning hype. When the 2019–20 season started, I didn't view them as a top title contender. More than anything, I was conditioned to expect something to go wrong.

During the preseason, something did. The Lakers were in China for exhibition games when Rockets general manager Daryl Morey posted his Twitter message in support of Hong Kong protesters. As the political circus unfolded, the Lakers were initially barred from meeting the press in China, and their preseason game was nearly canceled. "I don't want to get into a feud with Daryl Morey, but I believe he wasn't educated on the situation at hand and he spoke," James said, once the Lakers were back stateside. "So many people could have been harmed, not only financially but physically, emotionally, spiritually. Just be careful what we tweet, what we say and what we do. Yes, we have freedom of speech, but there can be a lot of negatives that come with that as well."

That commentary drew instant rebukes from Republican politicians, who accused James of prioritizing his business interests with companies like Nike over American values. Morey's tweet did have major financial ramifications for the league, as the Chinese government's television network refused to show NBA games for months and Chinese sponsors severed ties with the Rockets, costing the league some $200 million.

James was a veteran of controversies, even political ones, but this was no way for a new-look team to launch a season. Yet the Lakers stabilized themselves almost instantly. After an opening night loss to the Clippers, they rattled off a 24-3 start and looked like the Bizarro Lakers: drama-free, happy off the court, and committed to one another. James and Davis fit together brilliantly, and the Staples Center crowd roared back to life. The Lakers cruised along at the top of the standings and were an impressive 36-10 by the last week of January. Commentators were starting to look ahead to James's Lakers facing Kawhi Leonard's Clippers in the West finals or Giannis Antetokounmpo's Bucks in the Finals.

I woke up early on the morning of January 26 in New Orleans, where I was covering Zion Williamson's long-anticipated debut. The rookie sensation was playing the Boston Celtics in the third game of his career that night, a Sunday, and I had booked a morning swamp tour hoping to see some alligators before it was time to go to the arena. When bad weather intervened, I moped around my hotel room until a TMZ.com headline flashed across Twitter: "BREAKING: Kobe Bryant Has Died In A Helicopter Crash."

Like everyone else, I thought, or hoped, that it was a hoax. I knew Bryant loved traveling by helicopter to avoid Los Angeles's infamous traffic, and TMZ had a strong track record of breaking celebrity news. The next few hours were a blur, as word spread throughout the NBA community. By the time I arrived to watch the Pelicans play the Celtics, coaches and players were fighting back tears and the tributes were pouring in. Adam Silver, Michael Jordan, Shaquille O'Neal, and many others expressed their condolences, shock, and sadness, while the league office briefly considered postponing the nine games scheduled for Sunday.

I knew the city of Los Angeles and the Lakers would be devastated, and that mass grief would greet me when I flew home the next day. Lakers owner Jeanie Buss had known Bryant for decades and often referred to him as a brother. GM Rob Pelinka was Bryant's longtime agent and close friend. James and Bryant were rivals on the court, but Bryant did his part to welcome James to the Lakers. In his final tweet, Bryant saluted James for passing him to claim third place on the NBA's all-time scoring list. "Continuing to move the game forward," Bryant wrote on the night before his death. "Much respect my brother."

The ties between Bryant and the Lakers were endless. Bryant and Davis were USA Basketball teammates during the 2012 Olympics. The Lakers retired both of Bryant's jerseys, and they were expected to build a statue of him outside Staples Center. Bryant was seventeen when he was drafted and thirty-seven when he scored 60 points in that memorable finale. His wife, Vanessa, and children were well-known to Lakers fans, and his thirteen-year-old daughter, Gianna, was on the helicopter with him. All nine people, including the pilot, died in the crash, which occurred on a cloudy morning.

Father and daughter were heading to a basketball tournament when their helicopter crashed into a hillside in Calabasas, about thirty miles northwest of downtown Los Angeles. One month before their deaths, I photographed Kobe and Gianna Bryant sitting courtside at a Lakers game so that Gianna could meet Dallas Mavericks star Luka Doncic. Looking back at the pictures made the tragic crash feel even more impossible. Kobe and Gianna Bryant were way too young.

My first stop back in Los Angeles was to see the crash site for myself. From the parking lot of the Church in the Canyon, a small Presbyterian church, I looked up at the damaged hillside. I had hiked through similar hills many times. How could this have happened?

I met with church pastor Bob Bjerkaas in his office, which overflowed with books. Bjerkaas described the fateful morning: A loud crash interrupted Sunday school, a huge blaze covered the hill, firefighters responded quickly, and then the media arrived in droves. Mourning Lakers fans descended upon the church to hold vigils, and Bjerkaas and his staff provided snacks and restroom access to the visitors. Thousands came that week, many leaving flowers and Lakers merchandise to honor the Bryants. Some took refuge in the Church of the Canyon's sanctuary.

"The Bible says we're to practice hospitality," Bjerkaas said. "That's what we did. We prayed with people who were emotionally overwhelmed, in tears and in open grief. Sometimes all people need is a hug, a 'God bless you,' a short prayer, and a cup of water. I've always believed more good is done in this life if you can get close to the ground and share life with the people around you."

The entire city became a tribute to Bryant. Public buses bore his name, LAX's airport lights were lit purple and gold in his honor, and street corner vendors sold T-shirts with Bryant's image. The Lakers' practice facility set up temporary walls where thousands of fans wrote messages of gratitude. Downtown, ankle-deep piles of purple and gold bouquets covered the L.A. Live entertainment district. So many murals to Bryant popped up that a fan launched the @KobeMural Instagram account to track them all.

The NBA postponed the Lakers' first game after Bryant's death, and the players were shielded from the media for days. On Friday, January 31, the Lakers hosted the Blazers and held an extended tribute to Bryant. Red roses were placed on a pair of courtside seats, alongside jerseys belonging to Kobe and Gianna Bryant. Usher, the pop star, sang "Amazing Grace," and an extended video montage of Bryant's career played on the jumbotron. Bryant's jerseys were lit up in the rafters, and the Lakers held a 24.2-second moment of silence in recognition of Kobe Bryant's No. 24 jersey and Gianna Bryant's No. 2. StubHub's cheapest seats for the impromptu celebration of life ran $700 on the day before the game, and courtside seats fetched more than $15,000 apiece.

James tattooed Bryant's jerseys and an image of a snake—nodding to Bryant's Black Mamba moniker—on his leg as tribute. He stepped to center court before the game against the Blazers, wearing Bryant's jersey and telling the crowd that he was scrapping his planned remarks, as he dropped a piece of paper to the court. James hailed Bryant's determination and the outpouring of support in the wake of his death. When he finished, James recalled Bryant's famous line after his 60-point finale. "In the words of Kobe Bryant, 'Mamba out,'" he said. "But in the words of us: 'Not forgotten.' Live on, brother."

The Lakers lost to the Blazers, and coach Frank Vogel described it as "definitely the heaviest game I've been a part of." James hid his eyes behind dark sunglasses for the postgame press conference, the first time he had addressed the media since Bryant's death. "I felt like the last three years were the happiest I've ever seen him," James said. "Being able to be with his daughters and his family. When we're done for the day, make sure you hug the shit out of your family. If you have kids, tell them you love them."

The tributes to Bryant continued for weeks, culminating with a Staples Center memorial held on February 24, a date chosen to recognize Kobe and Gianna Bryant's jersey numbers. ABC's Jimmy Kimmel was the emcee, Beyoncé and Alicia Keys performed, and Vanessa Bryant remembered her daughter as "sunshine" and "a daddy's girl who I know loved her mama."

Jordan got emotional as he described Bryant as a "little brother" who would quiz him about basketball at all hours. "He used to call me at 3 o'clock in the morning to talk about post-up moves, footwork, the triangle," he said. "At first it was an aggravation. But then it turned into a certain passion. This kid had passion like you would never know." Jordan couldn't hold back the tears. "When Kobe Bryant died, a piece of me died," he said. "When I look in this arena, or across the globe, a piece of you died. That's what Kobe Bryant does to me. He knows how to get to you in a way that affects you personally, even if he's being a pain in the ass."

Bryant's death got to me. I had lost all four of my grandparents in the span of about five years, and little things—sugar cookies, corn on the cob, train rides, Lake Michigan whitecaps—randomly triggered grief's painful sting. In Los Angeles, memories of the tragedy were everywhere. In every barbershop conversation, on every street corner, at every game. Twice that month, I drove out to Palm Springs and walked around the barren Joshua Tree National Park to find some space to breathe.

I knew the Lakers had it much worse, and I wasn't sure whether any team could weather this blow. Soon, media members and fans were wondering whether the Lakers might "Do it for Kobe" and rally around his memory for a title push. I couldn't get there. It felt way too soon, and a championship was minuscule next to the Bryants' lives. Yet I knew the narrative would hang over the Lakers for the rest of the season, and I was certain they would find as many ways as possible to honor him as they went.

Vogel, James, and Davis did an impressive job of keeping the team together. For all the talk about the Lakers' superstar talent in the bubble, their excellent chemistry from top to bottom was a crucial factor all season. In early March, the Lakers scored back-to-back wins over Antetokounmpo's Bucks and Leonard's Clippers. Los Angeles was peaking, not collapsing, and James was ramping up for another deep postseason run. The Lakers went 13-4 between Bryant's death and March 11, when the NBA shut down due to the coronavirus. James never saw the pandemic coming, and he initially said that he wouldn't take the court if fans weren't in the stands.

When talk of the bubble first percolated, I was certain that James and the Lakers would want in. Bryant's death brought unspeakable pain—Pelinka called it an "amputation of part of my soul"—and the coronavirus was now inflicting another layer of cruelty. After everything the Lakers went through, from Johnson's resignation to Davis's trade to Bryant's death, their season needed a resolution and something that might approximate closure.

As the Lakers progressed deeper in the playoffs, James's words from earlier in the year kept coming back to me. "Hug your family," he had advised after Bryant's death in January, only to enter a restricted campus 3,000 miles away from his wife and children. "I play for the fans," he had declared before the March shutdown, only to compete in front of a few hundred people for three months straight. The bubble had separated the sport's most powerful player from his family and prevented Lakers fans from experiencing a long-awaited title push in person.

Nevertheless, I was beyond excited for the Western Conference finals. As a born-and-raised West Coaster, I jokingly dubbed myself a "Western Conference Elitist." The West was 14–7 in the Finals since Jordan's retirement, and the Western Conference was consistently deeper in superstar talent and quality teams. I spent years advocating for the NBA to get rid of conference designations based on geography in the playoffs so that better West teams could supplant weaker East teams, and I liked to point out that the Western Conference finals, not the NBA Finals, often featured the postseason's best matchup.

While Nikola Jokic, Jamal Murray, and the Nuggets spoiled the all–Los Angeles showdown, the Lakers' presence in the West finals had an order-restoring quality. The Lakers advanced to the West finals eighteen times between 1980 and 2010. James, meanwhile, went to the East finals every year from 2011 to 2018 before missing the playoffs entirely in 2019. An all-time franchise and an all-time player were back on a familiar stage.

The series opened with a thumping. Los Angeles, enjoying five days of rest after dispatching Houston, jumped Denver with a 126–114 win in Game 1. The Nuggets had just two days to prepare, and Jokic dealt with severe foul trouble as they trailed the Lakers by as many as 27 points.

The matchups were all wrong for the Nuggets, who lacked elite frontcourt defenders. Paul Millsap, a heady veteran with plenty of experience battling James in the playoffs, looked overmatched at age thirty-five. Jerami Grant and Denver's other younger options lacked the size and strength to contain James. Meanwhile, Jokic and Mason Plumlee were no match for Davis's quickness and versatility, while Dwight Howard and Davis were able to frustrate Jokic when Denver had the ball. This looked like it might be a quick series.

The Nuggets pushed back hard in Game 2, boosted by 15 points off the bench from Michael Porter Jr. No one besides Jokic and Murray had anything going, but the Lakers were busy shooting themselves in the foot with uncharacteristically sloppy play. James committed six turnovers, Rajon Rondo added five, Kyle Kuzma had four, and that should have been enough to even the series. Jokic backed down on Davis in the game's final minute, using his girth to work deep into the paint for a pretty jump hook. The Nuggets held a 103–102 lead with twenty seconds left.

On the Lakers' ensuing possession, a James drive to the hoop set up an open look for Alex Caruso at the top of the key. Caruso missed, and the scramble for the rebound led Danny Green to toss up a desperation jumper from the left corner. Murray and Millsap hustled out to defend the shot, with Murray deflecting it out of bounds with 2.1 seconds left on the clock. Between Jokic's bucket and this impressive defensive stand, Denver deserved the win.

When Rondo inbounded the ball from the baseline for the final play, James barely moved. Green flashed to the hoop but was covered, and Kentavious Caldwell-Pope was stuck on the far side of the court. That left Davis, who came curling around the top of the key toward the left angle. Rondo flicked a bounce pass by Jokic that reached Davis, who somehow had a clean look. Denver's Mason Plumlee had started on Davis, but he inexplicably called for a switch with Grant as the play unfolded. Grant didn't react, leaving Jokic to rush out in a vain attempt to contest Davis's shot.

It was a terrible defensive miscue at the worst possible time, and Davis made the Nuggets pay by taking two quick steps to set his feet before rising from beyond the 3-point arc. The ball was out of his hands within a second, and it swished through the net as the buzzer sounded. Nuggets coach Michael Malone held his head in disbelief, Murray looked down at the court, a confused Porter scratched his head on the bench, and P. J. Dozier punched the ball with full force as the Lakers celebrated.

Initially, the Lakers acted like they had robbed a bank and were looking in the rearview mirror to see whether the cops were on their tail. Rondo and Caldwell-Pope walked around casually, while James and Green both raised their arms and stood still. But Davis, who posted a game-high 31 points, 9 rebounds, and 2 blocks, couldn't contain his glee. His game-winning, buzzer-beating jumper had given the Lakers a 105–103 win and a 2–0 series lead. More than that, it represented the signature moment of his career.

Davis had already won two playoff series in the bubble, more than the one he claimed during his seven seasons in New Orleans combined. Now he had given the Lakers total control of the West finals with a shot that displayed his range of skills: mobility, footwork, technique, shooting touch, and late-game confidence. The Lakers' bench came storming onto the court to mob Davis, who was so excited that he jumped in the air and sent rookie Talen Horton-Tucker crashing to the court.

As Davis raced to the Lakers' bench, wearing a black jersey that honored Bryant, a slow-motion replay captured him yelling one word:

"Kobe!" In the heat of the moment, during the highlight of his career to date, Davis's mind went instantly to Bryant. At once, Davis's shot was a tribute to Bryant's memory and an acknowledgment of the Lakers legend's reputation for clutch moments. Davis was honoring Bryant by channeling Bryant. "It was a Mamba shot," Vogel said. "A shot Kobe Bryant would hit. He came off just flying to the wing like that, catch-and-shoot with the biggest game of our season on the line, nothing but net."

Davis's heroic moment also capped a personal journey that dated back to his ugly exit from the Pelicans after a public trade request. The saga, orchestrated by agent Rich Paul, was awkward for all parties. New Orleans refused to be bullied into dealing Davis before the trade deadline despite a mountain of rumors, a decision that kept both the Pelicans and Lakers in purgatory for the rest of the 2018–19 season.

The Pelicans played Davis sparingly down the stretch of a lost campaign, hoping to avoid injury to preserve his trade value. Davis might have been shut down completely, except the NBA mandated that he take the court if healthy. The Lakers were consumed by the rumors, which involved several young prospects, and never mounted a playoff push. Collateral damage piled up: Davis was fined $50,000, the Pelicans fired GM Dell Demps, Lakers president Magic Johnson resigned, and Lakers coach Luke Walton was let go.

Meanwhile, Davis's reputation took a major hit. Critics accused him of quitting on the Pelicans midway through the season, and of overplaying his hand more than a year before he was scheduled to hit free agency. Davis wasn't a particularly visible star: He didn't have a postseason track record, a signature sneaker deal, or a big personality. His bushy unibrow had been his calling card since college, but Davis's narrative arc was stuck in neutral. Now he was trying to bail on the team that drafted him with strong-arm tactics.

During the 2019 All-Star Weekend in Charlotte, I wondered whether Davis knew what he was doing. He looked confused and overwhelmed by the intense media interest that followed his trade request, and he couldn't decide which teams were on his list of acceptable destinations.

He hardly seemed like an empowered superstar taking control of his career. He looked lost.

Yet the trade came together four months later, with David Griffin, Demps's successor, and Pelinka, Johnson's successor, crafting a package that included Brandon Ingram, Lonzo Ball, Josh Hart, and three first-round picks. The Lakers invested almost all their assets in a single player, and the Pelicans salvaged a quality return package, given Paul's desire to pair Davis with James.

Fast-forward a year, and the Mamba shot provided the ultimate validation for Davis's move and Paul's cutthroat strategy. Davis didn't shy from that fact. "It's for sure the biggest shot of my career," he said. "When I left [New Orleans], I just wanted to be able to compete for a championship, and I know that moments like this comes with it—especially being in L.A., the biggest market in basketball."

Critics of Davis's desire to leave and Paul's tough tactics saw the game winner as proof that the NBA's system was broken. If a superstar could force his way to a large market and be immediately rewarded, what hope did small markets have of retaining their talent? A $50,000 fine wasn't going to dissuade top players from following in Davis's footsteps and issuing trade requests of their own. The Lakers won Game 2, and the NBA's long-stated goal of competitive balance suffered a clear defeat.

James, for his part, was grateful that Paul's master plan saved him from a bad outing. "In the second half, shit, I leaned on [Davis] and he brought us home," he said, before pushing back on those who might knock Davis's move to Los Angeles.

"It's not about the doubters or the naysayers or the people who are going to try to talk to you and slander you and bring you down every single day," James said. "They have never been in the arena. They don't understand. [Davis] wanted to be here. I'm happy he wanted to be here, because if he didn't, we wouldn't have a moment like tonight. That's what it's all about. Anybody can talk from outside, but if they got into the ring or they got into the arena, probably ten times out of ten they would shit their pants."

The Lakers had no plans to apologize, not after everything they went through together. Even on this joyous night, James unexpectedly struck a bittersweet tone. "The one thing I wish AD had tonight with the shot he made, I wish we were playing at Staples," he said. "We miss our fans so much. That probably would have blown the roof off."

I had the same thought after Luka Doncic's step-back game winner to beat the Clippers and OG Anunoby's catch-and-shoot 3 to down the Celtics. Davis's shot was bound to be included on postseason highlight reels for years to come, and it was a shame that Jack Nicholson, Rihanna, and the other celebrities who turned up at Lakers games wouldn't be in the picture. The dogpile at center court was a beautiful and thrilling sight, but the Mamba shot deserved a crowd's spontaneous response.

In a better world, the Staples Center would have been total bedlam, and Kobe and Gianna Bryant would have been leading the cheers from courtside seats.

20

Old Man Game

Anthony Davis's Mamba shot didn't eliminate the Nuggets, but it effectively ended the West finals. The Nuggets cheated death multiple times against the Jazz and Clippers, and here was definitive proof that their luck had run out. They weren't going to beat the Lakers four out of five times, not after that.

But Jamal Murray and the Nuggets had every intention of pushing the Lakers. "All y'all better start giving this team some damn respect because we put in the work," Denver's point guard said after knocking out the Clippers in the second round. "We've got a resilient team. We shouldn't have been down 3–1, but to come back from 3–1 against the Clippers is a big achievement. It's fun just to change that narrative."

The Nuggets wanted no part of a "sweep" narrative against the Lakers, proving it early in Game 3. Murray led the way with 28 points and 12 assists, getting into a groove and rising high in the third for an eye-popping dunk, which wasn't exactly his specialty. LeBron James and Rajon Rondo struggled with turnovers for the second straight night, and the Lakers started flat with a quintessential let-up performance.

In the fourth quarter, the Nuggets committed six consecutive turnovers and failed to even attempt a shot for nearly three minutes of game time. The Lakers blitzed Murray and whittled a 20-point fourth-quarter deficit down to 3. A lesser team than Denver and a lesser player than Murray would have folded under the pressure or given into thoughts about freedom from the bubble.

Murray righted the ship, icing a 114–106 win with a pair of late 3-pointers and an assist for a Paul Millsap dunk. "We feel like we should be up 2–1 right now, to be honest," Murray said, acknowledging that the specter of Davis's shot still lingered over the series.

Denver coach Michael Malone loved the bully pulpit, and he sang his team's praises and singled out Murray's mature late-game response. "For some reason, we love this bubble," he said. "I can't explain that, but this team loves the bubble. Last year, we knew what we were getting from Nikola, but what kind of game would Jamal have? That's no longer the case. We have two superstars in Nikola and Jamal, and a lot of young, talented players behind them. The difference from last year to this year is just that consistency and the confidence that we all have in Jamal."

Murray could sense his own growth too. He arrived in Denver as a teenager in 2016, spent his rookie year coming off the bench, and wrenched the car keys away from another lottery pick, Emmanuel Mudiay, in his second season. Now in year four, he was standing shoulder-to-shoulder with Jokic, rather than walking in the center's shadow. "The most important part is the energy I bring," Murray said. "When I'm talking to my teammates, being the vocal leader, going up and down, and pushing everyone, they tend to follow."

Conjuring energy at this stage of the bubble wasn't easy, a fact of life made apparent on the day after Game 3. Kentucky attorney general Daniel Cameron announced September 23 that a grand jury had decided not to charge the three Louisville officers involved in Breonna Taylor's killing. The City of Louisville had previously reached a $12 million settlement with Taylor's family, but the officers' use of force was justified, according to Cameron, because Taylor's boyfriend, Kenneth Walker, had fired a weapon first. Walker's version of events differed from that account, and one of the officers involved was indicted on three counts of wanton endangerment for shooting into a nearby apartment.

Whenever I was asked about the players' advocacy that summer, I said that LeBron James was the No. 1 name in the bubble and Breonna Taylor was No. 2. The title chase revolved around the Lakers' superstar, but Taylor's senseless death united players, coaches, and media members. From the first days in July, players made a point to mention her death in postgame interviews. James explicitly asked for the Louisville officers to be arrested during his impromptu speech on gun control, and Murray wore shoes with her likeness.

There were four teams left in the bubble, and all four teams took the news hard. James wrote on Twitter that he was "devastated, hurt, sad, and mad." Lakers guard Danny Green said it was "disappointing," while Malone and the Nuggets coaches called a team meeting to address the ruling.

"I just put myself in Breonna Taylor's boyfriend's shoes," Malone said. "Somebody breaks into my house at 2 or 3 in the morning. I am going to feel like somebody should not be there. We've been using our platform down here to try to bring about education, especially speaking out on justice for Breonna Taylor. We have not gotten that justice. That's a shame. Hopefully that will change at some point."

The Celtics and Heat played Game 4 of the Eastern Conference finals a few hours after the ruling was announced. Boston's Jayson Tatum said the verdict was preordained—"We knew what was going to happen"—and called it a "sad, frustrating and tough day for all us." Jaylen Brown echoed his teammate's resignation. "This society, the way it's built, is not meant to protect and serve people of color," he said. "I knew the wrong decision would be made."

Miami's Jimmy Butler said the verdict weighed on players when they took the court. "It's always much bigger than basketball because that could be anybody," he said. "That could be me. That could be any African American. It's always on my heart because I just think it's some bull crap. Going into the game, you do have to compete. But at the end of the day, we're people first, not just athletes."

Heat coach Erik Spoelstra called the financial settlement "a ridiculously empty payoff," and Tyler Herro dismissed the idea that Taylor's family had been treated fairly by the system. "Money is not justice, and that's really it," Miami's rookie guard said.

The bubble's energy was noticeably different. Many players had fire in their eyes over Jacob Blake's shooting in August, and the Bucks couldn't bring themselves to take the court. A month later, several players looked to the ground in despair when they were asked about the lack of charges for Taylor's death. It had been a long, trying month. What's more, a broken system was a more daunting foe than a single police officer pulling the trigger. If Blake's shooting prompted outrage, Taylor's ruling inspired feelings of hopelessness.

The rest of the West finals was decided by James's ability to summon energy in the face of heartbreaking news and heavy legs. His turnover problems against Denver seemed born of fatigue, and his outside shot wavered a bit too. The twenty-three-year-old Murray kept coming in Game 4, floating through the air for a miraculous double-clutch layup past James. Meanwhile, the thirty-five-year-old James grasped the bottom of his shorts to catch his breath during a dead ball late in the game. Frank Vogel had masterfully limited James's workload throughout the postseason, but the Lakers' coach needed more from his superstar after Davis sprained his ankle early in Game 4.

Down the stretch of a tight contest, the six-foot-nine James regularly switched onto the six-foot-four Murray. The defensive move was reminiscent of a much younger James defending Bulls star Derrick Rose during his early days with the Heat. James's length and experience nullified Murray's quickness advantage: He pressured Murray into passing on the perimeter and wiped out one drive with a block. Murray still had 10 of his 32 points in the fourth quarter, but the Lakers came away with a gutsy 114–108 victory to take a 3–1 series lead. Davis, who hobbled around the court after the initial sprain, played through pain to score 34 points and pledged to take the court in Game 5.

"I've got pretty good energy when I'm on the floor all the time," James said afterward. "It's winning time, and I don't have a chance or time to be feeling tired. I'm tired now. That's when I'm tired, when it's zeros on the clock. That's when I'm tired. I'm not tired during the game."

I wasn't convinced. I saw a tired player. James shot 7-for-18 from the field and made just one basket in the final eighteen minutes. When he needed points late, he was forced to dig deep into his bag of tricks to get to the foul line. Earlier in the series, some of his turnovers resulted from wild drives. He wasn't quite getting to the spots he wanted, and his unmatched ability to read the action before it happened was slightly off. James looked vulnerable in a way that he hadn't against Portland or Houston.

But that developing narrative didn't hold. The greats toy with their opponents, luring them in and letting them get their hopes up before going for the kill. Michael Jordan loved to embark on fourth-quarter comebacks, one turnaround jumper at a time. Ditto for Kobe Bryant. It wasn't that different from an older brother spotting his younger brother 5 points in a game going to 11, to up the stakes and make things interesting. In Game 5, it became clear that James was simply biding his time. He reenacted Muhammad Ali's rope-a-dope on the hardwood, and he only needed twelve minutes to do it.

James shot just twice in the first quarter before working himself into the action with 14 points in the second quarter. The Lakers held a 10-point halftime lead, Davis was moving all right on his ankle, and the Nuggets were reeling. In the third, James largely deferred to Davis as Denver crept back within 3 points entering the fourth.

The final period was a blur with James as the axis of the action. He raced out in transition, finishing a layup through a touch foul. He manipulated Denver's defense in a high pick-and-roll, tucking into a soft spot for a leaning pull-up jumper. He drove hard across the paint for a fadeaway on the left baseline that splashed in. He used another high screen to step back into a long 2. He drove right on Murray, spun around back to his left, and drained a turnaround from the middle of the paint. He hesitated to freeze Grant and then buried a pull-up in his face. He looked off two defenders and hit a 3-pointer from a full step beyond the arc.

James's shot wasn't always there against Denver, but it was perfectly dialed in when he needed it in Game 5. The final damage: 38 points, 16 rebounds, and 10 assists in forty minutes. James played the entire fourth quarter, scoring 16 points on 7-for-10 shooting in the period. When Denver cut Los Angeles's lead to 4 points with less than five minutes to play, James scored or assisted on 12 straight Lakers points to put away the series.

There wasn't a single dunk, layup, or blow-by going to the basket. Everything was technique. Below-the-rim technique. Old man technique from James, whose overgrown beard had shown specks of gray. The same tough jumpers that turned Jordan and Bryant into legends. Steady control over all aspects of the game: defensive matchups, momentum, spacing on the court.

I had seen James play live roughly seventy-five times since Game 1 of the 2018 Finals, but this struck me as his most dominant individual performance since that 51-point masterpiece against the Warriors. The win improved James's career record in closeout games to 38-10, including 17 wins in his last 18 tries. This time, he finished off a younger, spunkier conference finals opponent with his head.

"My shoulders are wide enough to carry a lot of load, but my mind is stronger," James said after clinching the 117–107 victory to advance to his tenth Finals. "If we are in the fourth quarter and we have a chance to win, I do not want to play another game. I want to be just as desperate as my opponent."

James and Malone shared a mutual affection, and the Nuggets coach never needed to be pushed too hard to gush about the Lakers' star. After watching James torch a Nuggets team that had won six straight elimination games, Malone was effusive. "I know everybody wants to get caught up in the whole argument about the greatest of all time," he said. "That is an unwinnable debate. LeBron is one of the greatest to ever do it, and his résumé speaks for itself. When the game was hanging in the balance, who took over? The best player on the floor. That's what you've come to expect from him."

As James walked triumphantly toward the locker room with a camera crew in tow, he quoted Bryant's famous declaration during the 2009 Finals. "Job not done," James said, adding later that he was "one of the few that can understand" Bryant's mentality. "That drive to always want to be victorious, it stops you from sleeping and you sacrifice a lot of things. You sacrifice your family at times because you're so driven to be so great."

The Lakers rolled through the West playoffs with a 12-3 record and were set for a Finals date with the Heat. To claim his fourth title, James would need to beat his former team six years after leaving them to return to the Cavaliers. James left the West finals quoting Frank Sinatra—"I did it my way"—as he reflected on reaching the Finals with his third different franchise. Jimmy Butler, meanwhile, left the East finals saying that the Heat would "have to be damn near perfect" to beat the Lakers.

"It's been like this for a very long time," Butler said. "If you want to win, you're going to have to go through a LeBron James–led team. That's what it normally comes down to. That's what we've got to focus in on. You're going to get the same test over and over again until you pass, and that test is LeBron James."

21

Grand Opening, Grand Closing

Almost all my favorite basketball reporting memories have happened at the NBA Finals.

I realized immediately at my first Finals, in 2011, that the championship stakes and the global scope of the event was unlike anything that I had seen. The Finals felt more important, more dramatic, more tense, more everything. I looked forward to the championship series every year, and I wrote an entire column during the hiatus imagining the series that would have taken place if not for the pandemic. Of course, I didn't foresee the Heat winning the East to challenge the Lakers.

The Finals can be agonizing, jubilant, and heartbreaking, sometimes all in the matter of a few seconds. My introduction to Finals pressure came that first year when LeBron James faltered in big moments, prompting testy exchanges with media members. James was seething, the packed press conference room was awkward beyond belief, and the story lines twisted and turned at a dizzying rate.

Since then, I witnessed several all-time clutch plays—including Ray Allen's corner three in 2013 and James's chase-down block in 2016—and collected champagne corks from locker room celebrations. In 2014, I found myself wedged in a tiny, steaming locker room in San Antonio after the AT&T Center's air-conditioning gave out. Sweat from a cameraman, who was perched on a stool above me, dripped onto my head as we waited for James, who was receiving treatment for cramps and never showed. In 2019, I sat in a hockey press box, high in the rafters in Toronto, trying and failing to process Kevin Durant's devastating Achilles injury.

The typical Finals was an international celebration of basketball, drawing hundreds of reporters from around the globe, attracting raucous crowds filled with celebrities, and dominating the sports landscape for two weeks in June. Given the restrictive conditions, Drake wouldn't be sitting courtside and Hall of Famer Bill Russell wouldn't be there to present the Finals MVP trophy. With its exhausting run-up, altered calendar, and isolated locale, the bubble Finals felt more like the season finale of *Survivor*. Whichever team was left standing would get the trophy, and then everyone would go home.

"When the players first got here, there was a healthy level of skepticism and curiosity," NBA deputy commissioner Mark Tatum said before the Finals. "How is this thing going to work and feel? Then there was a settling in, and everyone got into routines. Fast-forward and there's obviously a very different feel on campus now that there are only two teams, but the Lakers and Heat are zoned in and energized. They can see the finish line, and they recognize that all that sacrifice over these last few months is for the chance to win an NBA championship."

I had worried for months that the NBA wouldn't be able to resume the playoffs, so I was thrilled that the Finals arrived on schedule and without any health crises. I felt fortunate to be attending my tenth in a row during a year in which nothing else went according to plan, and I appreciated the NBA's efforts to inject a little pomp and circumstance.

Commissioner Adam Silver arrived in Orlando and completed a quarantine in time to give his customary address before the start of Game 1. Soon, he was briskly jogging the campus loop. The Advent-Health Arena was decorated with images of the golden Larry O'Brien Trophy in every direction: on the court, on the sideline videoboards, and in the tunnels to the locker room.

An NBA Entertainment photographer arranged for group and individual pictures for all media members in attendance, and the Disney gift shop offered Finals-specific shirts, water bottles, and other knick-knacks. The league also released staggering statistics that put the bubble's daily frenzy into perspective: Over three months, there were 3,600 virtual media interviews involving players and coaches, 115 charter buses and vans used for safe transportation, 525 guided fishing tours, and 106,000 total hotel room night stays.

Despite my best efforts, I suffered from senioritis by the time the Finals opened on September 30. I had shipped home almost all my belongings, bought bags full of souvenirs, exhausted the room service menu, walked every square inch of the bubble property, and taken plenty of pictures of Mikey the egret. The Lakers and Heat inspired a strong sense of anticipation, but so did the idea of going home. Everyone felt it. The NBA came, saw, and conquered Disney World, and the usual desire to savor every moment of the Finals wasn't quite there.

"It's probably been the most challenging thing I've ever done as a professional as far as committing to something and actually making it through," James said on the day before Game 1. "The toll that it would take on your mind and your body and everything else, it's been extremely tough."

While I didn't allow myself to count down the days during August or early September, it was unavoidable now. I looked at possible flights home and started to think about reentering society, a daunting proposition because the pandemic had only worsened since July. Hopes that the bubble would be a bridge to a safer future for the league and for my life hadn't materialized. All these months later, there was no end in sight.

For the NBA's leadership team, the excitement of the Finals came wrapped in a heightened vigilance about the coronavirus. The league's decision makers anticipated that a perfect track record would come to define the bubble experiment. Even if the television ratings were down and the players struggled with adjusting to the isolation, at least the bubble kept its inhabitants out of harm's way and allowed games to continue.

But that argument relied on maintaining no positive cases until the conclusion of the Finals, a fact that wasn't lost on the league's leaders. Silver told CNN that his "favorite emoji has become the fingers crossed one," and Tatum preached caution too.

"We've been able to demonstrate a model for how you could operate a business successfully in the pandemic," he said. "We're very proud of that. We're excited to get where we are, but we still have work to do. The virus is so unpredictable that we can't have anybody let their guards down. That's important for us to collectively reinforce. We're trying to crown an NBA champion, and we have one more series to go. We owe it to the teams, the players, the staff, and the employees who have sacrificed so much."

With Silver in town, the tight rules were cinched even tighter. Eating food was barred during games. Reporters were put through a mandatory check of their proximity alarms before entering the arena. A barrage of text messages came in every day reminding bubble dwellers about various health protocols. The postgame press conference rooms were dolled up, with players and coaches sitting on a raised stage rather than a normal chair while reporters sat farther apart.

These were still intimate gatherings, given that the media contingent was strictly limited, but there was now room for league and union officials to listen in on the proceedings. Most importantly, the social distancing between the players and everyone else was larger than ever before. It struck me that the NBA's leaders were acting like a coach whose team held a 10-point lead in the final four minutes. They were doing everything in their power to protect their lead to ensure health, maintain television ratings, and avoid a public relations black eye.

As for the series, the Lakers were clear favorites in my view. James and Anthony Davis were the two best players, and both entered the Finals with momentum after Los Angeles's convincing showing against Denver. Although the Heat were overmatched and lacked the top-shelf talent usually required to win the title, they matched up well with the Lakers' stars on paper. Jimmy Butler wouldn't back down from James, and he was seeking revenge for previous head-to-head losses in the 2013 and 2015 playoffs. Bam Adebayo was one of the few NBA big men with enough speed, length, and athleticism to keep up with Davis. The Heat's underdog bid would rely on making James and Davis work for their points while hoping that their egalitarian offense could outgun the Lakers' supporting cast.

On the afternoon of Game 1, I ironed a dress shirt and eagerly broke out one of the three suits that I had been saving for months. I hate ties, but I looped one around my neck without thinking twice. After wearing sneakers all summer, I dusted off my one pair of dress shoes. The Finals.

The NBA was making the best out of a bad situation, and I sought to do the same. After all, Butler was the subject of my first cover story for *Sports Illustrated*, in 2015, and James was my final cover, in 2018, before I joined the *Washington Post*. I attended their most recent playoff matchup when James's Cavaliers defeated Butler's Bulls in an excellent 2015 second-round series. I grinned when I arrived at AdventHealth Arena, and I felt butterflies as I looked around. It wasn't a normal Finals, but it was still the Finals.

"It's been the longest season in NBA history," Silver said during his state of the union address before Game 1, nodding to the deaths of Kobe Bryant and David Stern, the four-month shutdown, and the bubble odyssey. "Being here has taken extraordinary sacrifices by everyone involved."

Just a few hours later, the whole thing felt over. Like Jay-Z once said, "Grand opening, grand closing." The Heat raced to a 23–10 lead, raising hopes that they might be able to push the Lakers to their limits. But then wheel after wheel after wheel fell off Miami's wagon. Butler rolled his left ankle and moved gingerly afterward. Goran Dragic suffered a foot injury and didn't play in the game's final twenty-eight minutes. Adebayo suffered a shoulder injury in the second half and departed for good midway through the third quarter.

The Heat's three most important players were all making their Finals debuts, and they all suffered significant injuries in the first three quarters of Game 1. This felt like indisputable evidence of a cursed season, a cursed year, a cursed planet. The Lakers mercilessly erased their early deficit and built a 32-point lead in the third quarter before coasting to a 116–98 victory. Things got so ugly in the second half that I did something I never do: I filed my game story before the fourth quarter even started.

"They smacked us in the mouth," said James, who posted 25 points, 13 rebounds, and 9 assists. "From that moment when it was 23–10, we started to play to our capabilities. We started flying around. We started getting defensive stops. We started sharing the ball a lot better offensively and just got into a really good groove. Fans or no fans, because of the inner challenge for myself and the way I prepare, it felt amazing to be playing in the Finals once again."

James was on the other side of this equation with the 2015 Cavaliers, losing Kyrie Irving in Game 1 of the Finals before falling to the Warriors in six games. Then, as now, the series would move on without the injured. The Heat needed to fill their rotation holes and deal with a heavy psychological burden. Three injuries in one game? How was that fair? For the Heat, the games would be coming too fast. For the Lakers, the games couldn't come fast enough. "I want to be mentioned in the category of champions," said Davis, after finishing with 34 points and 9 rebounds. "That's the next step."

As Heat coach Erik Spoelstra awaited updates on his key players, he pledged to reporters that his team was "better than we showed tonight." I knew that was true in spirit, but I wasn't so sure that it would play out that way in reality.

A limping Butler was no match for James. Dragic was the Heat's best initiator, and he arguably represented their biggest positional advantage. Adebayo was an essential ingredient for an upset bid, as Miami's other frontcourt options were lacking. Kelly Olynyk and Meyers Leonard stood no chance of defending Davis during a seven-game series. The Heat couldn't count on a home-court boost in Game 3 and Game 4. This was shaping up to be a sweep.

After dropping Game 1 on Wednesday, Miami had to collect itself for Game 2 on Friday. The NBA had gone four months without basketball, but now there were just forty-eight hours for the Heat to work on Butler, Dragic, and Adebayo. While Butler was able to play through the pain, Dragic and Adebayo were not.

"I had to play the role of not just head coach, but almost of a parent the last 24 hours," Spoelstra said during his media session before Game 2. "[Dragic and Adebayo] are really amazing. Like everybody in our locker room, there's a real special sense of brotherhood and responsibility. They were both lobbying to play, and we ultimately had to take the decision out of their hands."

Spoelstra was left to start Butler, Tyler Herro, Jae Crowder, Duncan Robinson, and Leonard. Seeing that group go out for tip-off added another layer to the surreal bubble experience. Butler was a legit star, but Herro was a rookie, Crowder was a well-traveled veteran, Robinson was in his second season, and Leonard appeared in only one of Miami's previous sixteen playoff games.

I couldn't remember another Finals team in such desperate straits in my lifetime. Nothing in the ten series I had covered came close. The 2015 Cavaliers still had James in his prime to make up for Irving's absence. The 2019 Warriors still had Stephen Curry and Draymond Green when they lost Durant and Klay Thompson late in the series.

The Lakers rolled again in Game 2, controlling the contest from the outset to win 124–114. James had 33 points, 9 rebounds, and 9 assists, while Davis made fourteen of his first fifteen shots to finish with 32 points and 14 rebounds. Lakers owner Jeanie Buss and Rich Paul, Davis's agent, had both arrived at the bubble and were in attendance for Game 2. The coronation was on, and the celebration was only two wins away. "I want a ring, and he has three of them," Davis said of James, not worried about risking a jinx. "Hopefully, I don't have to be envious of that much longer."

There was no tension to Game 2, and I really felt the emptiness of the arena for the first time in weeks. The Lakers only needed to go through the motions that night to win, and my excitement from earlier in the week evaporated. This was plain sad. Miami's valiant run was frozen by injuries, leaving Los Angeles to worry more about complacency than its depleted opponent. Spoelstra and Butler were stone-faced and stubborn in defeat. "We don't give a shit what everybody else thinks," Spoelstra said. "What will it take? Whatever is necessary. It's as simple as that. If you want something badly enough, you'll figure it out."

Spoelstra would never concede an inch, but I saw no path forward for the Heat. After I sent in my story, I called Delta Air Lines. Game 4 was set for October 6, so I booked a one-way flight from Orlando to Los Angeles departing on October 7.

The "longest season ever" was about to conclude with the shortest possible Finals. I would be home in five days. I was sure of it.

22

Not So Fast

When I profiled Jimmy Butler for *Sports Illustrated* in 2015, I chatted briefly with Tom Thibodeau, then the coach of the Chicago Bulls, at the University of San Francisco during a road trip. Butler was twenty-five years old and enjoying a breakout campaign that saw him earn Most Improved Player honors. Thibodeau had coached Butler for four years, watching him blossom from a seldom-used defensive specialist into an All-Star playmaker. Coach and player were both straight-talking workaholics, and Thibodeau was eager to sing Butler's praises. "If they don't bite as puppies, they usually don't bite," Thibodeau said. "Jimmy was biting right from the start."

Butler loved to laugh about his frisky beginnings. During a sit-down interview at a luxury hotel in Portland, he told me that he spent his rookie season begging Thibodeau for playing time. By the end of his second season, Butler was a full-time starter in the playoffs. There was only one problem: The old-school Thibodeau, who didn't believe in minutes limits, barely took Butler off the court. During a five-day stretch in the 2013 postseason, Butler played every single second in three consecutive games. Fatigue wasn't an option.

"I used to always complain to Thibs," Butler said. "I would tell him, 'I want to play, I want to play, I want to play.' It got to the point where I was annoying my damn self by how much I was talking to him about playing. The first time he played me all 48 minutes, I was like, 'Don't complain. Your rookie year, you were always asking to play.' I was gassed, tired, but I got what I asked for."

Those playoffs represented Butler's introduction to a national television audience. In a second-round series against the Heat, a twenty-three-year-old Butler shadowed LeBron James everywhere he went. Butler played all forty-eight minutes three times in the five-game series, and he keyed a Game 1 upset with 21 points and 14 rebounds. While he didn't resort to cheap tactics like blowing in James's ear, as Indiana's Lance Stephenson did in 2014, Butler was a pest. James was at the peak of his athletic powers at age twenty-eight, and he intimidated many of his opponents. Yet Butler was fearless, crowding James when possible and doing his best to body him despite a sizable height and weight difference. Miami won the series without too much trouble, but Butler was on the map.

In 2015, Butler and James met again in the second round. James was back on the Cavaliers, who were dealing with serious injury issues and questionable decisions from rookie coach David Blatt. The Bulls took a 2–1 series lead into Game 4 at the United Center thanks to Derrick Rose, who banked in a miraculous 3-pointer at the Game 3 buzzer. A tireless Butler again found himself logging more than forty minutes per game defending James. The Bulls and Cavaliers enjoyed memorable playoff battles throughout Michael Jordan's career, and Chicago would have loved to spoil James's homecoming.

James had other ideas. With the score tied at 84 and 1.5 seconds remaining, Butler lined up against James as Cleveland inbounded from the left baseline. James nudged Butler toward the basket, broke free to the left corner, set his feet, and drilled the game winner as time expired. Butler recovered to get his left hand up in James's face, only to turn around and slump his shoulders as the ball dropped cleanly through the net. The United Center sat in stunned silence, just two days after it had erupted for Rose's heroics.

During the postgame interview, James added another layer to the shot's legend by informing reporters that he "scratched" Blatt's play call. The coach wanted James to inbound the ball, but James wanted the shot and he got the shot.

Butler took the loss hard, and Chicago went down in six games. Thibodeau was fired less than three weeks later, and Butler didn't win another playoff series until 2019 with the Philadelphia 76ers. James's shot over Butler had effectively ended Chicago's 2014–15 season,

Thibodeau's five-year Bulls tenure, and Butler's run of modest post-season success in the Windy City. That type of loss left a mark.

Butler's "puppy" days were long gone by 2020, and he waited for another shot at James throughout a six-year journey that took him from Chicago to Minnesota to Philadelphia to Miami. With a 2–0 series lead in the Finals, James was now 10–3 head-to-head against Butler in the postseason, with five consecutive victories dating back to his 2015 buzzer-beater.

But in Game 3 of the Finals, Butler turned in the defining performance of his career. He was sick of losing to James, sick of the media assuming that the Heat would lose, and sick of hearing about how injuries ruined the Finals. Butler was raging against the world, but it was a controlled rage that encapsulated his many virtues: physicality, indefatigability, stubbornness, bravery, intelligence, pride.

The Lakers were a soft target that night, a little caught up in their own hype and unbelievably careless with the ball. Butler, still without Goran Dragic and Bam Adebayo due to injury, pounded and pounded and pounded. In an early flurry, he drove hard for a dunk, threaded a pass to a cutter, and poked the ball free from James to race ahead for a slam. When matched up against smaller or less physical Lakers defenders, Butler bullied his way into the paint for pull-up jumpers, tough runners, and free-throw attempts. Much of Miami's offense boiled down to four guys spotting up around the perimeter as Butler put his head down and barreled to the basket.

Butler was never a great 3-point shooter, and he didn't attempt a single one all night. This performance was straight out of the 1990s: backing down defenders in the post, banking in shots, and hitting tough fadeaways like Michael Jordan. In 2014, Butler told me that he would jokingly call himself "Baby Mike" when he hit jumpers from the mid-post during Bulls practices. Game 3 was pure Baby Mike.

As Miami took control in the second half, Butler barked at James when the two teams left the court for a timeout. Butler explained later that James had told him that the Heat were "in trouble" at the end of the first quarter. As Miami closed in on its 115–104 victory, Butler shouted the same words back at James in the fourth quarter.

"LeBron has gotten the best of me way too many times," Butler said after finishing with 40 points, 11 rebounds, and 13 assists in forty-four minutes. "I respect the guy for it, but this is a different time now and a different group of guys around me. We're here to win. We're not going to lay down. We're going to fight back in this thing and even it up 2–2."

Butler's game and demeanor reminded me of Philadelphia's Allen Iverson in the 2001 Finals. The Sixers were overmatched against Shaquille O'Neal, Kobe Bryant, and the Lakers, but Iverson scored 48 points in fifty-two minutes and hit his famous step-over jumper on Tyronn Lue in an overtime Game 1 victory. Los Angeles went on to win the series, but Iverson's force of personality demanded respect. Butler found himself in a similar spot.

"I'm ready for this," Butler said. "On the biggest stage, whatever you ask me to do, I can do. Obviously y'all are picking us to lose. Nobody's picking us, and we really don't care. We're going to stay confident because we know we're a good team."

So much for that flight home. I called Delta and pushed back my flight until October 10, the day after Game 5. Miami's victory had bought everyone in the bubble at least three more days at Disney World, due to an extra off day in between Games 4 and 5. "I just want to fucking go home," one of my writing colleagues told me on the way to the shuttle bus that night. "But Jimmy was something else," I offered in reply. "I just want to fucking go home," he said again.

That exchange clinched Game 3 as the quintessential game of Butler's career. Great players and quality teams tapped out of the bubble under far less adversity than Butler's Heat faced in Game 3. Again, he was surrounded by Tyler Herro, Jae Crowder, Duncan Robinson, and Meyers Leonard in the starting lineup. None of them played especially well, leaving Kelly Olynyk, who hadn't seen much playoff action before the Finals, to emerge as Butler's sidekick with 17 points off the bench.

Butler loved to punish himself. He was famous for rising early to get in pre-sunrise workouts, and he disconnected his cable and Internet connections during the summer of 2014 to ensure that he had nothing to do except go to the gym three times a day. Now he was punishing everyone in the bubble by refusing to crack when Miami was well past its breaking point. It was perfect.

The Lakers blamed their sloppy play and lack of urgency for the loss, and James was downright dismissive in defeat. "I don't feel like we're concerned," he said, before firming up the sentiment. "We're not concerned." Prior to Game 4, James sent a group text to his Lakers teammates stressing that it was a "must-win" despite their 2–1 series lead.

Years earlier, I did a wide-ranging interview with Shavlik Randolph, a high-profile high school prospect whose professional career included stops in the NBA, Puerto Rico, China, and Japan. The topic turned to a training camp he spent with James soon after the Heatles formed in Miami. Randolph was a McDonald's All-American who spent three years at Duke and played with All-Star Brandon Roy on the Portland Trail Blazers, but he claimed that he had no frame of reference for what it was like to share a court with James.

According to Randolph, James was the best player in every category and the top-performer in every drill. He was the quickest, fastest, strongest, smartest. He was the best scorer, passer, on-ball defender, off-ball defender, leaper, and leader. Randolph put it this way: James was, almost without exception, better at your best skill than you were, no matter who you were and no matter the skill. To top it off, James knew it and everyone else knew it too. Every scrimmage began with James possessing those inherent advantages and with his opponents left hoping that today would be their lucky day.

That was still mostly true a decade later. Importantly, James was just as competitive as Butler. He hated losing just as much as Butler. He was just as tireless as Butler.

The Lakers came ready for a fight in Game 4. At last, the series felt like both teams were playing at Finals-level intensity. James lashed out at the referees over multiple missed calls, and his screams bounced around the empty gym. Although he struggled with turnovers again early, James took a page out of Butler's book late in the game. Needing to grind out fourth-quarter points, he went to the post, earned trips to the free-throw line, and bided his time to take advantage of narrow openings.

With a little more than three minutes to go and Los Angeles clinging to a 90–88 lead, James grabbed the rebound on a Butler miss and pushed the ball up the court. Drawing three defenders as he approached the free-throw line, James dished quickly out to Kentavious Caldwell-Pope in the right corner. Caldwell-Pope, an unsung hero throughout the playoffs, buried the open 3 to stretch Los Angeles's lead to 5 points. Randolph's portrait of James emerged in that decisive moment: unparalleled pace, strength, and smarts, with the ability to make a perfect, unselfish read at full speed in a high-pressure moment.

"That's the best part about it: It's a chess match," James said. "When you get to this point in your career, having your mind at a high level is so much more important than the physical. To be able to think through the game, see the adjustments, and make plays before they even seem possible, that's the best part for me personally."

There was another telling sequence late in the third quarter. An uncertain Kyle Kuzma shoveled a lazy pass to James on the perimeter, and Butler jumped the play to poke the ball free and take off in transition. James sprinted back to try to block Butler's layup, but he was whistled for a foul. In one spinning motion, James argued the call and then shouted at Kuzma to be more careful.

As soon as Kuzma tossed the pass, I knew James would rip into him. The middle of a one-possession game in the Finals was no time for hesitation and half-heartedness. But I didn't expect what happened on the Lakers' next possession: Rather than ice out Kuzma or take back control of the action, James set up his teammate for a 3-pointer, and Kuzma delivered. In a fraught contest, James proved to be the most composed player on the court too. Los Angeles held on for a 102–96 victory, as James played the entire fourth quarter and finished with 28 points, 12 rebounds, and 8 assists.

"This was one of the biggest games of my career," James said, pleased with the 3–1 series lead. "I don't care about rest. I really don't. I don't care about resting. I can rest in a week, max. I can rest for a month straight."

James had played in bigger games: Game 6 against the Celtics in 2012, Game 7 against the Spurs in 2013, and Game 7 against the Warriors in 2016, to name three. But I understood why he weighed the stakes differently. Butler was playing the best basketball of his career, Adebayo had returned from injury, and momentum was fickle. Blowing a 2–0 lead as a heavy favorite in the Finals would be disastrous for James's legacy and his pursuit of Jordan's six championship rings. James and the Lakers would have faced all the pressure if the series were tied. Staying at Disney World for this long only to go home without a ring had to be a sickening thought.

Anthony Davis played no small role in the pivotal victory. Lakers coach Frank Vogel gave him the assignment of guarding Butler, an unconventional cross matchup that asked the taller and longer Davis to slow the Miami star's powerful drives to the basket. In the second round, Milwaukee was reluctant to switch Giannis Antetokounmpo, the 2020 Defensive Player of the Year, onto Butler. Davis, who finished second to Antetokounmpo in the award voting, took the challenge in the Finals.

While Butler still finished with 22 points, 10 rebounds, and 9 assists, Davis prevented him from exploding again. "When I was in New Orleans, [coach Alvin Gentry] used to say it all the time, he used to preach defense," said Davis, who posted 22 points, 9 rebounds, and 4 blocks. "I had the best offensive team. We would score 130 and would never get past the second round because we didn't play defense. You hear the cliché all the time, defense wins championships."

In the game's final minute, Davis also delivered a dagger 3-pointer over Adebayo to stretch the Lakers' lead from 6 points to 9. James began celebrating as soon as Davis released the shot, and he swung his arm for a high five as both players shouted toward the sideline cameras with fierce relief. "He's a big shot-maker late in the shot clock, early in the shot clock, fourth quarter, first quarter, everything in between," James said of Davis. "He knew it was late in the shot clock and he obviously trusted his shot that he works on consistently. Big-time shot, big-time play for our team to be able to put the game away."

The Lakers could taste their title, and the prospect of their closeout win set into motion a wave of preparations. Checkout instructions went out to all reporters. Black cars for safe transportation to the airport were scheduled for October 10, the morning after Game 5. I packed my remaining belongings into two suitcases and checked into my flight home to Los Angeles a few hours before tip-off. Davis took the court in gold Nike sneakers—an apparent homage to the Larry O'Brien Trophy—and the Lakers wore their black tribute jerseys to Kobe Bryant. They were writing their own ending to a marathon season, and it wasn't particularly subtle.

Once again, Butler intervened. Game 5, like Game 4, was a slugfest, except this time Butler had a little more help. Duncan Robinson, a twenty-six-year-old wing, had looked overwhelmed for much of the series. He was a long way from Division III, where he began his collegiate career at Williams College, and the G-League, where he landed after going undrafted in 2018. Now in his second season in Miami, the shooting specialist was starting in the Finals against James and Davis.

In Game 1, Robinson took only three shots in twenty-seven minutes and missed them all. In Game 2, he went 2-for-7. During one dead ball early in the series, media members could hear Spoelstra imploring Robinson with colorful language to shoot the ball. Miami couldn't afford one of the league's best marksmen to have stage fright. After the Heat's Game 3 win, in which Robinson shot 4-for-12 and again appeared hesitant, Butler applied public pressure.

"Duncan needs to shoot the ball a lot more," he said. "He needs to hunt shots because he's going to be a reason that we win one of these games. He's going to hit six or seven three-pointers and I'm going to jump up and down and I'm going to give him a big hug, maybe a slight kiss on the back of his head. I know how important that guy is to our team."

Butler was riding high when he delivered that prediction thanks to his 40-point triple-double, but he looked clairvoyant in Game 6. Davis went down with an apparent right foot injury in the first quarter, prompting flashbacks to Kevin Durant's Achilles tear in the 2019 Finals. Thankfully, Davis never went to the locker room and avoided serious injury, though he was sidelined long enough for Butler to get into a groove.

Without Davis to defend him, Butler was able to replicate his sledgehammer approach from Game 3. As he attacked inside, opportunities opened outside for Robinson. By night's end, Robinson scored a postseason career-high 26 points and hit seven 3-pointers, just as Butler predicted. That was enough for Miami to withstand a 40-point performance from James, who was gunning hard to end the series.

"I thought I was a little more persistent tonight getting to the ball and getting to my spots," Robinson said. "That helped, and it helps to see some fall in. That helped build confidence more. [Butler] took us home. He does whatever it takes to win. He hit some shots. He made plays on both sides of the court. He willed it. It's not always pretty, but he always finds a way."

The late-game sequence was a classic mano-a-mano showdown between Butler and James that reminded me of the blacktop battles between Jake and Jesus Shuttlesworth in Spike Lee's *He Got Game*. Indeed, the fourth quarter of Game 5 represented the most intense basketball of the entire bubble. Writing on a print deadline, unsure whether I was going to be covering a title celebration or not, I had to loosen my tie and undo the top button of my dress shirt in the final period. The adrenaline that I felt down the stretch of Game 5 rivaled previous Finals, even without any fans in the building.

As the final three minutes approached, Butler set up Robinson for a go-ahead 3. James answered with two free throws. Butler answered with a midrange jumper over Davis. James replied with a double-clutch layup and the foul, flexing toward the baseline camera. Butler answered again with a spinning baseline turnaround, to give Miami a 105–104 lead with a little over a minute to play. James immediately took Butler into the post and backed his way down for a go-ahead layup.

Trailing by 1 with fifty seconds left, Butler dribbled straight into the teeth of the Lakers' defense and drew a foul going to the basket. Once he realized that the whistle had blown, he walked to the baseline and doubled his body over a waist-high electronic sign that surrounded the court.

Butler put his head between his forearms and rested his forehead on the padded wall, his chest heaving. He stayed there for perhaps ten seconds, enough time for Dan Woike of the *Los Angeles Times*, seated on the baseline, to snap a stellar picture of Butler with his head down and arms limp from exhaustion. "Right away I knew it was a special image, the thing that captured the night as [well] as any words would," Woike wrote. "I tweeted it with a one-word caption: Monster."

Butler caught his breath during a timeout and made both of his free throws to give Miami a 107–106 lead. During a roughly two-minute stretch of action, James had scored 7 straight points for the Lakers and Butler had score 6 straight for the Heat. No one else on the court had scored, and only one other player had even attempted a shot.

Even though Butler could barely stand up, the Lakers cracked first. On the game's deciding possession, James drove hard to his right with ten seconds left and drew four defenders as he went to the basket. The fifth, Andre Iguodala, wasn't all that far away either. James whipped a pass over his head to Danny Green, who was wide open at the top of the arc.

This was a vintage James decision, as he always insisted on calculating the right basketball play rather than taking every game-deciding shot himself. Green was a career 40 percent 3-point shooter, and there wasn't a defender within ten feet of him when he caught James's pass, which arrived a bit off-target.

Green had struggled throughout the playoffs, though, and he short-armed the potential championship-clinching jumper. James to Green wouldn't go down alongside Michael Jordan to Steve Kerr. Talking heads spent the next forty-eight hours arguing whether James should have trusted his teammate on the final play, given Green's shakiness throughout the postseason.

"I was able to draw two defenders below the free-throw line and find one of our shooters at the top of a key for a wide open three to win a championship," James explained. "I trusted him. I know he wishes he could have it again. I wish I could make a better pass. You live with it."

The offensive rebound from Green's miss bounced to Markieff Morris with five seconds left. James was open and calling for the ball on the right wing, but Morris panicked with the clock ticking down and tried to force a pass inside to Davis, who was battling with Adebayo. The ball sailed out of bounds, and Miami escaped with a 111–108 victory. The confetti cannons that were rolled out near the court went unused, and Davis didn't go home with the gold trophy to match his gold shoes.

Butler's 35 points, 12 rebounds, 11 assists, and 5 steals were just enough to overcome James's 40 points, 13 rebounds, 7 assists, and 3 steals. "No matter how they guard me, I'm going to make the right play," Butler said. "I'm sure they wanted to win and thought they were going to win coming into it. The next one is going to be even harder for us, but I like our chances."

The postgame scene was déjà vu from Game 3, except the collective animosity was ratcheted up a notch. Butler had extended everyone's stays again, leaving exhausted reporters stumbling around in a daze. I called Delta and pushed back my flight home for a second time, and the NBA informed me that my car to the airport was rescheduled. There was moping on the bus ride back to the hotel: Some reporters had black cars lined up to take them home that same night. Instead, they were held captive for another two days before Game 6 on October 11. "I can't believe this shit," muttered one reporter, who had planned to stay up all night and catch a 6:00 a.m. flight out of Orlando.

I couldn't believe it either. There was no explanation for the Lakers dropping two games to the injured Heat, other than Butler's out-of-body experiences. Davis said the Lakers felt "no pressure," but my mind started playing out scenarios that seemed impossible when they were up 2–0. What if Los Angeles blew a 3–1 lead to Miami? James would fall to 3–7 in the Finals, and 2020 would supplant 2011 as the worst championship series loss of his career. This would be his biggest playoff failure ever and a rotten bookend to Cleveland's incredible 3–1 comeback against Golden State in 2016.

Butler was doing his best to manifest that inconceivable twist of fate. "We're here to win," he said after Game 5. "These next two, we're in the trenches."

23

Champagne at Last

Anthony Davis met the Los Angeles media for the first time as a member of the Lakers all the way back in July 2019. During that press conference, he made it clear that he viewed himself as a power forward rather than a center, no matter how much the NBA was trending toward smaller and more versatile lineups. "I'm not even going to sugarcoat it," Davis said. "I like playing the four. I don't really like playing the five."

Lakers coach Frank Vogel was sitting to Davis's left, so the All-Star tacked on an addendum directed specifically to his new boss. "If it comes down to it and you need me to play the five," he said, "then I'll play the five."

Davis wasn't alone in his preference: Many hybrid big men preferred to play power forward alongside a traditional center to avoid prolonged exposure to the wear and tear that accompanied the most physical interior matchups. Vogel believed that starting Davis alongside a true center like JaVale McGee or Dwight Howard gave Los Angeles the ability to punish teams in the paint and on the glass. The Lakers sacrificed some shooting and spacing with these looks, but it was hard to argue with the results after they claimed the West's top seed and stormed to the Finals. McGee's effectiveness waned as the playoffs went on, but Howard provided valuable minutes against Nikola Jokic, Denver's big-bodied center.

Vogel started Davis at center twice in the playoffs before the Finals: during Game 4 and Game 5 of the second round against the Rockets. Houston was the smallest team in the postseason field, and Los Angeles's shift downward set up a pair of convincing wins. When the Lakers went small, James enjoyed more room to attack the basket, Davis had the paint to himself, and the two superstars were surrounded by three shooting threats for maximum spacing. On defense, Los Angeles played even faster and fiercer than usual, pressuring opponents into turnovers and racing out in transition.

"I don't look at it as a small lineup," James said. "We all have this wingspan and we play hard. When you have that type of length and athleticism from guys, it definitely helps clean the glass, defend, and rotate. If something breaks down, you have guys that can fly around. It's a good lineup for us."

The Lakers' traditional centers weren't much use in the Finals because Bam Adebayo and the Heat's other big men spent so much time on the perimeter. In fact, McGee didn't play at all against Miami, and Howard hadn't seen many important minutes. With a title in reach, a patient Vogel revealed the ace up his sleeve. Fifteen months after the initial press conference, the coach finally needed Davis to play center.

Against Houston, Vogel inserted Markieff Morris into the starting lineup in place of McGee. Up 3–2 against the Heat, Vogel benched Howard in favor of Alex Caruso. The third-year guard was a fan favorite, a balding, headband-wearing Texas native who went undrafted and worked his way onto the Lakers' roster after stints in the G-League. Caruso earned James's respect with his intelligence and unselfishness, and at six feet five he surprised observers with the occasional highlight dunk. The Lakers planned to counter the Heat's gutsy Game 5 win with pure speed.

It was a masterstroke. Miami kept pace for a quarter and received an emotional boost from Goran Dragic, who returned for the first time since Game 1. After that, it was over. During a seven-minute span, the Lakers went on a 26–7 run to take a stunning 64–36 lead into the break. Davis pounded away inside, Kentavious Caldwell-Pope drained 3-pointers, Caruso ran out in transition, and James and Rajon Rondo took turns orchestrating. The drama that defined the previous three games had completely dissolved.

There was no need to worry about complacency or another late flurry from Jimmy Butler. The Heat were done. Los Angeles's small ball lineup kept the points flowing after halftime, scoring on four straight possessions to push the lead to 36 points. For the second time in the series, I filed my game story before the fourth quarter began.

It dawned on me that this was it. There wouldn't be a Game 7. There wouldn't be another late-night call to Delta reservations. There wouldn't be another rescheduled ride to the airport. There would be a title celebration. There would be a black car waiting the next day. There would be a flight home. This was the end of the bubble.

Whether out of nostalgia or nerves, I took one final lap around AdventHealth Arena during the fourth quarter. I walked down the hallway where I waited for the Bucks during their protest, past the press conference rooms where I spent untold hours, up the stairs to the bathrooms where the faucets sprayed water twice as hard as necessary, and back to the front entrance where a video control center beamed the action all over the world. I peeked in the curtains at the made-for-television court and saw the clock ticking down, victory getting closer. I looked across to the Lakers' fan section, which was overflowing with anticipation. A few dozen wives, girlfriends, and children had been in the bubble for more than a month, and they were savoring the long-awaited conclusion. The Heat's smaller family section looked crestfallen.

I thought back to a phone conversation that I had with the author Thomas Beller during the Western Conference finals. We spent about fifteen minutes gushing over Jokic's creativity and clutch play against the Clippers, and I noted how the Serbian big man had ended long-running debates about whether he was the NBA's best center. Joel Embiid, Karl-Anthony Towns, Rudy Gobert, and the rest were all competing for second.

Then the topic turned to Jokic's play against the Lakers and Davis's play against the Nuggets. While Los Angeles had some success using Howard to harass Jokic, Denver couldn't slow down Davis, who hit the Game 2 buzzer-beater and was a reliable scoring threat late in the series. I stopped myself mid-thought and said: "Actually, the NBA's best center is the one who doesn't want to call himself a center."

I returned to my seat in time to see Davis choking back tears of happiness in the game's closing minutes. His much-maligned trade request was paying off in full, more than eighteen months after he looked lost at the 2019 All-Star Weekend. James came over to tease him about the crying, and they shared a moment. They both understood the parallels at work. James, who now had four rings, left Cleveland to win his first title in Miami at age twenty-seven. Davis departed New Orleans and was claiming his first title with Los Angeles at age twenty-seven.

The Lakers won 106–93, a score made more palatable by a meaningless Heat run in the game's closing minutes. They clinched in six games, completing a 16-5 run to the bubble title. Davis finished with 19 points, 15 rebounds, 3 assists, and 2 blocks, and his shift to center finally broke the Heat. James capped a magnificent playoff run with 28 points, 14 rebounds, and 10 assists, a triple-double that sealed his fourth career Finals MVP award. Back in Los Angeles, the Staples Center, the Santa Monica boardwalk, and other landmarks were lit up with purple and gold lights in recognition of the franchise's seventeenth championship. As a Western Conference Elitist, I couldn't help but note on Twitter that the West had now won fifteen of the last twenty-two titles.

Purple and gold confetti flew into the air when the buzzer sounded. A jubilant James, with his jersey untucked and cameras trained on his every move, exchanged handshakes with his teammates as league officials set up the trophy presentation ceremony on the court. The Larry O'Brien Trophy was removed from its custom Louis Vuitton travel case, and I made my way down the sideline for a better angle. As NBA commissioner Adam Silver, Lakers owner Jeanie Buss, GM Rob Pelinka, adviser Kurt Rambis, and the family section joined the players and coaches on the court, I congratulated NBA and NBPA officials on accomplishing their months-long goal.

As I feared, the trophy celebration was a bit lacking without a crowd and without Bill Russell's gravitas. Just as James wished that Davis's Mamba shot had come at Staples Center, I wished that the Lakers could have shared their title moment with a full building. But the Lakers were thrilled, donning the traditional championship T-shirts and hats as they raised the Larry O'Brien Trophy in the air.

Rachel Nichols of ESPN emceed the trophy presentation, later noting the feeling of achievement that resonated in the building for the Lakers, the league, and everyone else who lived in the bubble. "As I was throwing it to the commissioner, it was impossible not to feel some sense of grandiose human capability, what people can do when challenged," Nichols said on the *ESPN Daily* podcast. "I know it's just a game, I do. I'm not pretending that this is solving world hunger. This was a bunch of people, in a bunch of cities across the country, with a bunch of different jobs working together to pull something big off."

That night, October 11, was my ninety-second at Disney World. I didn't need to report for a mandatory COVID-19 test in the morning. The league wanted me to give back my proximity alarm. I wouldn't be using my credential to get into any more games. There were no more games. I was checked into my flight. I would be leaving on Day 93.

The Lakers were reaching similar conclusions. James held up his Finals MVP trophy to loud applause from his teammates, and Davis shoved him so hard that he nearly lost his balance. They were the two most talented players in the bubble, but they also epitomized the Lakers' mental and physical toughness during a season that was marked by Kobe Bryant's tragic death and nearly scuttled by the coronavirus.

Davis fought through injuries and raised his game in high-pressure moments. James simply did it all in a way that no other modern NBA player could match. "I've never missed a playoff game in my career," James noted in his postgame speech from the court. "The best thing you could do for your teammates is to be available."

That sentiment mirrored a line that a decorated scout had told me soon after I first started covering the NBA, in 2007. "The greatest ability is availability," he advised, underscoring the importance of health, durability, and consistency when evaluating players. It remained one of my most prized basketball maxims, and James's time in the bubble redefined and broadened my understanding of availability.

Yes, he appeared in all 21 of the Lakers' playoff games, adding to his career tally of 260. But he was also the bubble's central force from start to finish. Fellow stars like Damian Lillard showed up to watch him play on opening night. He led the charge on social justice activism, speaking fearlessly on Donald Trump, gun control, and Breonna Taylor. He gave thoughtful interviews and choice sound bites during dozens of interviews, welcomed a camera crew to document his journey, and opined repeatedly on the bubble's mental and physical toll.

Day after day, night after night, James displayed championship habits and rigorous routines. He invested hours into the quiet work before tip-off in an empty gym thousands of miles from his family. There, he found the discipline and internal motivation to keep going when his top rivals cracked one by one. He put on the pregame dunk contest against the Rockets, finished off the Nuggets with the old man game, and prevailed after some memorable battles with Jimmy Butler.

Before that, James helped gather the league's stars to present a unified front as they pursued the bubble. He masterfully supported Davis and put his other teammates in position to succeed. He stepped forward in the aftermath of Bryant's death and brought a title to Los Angeles.

There he was, at center court, clutching the Larry O'Brien Trophy in his right hand and the Finals MVP trophy in his left. His grin stretched from ear to ear, and he danced a little two-step, bending deep at the knees and swinging his hips from side to side, much to his teammates' delight. When the Lakers posed for their team photo with the trophies, James sat in front and raised one finger to the sky. It had been an incredible run, and it was time to party.

In a break from tradition, media members were not allowed in the Lakers' locker room, due to the league's coronavirus protocols. I did the best that I could, staking out a front-row position just to the right of the locker room's door. "I'm free," Danny Green said, running down the hallway with his hat turned backward. "I'm free out this bitch. I'm fucking free!"

Indeed, the Lakers had two reasons to celebrate: they won the title, but they also earned the right to go home as winners. Within seconds, the players were banging on the lockers and locating the nearest champagne bottles. James walked triumphantly down the hallway, and then briefly detoured when he saw his teammates. "Goggles! I need some goggles! Fuck no. No sir, you're not about to spray me and burn my fucking eyes," he said, with the experience of a four-time champion. "Where's the goggles?"

Unfortunately, I wasn't a four-time champion, and I hadn't thought to pack goggles. Or a poncho. Green popped out of the locker room first, letting off streams of champagne from two bottles in every direction. My suit jacket caught a few droplets, and I took a selfie as a keepsake.

Three minutes later, James emerged from the locker room with a full bottle. I was smart enough to keep my iPhone camera rolling but not smart enough to anticipate what was about to happen. As writers shouted and ducked out of the way, I stood tall and absorbed ounces of champagne straight to the face. My glasses were fogged up, my mask was wet, my iPhone's lens was soaked, and my suit jacket and tie were an utter mess.

I stopped drinking alcohol in 2007 as I prepared for heart surgery, so the smell and light taste of the champagne that lingered on my mask was disorienting. Watching the video back, I could hear myself giggling. It had been a long three months. A long year. I started giggling again watching it back.

The documentary crew was over James's shoulder and caught the whole thing. I could now look forward to making a regrettable cameo in an awesome movie sometime in the future. I sent out my video on Twitter with the caption: "This is what it looks like to be sprayed with champagne by Lakers' LeBron James after he wins a title." The replies kept coming for days, and I still haven't heard the end of it.

James then took his festivities down the hall, lying on his back in the concourse with Nike goggles over his eyes, a cigar in his left hand, and a phone in his right hand. I hesitated for a moment, wondering whether calls with his children and his mother, Gloria James, were better left off the record. As James puffed his cigar and shouted his greetings, I realized this was a scene that he wanted the world to see.

"Mama! Mama!" James said. "Hey, Mama! I had to leave the locker room. They're going crazy right now. I had to get away. There's nothing that can stop me because this shit is nothing compared to the shit you had to go through."

"God is good," Gloria replied.

"God is good," James repeated. "God is great. I hope I continue to make you proud, Mom."

"Man, are you kidding me?" Gloria asked.

That beautiful moment between a single mother and her only child passed quickly, as Caldwell-Pope came by to reload James's champagne supply. Before long, the NBA's public relations staff intervened so that James could begin a long list of interviews with media partners. James chomped on his cigar on his way back to the court, and his teammates circled him. "You want to know what a champ looks like?" Morris asked, addressing no one in particular. "Look at me, motherfuckers!"

James composed himself for his official postgame press conference, although he blew huge plumes of smoke as he listened to the questions and weighed his answers. He said that he was "fueled" by "little rumblings of doubt or comparing me to the history of the game," a possible allusion to the endless Michael Jordan debates, refueled by *The Last Dance*.

Most of James's interview, though, was spent reflecting on the Disney World experience. "You wouldn't be human if you didn't have ups and downs in the bubble," he said. "At times I was questioning myself. Should I be here? Is this worth sacrificing my family? So many things. I've never been without my family this long. Missing the days of my daughter being in kindergarten, even though it's through Zoom. Missing my son's sixteenth birthday, which we all know is a big birthday if you have kids. Seeing my middle child continue to grow and be who he is."

James paused his sentimental stroll for a punchline: "Big-time shoutout to the late, great Steve Jobs. Without him, without his vision, those FaceTime calls wouldn't be possible."

After watching the entire playoffs, I left confident that the Lakers' title wouldn't bear an asterisk. They were clearly the best team, and

James was clearly the best player. More importantly, the quality of play was excellent for months. The choppy games I feared during the hiatus hadn't come to fruition. Instead, there were plenty of competitive series and memorable scoring performances.

"This was very challenging and difficult," James said. "It played with your mind. It played with your body. You're away from some of the things that you're so accustomed to that make you the professional that you are. I heard some rumblings from people that are not in the bubble that we don't have to travel or whatever. People just doubting what goes on in here. This is right up there with one of the greatest accomplishments I've had."

The interviews continued for two hours after the final buzzer, but the arena started to empty around midnight. I didn't want to leave. I took pictures of the confetti on the court, of James's Finals MVP trophy, and of a few media members who wanted a final bubble souvenir. With nothing left to do, I returned to my hotel room, where I could hear the Lakers' party continuing at the restaurant across the lake until deep into the night. Some of my media colleagues had already checked out and hit the road.

Whenever a season ends, it's impossible to sleep. My mind raced to recount all the pivotal moments. I thought back to Davis's blockbuster trade, the Hong Kong controversy, Bryant's death, and the All-Star Weekend in Chicago where no one realized that the coronavirus was about to change the country forever. I remembered Rudy Gobert's positive test, the endless hiatus, and all those hours walking my neighborhood, watching *The Last Dance*, and praying for a resolution to the season.

I recalled the endless planning meetings for the bubble, the long wait for the credential approval, my stressful health clearance, and pacing in my hotel room during the quarantine. I rewatched OG Anunoby's game winner, Davis's buzzer-beater, and highlights of Butler's 40-point night. I grimaced at all those hours I circled the loop, chased Mikey the egret, and waved at some of the NBA's most respected figures. I pondered the Bucks' protest and premature exit, the Clippers' collapse, and the Heat's valiant effort. I thought about my ninety-two COVID-19 tests, and how there wasn't a single positive test inside the bubble.

I watched a video of Erik Spoelstra, who was overcome with emotion after Miami's season-ending loss. The coach wiped away tears and took more than thirty seconds to collect his thoughts. "We didn't get the final result that we wanted," he said. "These are going to be lifetime memories that we have together. We're going to remember this year, this season, this experience, and that locker room brotherhood for the rest of our lives.

"You're in this business to be able to be around people like this. We had several guys that were not even close to being 100 percent, probably shouldn't have been playing. But that's how this group was. They wanted to do it for each other. I'm really bummed that we couldn't find a way to get over the hump and finish the season with a win."

Spoelstra's pain was as raw as James's joy. Two sides to the same competitive coin.

This wasn't the most dramatic Finals that I had covered, and I certainly had seen better championship-clinching games and heard more enthusiastic crowds. But that Sunday at Disney World was the most memorable, gratifying, and fun night of my career. The Lakers' celebration was equal parts college graduation and New Year's Eve party, and the unexpected champagne bath was the perfect ending to three quirky months. My suit smelled horrible, in the best way.

Exhaustion had gotten the best of me a few times, but I pushed myself as hard as I could, and I saw it through to the end. I accomplished my goal of attending every playoff game from the second round on, and I observed James's fourth title from the closest imaginable vantage point. I still wasn't quite ready to place him above Jordan in the GOAT debate, but he made one heck of a case.

The NBA bubble was an incredible public health story, an incredible business story, and an incredible basketball story. As the 2020 playoffs reached their conclusion, the NBA was competing for television eyeballs with the National Hockey League, National Football League, Major League Baseball, Major League Soccer, and college football. Basketball's ratings suffered, and some of the NBA's magic got lost in the oversaturated sports landscape, the pandemic's ongoing suffering, and the final stages of the presidential election.

I realized that night that I might never get a professional thrill that matched the bubble experience, or a longer, better look at greatness. The place was information and sensory overload, so intense, so small, so immersive, so taxing. James, its star, was so overpowering, so skilled, so thoughtful, so focused, so available.

The bubble was for the diehards, and the diehards should never forget it.

Afterword

There was no championship hangover. I woke up early on October 12, treating it like Christmas morning. With my bags already packed and an afternoon flight, I killed the empty hours by taking one final walk around campus.

If the Coronado Springs Resort started feeling deserted in September, it now felt postapocalyptic. I walked the entire 1.5-mile loop three times and didn't encounter another person, save a few security guards driving by in SUVs. The Casitas were lifeless: No one was lounging by the pool, no one was queued up at the testing rooms, no one was playing pickleball, and no one was working in the media dining room. The Disney employees who spent months serving us food were nowhere to be found. Evidently, their short-term work assignments were over.

The checkout rules were explicit: (1) You don't have to go home, but you have to get out of Disney World. (2) Feel free to leave anything you don't want to take with you in your room. (3) Call a phone number to confirm once you've departed campus.

I left a cheap computer monitor, a bulky microphone stand, a pair of beat-up Air Maxes, three unopened boxes of Wheat Thins, and a bag of half-used toiletries. At the appointed time, I snapped one final photo next to Casitas 4432—my home away from home—and then hopped in the waiting town car. I pledged then and there to never return to Disney World unless a work assignment brought me back.

The ride to the airport was uncomfortably fast. The driver wasn't speeding, but I was accustomed to the meandering charter buses. I made the mandated phone call, and then took off my encumbrances piece by piece. The NBA had reclaimed my proximity alarm the previous night, so my credential was lighter than usual. I removed that from around my neck and tucked it into my backpack for safekeeping. Then

I slipped my Oura tracking ring off my finger. Finally, I peeled the MagicBand off my right wrist. I wouldn't need to swipe into my apartment when I got home. Thank God.

I felt naked, so I put the ring back on. As the airport drew closer, I braced for my first contact with the real world in months. Florida's handling of the coronavirus wasn't going well, and I had no idea what to expect at the Orlando airport. Would people be following the rules and wearing masks? Would anyone care about social distancing? I knew the rest of the travelers couldn't possibly have lived with bubble-like diligence. There was bound to be a culture clash.

It hit immediately. There were comforting signs and markers on the ground to encourage distancing, but I was overwhelmed from the minute that I stepped foot into the airport. While it wasn't particularly busy for an airport, it was far busier than anything that I had experienced since the pandemic started. Efforts to maintain distance were half-hearted at best, crowds of people gathered in all directions, and mask discipline wasn't top-notch.

To my chagrin, I found myself stuck in a long, cramped line because only a few of the security checkpoints were open. For whatever reason, a TSA employee decided he needed to pat me down from shoulder to ankle. This was hell. I closed my eyes and tried to calculate whether the TSA employee had more close physical contacts in a day than I had had in the previous three months combined. It seemed likely. He finally cleared me. I missed the bubble already.

I retreated to the Delta lounge and hid in the far corner. There were a few hand sanitizer stations scattered around, but some were empty. Whenever a passenger coughed, I noticed people got up and moved away quickly. Before long, it was time to board. I had an entire row to myself, my tension eased, and I made it home without further incident.

Los Angeles hadn't changed much, although I noticed a local coffee shop had gone out of business and a few restaurants had erected makeshift outdoor seating on sidewalks. My neighbors were all religiously wearing masks, and street traffic was still a fraction of what it had been prior to the pandemic. My neighborhood wasn't quite the bubble, but

I was grateful that it was operating at a much higher level than the Orlando airport.

Still, the coronavirus raged on. There were 66,281 new cases on July 12, the day I checked into the bubble. When I checked out on October 12, the number was 53,055. But any progress was fleeting, as the country was on the verge of a massive autumn wave. By Election Day, November 3, the number was 75,888. By Thanksgiving, November 26, it was up to 165,091. By Christmas, it reached 221,145. For the first time in my adult life, I spent the holidays apart from my parents and siblings. Travel was out of the question. The national death toll surpassed 337,000 by the end of 2020. Less than a week later, it passed 350,000. Only the vaccines could save us now.

The bubble finished with a perfect health and safety record, an achievement that has gotten more impressive with time. In late October, Justin Turner of the Los Angeles Dodgers tested positive for COVID-19 during Game 6 of the World Series. Shortly after MLB commissioner Rob Manfred handed out the championship trophy, a mask-less Turner joined his teammates and their families on the field to celebrate their title. The nauseating scene prompted a severe public outcry, and it made the NBA's strict rules and ramped-up enforcement during the Finals look prescient.

Despite the bubble's health successes, the NBA and the players union moved on immediately as they plotted how, when, and where to hold the 2020–21 season. NBA commissioner Adam Silver said in December that the prospect of living on a campus for an eight-month season was "untenable" due to the "long stretches of isolation." There was more to health and safety than just protecting players from the coronavirus, and the NBA and its teams were feeling significant financial pressure to return to a more normal gameplay experience. As one team executive told me, "The owners wanted their arenas back and the players wanted their lives back."

From a financial standpoint, the bubble was a success. ESPN.com reported in October that the bubble, which had cost nearly $200 million, saved the league from $1.5 billion in lost revenue. Revenues for the year were still down 10 percent. Even tougher times lay ahead, with the possibility that revenue could drop 40 percent in 2020–21—a loss that could reach $4 billion—if fans were unable to return to arenas en masse.

Meanwhile, the NBA saw its average television viewership in the Finals drop from 15.1 million in 2019 to 7.5 million in 2020. This sharp decrease was in line with pandemic-related declines across other professional sports, but NBA executives were quick to point out the harrowing alternatives if there hadn't been a bubble. Declining ratings were far better than no ratings, and the league aired more than 1,000 hours of games and generated more than 5 billion video views across five social media platforms.

Even though the bubble playoffs had unfolded in unusual circumstances, teams that came up short treated the results like a typical postseason. The Bucks traded Eric Bledsoe. The Rockets let go of Mike D'Antoni and traded both Russell Westbrook and James Harden. The Clippers fired Doc Rivers. The Pelicans fired Stan Van Gundy. The 76ers fired Brett Brown and hired Daryl Morey. There were real consequences across the league.

Meanwhile, plenty of bubble standouts were rewarded in free agency. Feeling good about their title, LeBron James and Anthony Davis re-signed multiyear maximum contracts with the Lakers. Giannis Antetokounmpo inked a five-year supermax extension with the Bucks to continue chasing his first championship, while Bam Adebayo, Goran Dragic, Donovan Mitchell, Jayson Tatum, Fred VanVleet, and Jerami Grant were among the other players who cashed out after playing well in Florida. With his COVID-19 saga behind him, Rudy Gobert signed a five-year, $205 million contract to remain with the Jazz.

Many prominent members of the NBA community, including some of the loudest activist voices in the bubble, cheered Joe Biden's victory over Donald Trump in the presidential election. After NBA players spent months encouraging voter turnout and campaigning for arenas to be used as polling locations, Biden's strong performances in four predominantly Black cities with NBA franchises—Milwaukee,

Philadelphia, Atlanta, and Detroit—helped him claim crucial swing states. After my endless summer at Disney World, I wasn't surprised that Trump carried Florida.

NBA and WNBA players watched with satisfaction on January 5 as Raphael Warnock, a Black pastor, defeated Kelly Loeffler, the Trump-supported white owner of the WNBA's Atlanta Dream, in a Senate runoff. With wins in Georgia by Warnock and Jon Ossoff, which were boosted by Black voters, the Democrats claimed control of the Senate.

On January 6, a pro-Trump mob stormed the Capitol Building in Washington, seeking to obstruct congressional certification of Biden's victory. Five people, including a Capitol Police officer who was struck with a fire extinguisher, died in the siege. NBA coaches and players pointed to a double standard in law enforcement's response to the insurrectionists and to Black Lives Matter protesters, and they noted that the police officer who shot Jacob Blake in Kenosha was let off without charges, just like the officers in the Breonna Taylor case. "There's two different Americas," Celtics forward Jaylen Brown said, citing Martin Luther King Jr. "In one America, you get killed by sleeping in your car, selling cigarettes, or playing in your backyard. And then in another America, you get to storm the Capitol and no tear gas, no massive arrests, none of that."

Some aspects of the league's social justice work didn't last after the bubble. When the 2020–21 season opened, the jersey slogans were gone and players generally stood for the national anthem, although several teams did kneel to protest the Capitol mayhem and the decision in the Blake case. Silver said that the league was "not focused in any way right now on discipline" if players chose to kneel, noting that it remained a "very emotional issue on both sides of the equation in America right now."

However, the NBA moved forward with its plans for the $300 million foundation, which sought to support career development and employment opportunities in Black communities. The league also appointed members to its new social justice coalition, which was tasked with increasing Black representation throughout the business of professional basketball.

The NBA and the NBPA spent weeks hashing out the details for the 2020–21 season, ultimately deciding on a condensed seventy-two-game schedule that began on December 22. All teams would play games in their home markets, except the Toronto Raptors, who were forced to relocate to Tampa Bay due to the pandemic.

Money played a central role in the major decisions that governed the first post-bubble season. Starting in December, rather than waiting until January or February, allowed the NBA to air its traditional Christmas showcase games and wrap up the Finals in July before the scheduled start of the 2021 Olympics. The shortened season enabled the playoffs to be held in May, June, and July, returning the league's schedule closer to its typical calendar while setting up the 2021–22 season to begin in the fall like usual.

Using home arenas instead of a restricted campus environment let players live with their families, and it allowed owners to get ready to collect gate revenue. Six teams opened the season with limited fans in attendance—the Cavaliers, Jazz, Magic, Pelicans, and Rockets, plus the Raptors in Tampa Bay—while the rest held their made-for-television games in empty, cavernous arenas.

Per the NBA's new health guidelines, media members were barred from the lower bowl of the arenas and team practice facilities. Reporters were not allowed to eat or drink in the arenas, and they had to settle for virtual press conferences, as all in-person interviews with players and coaches were banned. The players, meanwhile, were not allowed to use public transportation, go to restaurants or clubs while traveling, or invite large groups of friends to their hotel rooms during road trips.

Out of 546 players, 48 (8.8 percent) tested positive for COVID-19 when they first reported to preseason, a higher percentage than tested positive before the bubble. Silver acknowledged that the NBA was "anticipating that there will be bumps in the road along the way," given the extensive cross-country travel and lack of a protective bubble. All told, the NBA announced that a total of 128 players, or nearly one-quarter of the league, had tested positive between June 26, 2020, and January 20, 2021.

Timberwolves center Karl-Anthony Towns returned to the court in December, still grappling with his mother's death eight months earlier. "I only know what happened from April 13 on," Towns said, revealing that he had six additional family members die from COVID-19. "You may see me smiling and stuff, but that Karl died on April 13. He's never coming back. I don't remember that man. I don't know that man. You're talking to the physical me, but my soul has been killed off a long time ago." On January 15, Towns himself tested positive for COVID-19. "To my niece and nephew, Jolani and Max, I promise you I will not end up in a box next to grandma," he wrote on Twitter.

In preparation for games impacted by the virus, the NBA released only the first half of its schedule before the season started, to allow for possible alterations if positive tests led to postponed or canceled games. On the second night of the season, a game between the Houston Rockets and Oklahoma City Thunder was postponed when multiple Rockets players tested positive or inconclusively, and others were held out due to a contact tracing program that was instituted to limit spread within teams. Games proceeded like normal until mid-January, when the NBA, which mandated that each team needed at least eight available players for every game, was forced to postpone twelve games in an eight-day period due to positive tests and contact tracing absences.

Speculation mounted that basketball might need to be put on pause, and the NBA and NBPA responded by tightening the health protocols: eliminating all hotel visitors, cutting down on pregame and postgame contact between players on opposing teams, and barring players from nonessential activities in public when in their home markets. As it sought to enforce its guidelines, the NBA fined James Harden and Kyrie Irving $50,000 each for going to clubs without wearing masks and dinged Rivers $10,000 for lowering his mask too often during a game while coaching the 76ers.

Still wary from the backlash to its early access to COVID-19 tests in the opening stages of the pandemic, Silver said that the NBA would not "cut the line" to obtain vaccines for its players. He added that "mass distribution" of the vaccine would likely be required for games to return to full capacity, while leaving open the possibility that a bubble environment could be utilized for the 2021 playoffs if the home market approach wasn't working out as expected.

The NBA's quick turnaround left me exhausted. Like the Lakers and Heat, I had only ten weeks to regroup between the end of the Finals at Disney World and opening night. I spent the first few weeks coming to terms with what would be the shortest off-season in league history. Everything was different and rushed: The NBA Draft was held virtually in November, free agency took about two weeks to play out, and the preseason was over in the blink of an eye.

When the Lakers' new season opened at Staples Center, LeBron James, Anthony Davis, and the other returning players received their championship rings from Silver in an empty stadium. "To the Lakers fans, we'll make it up to you. We'll do this again when fans are back in the building," the commissioner promised. With their family members barred from the building, the Lakers were honored with video messages from their loved ones on the jumbotron. "Just a weird day to say the least," James said. "It was a pretty cool moment, but you would love to do that with our fans and our family. They sacrificed throughout the season. I was happy to be a part of it, but it was bittersweet."

I have fond memories of the bubble, but I don't miss it. In hindsight, it was exactly as hard as the players kept saying. During my first few weeks at home in October, I took my own temperature and blood oxygen reading every morning out of habit and a desire for peace of mind. Once I realized that I wasn't going anywhere or seeing anyone, I settled back into my pre-bubble routines. As it turned out, the daily discipline required to live and work in an isolated bubble was perfect practice for writing a book.

Since leaving Disney World, I've received three questions more than any others. What was it like to get sprayed with champagne by LeBron James? Would I live in a bubble again? Why did the NBA give up on the bubble and return to its arenas after the experiment worked so well?

Hopefully, the last chapter of this book covered the champagne scene. As for the second query, I would return to a bubble without hesitation if I knew the duration of the stay ahead of time. As challenging as it was, I think I could handle another three months, especially if it meant covering the Finals again.

The answer to the third question was straightforward: The players had enough. In their view, the quality-of-life compromises required by a bubble were not worth the payoff of zero positive tests. The idea of eight months in isolation was too daunting. For better or worse, the players became more accustomed to living with the virus, just like the rest of the country. Their decision was surely shaped by the fact that most players who tested positive were asymptomatic, only a few reported serious symptoms, and none died.

I respected their conclusion. At the same time, I wouldn't have been comfortable agreeing to seventy-two games' worth of cross-country travel with the pandemic reaching new record highs. Given the strict media access limitations and the virus's spread, I plan to spend the 2020–21 season working from home and attending games in Los Angeles sparingly. I wish the players, coaches, team staffers, arena workers, and traveling media members all the best.

In the final analysis, the 2019–20 NBA season was rocked by the coronavirus, but not broken by it. The bubble was defined by ingenuity and perseverance, and the league and its players will need both qualities as they proceed through the rest of the pandemic and prepare for whatever comes next.

My head is still spinning thanks to the craziest year of my life and the longest season in NBA history. There was no opportunity to detach from basketball's grasp, but that's OK. The NBA raced into its new season hoping to make up for lost time and lost money, and I don't want to be left behind.

Ben Golliver
Playa Del Rey, California
January 17, 2021

Acknowledgments

I want to thank Matt Vita and Matt Rennie at the *Washington Post* for supporting this project, NBA editors Glenn Yoder, Sarah Larimer, and Jason Murray, and everyone else in the Sports department.

I'm indebted to Jamison Stoltz and Abrams Books for taking a chance on *Bubbleball*, and to Tim Wojcik of Levine Greenberg Rostan, whose "Hello from an Agent" email made this book possible.

Thanks to the many editors and writers who have provided guidance over the past thirteen years: Dave Deckard, Dwight Jaynes, Kerry Eggers, Wayne Thompson, Chris Haynes, Matt Moore, Sergio Gonzalez, Kevin Pelton, Royce Young, Lee Jenkins, Chris Ballard, Rob Mahoney, Zach Lowe, Marc Stein, Rachel Nichols, Thomas Beller, Chris Stone, Ryan Hunt, Brad Weinstein, Mark Bechtel, Matt Dollinger, DeAntae Prince, and Jarrel Harris. Rest in peace, Sekou Smith.

I will always appreciate the responsiveness and dedication of the NBA's public relations team and bubble crew, including Tim Frank, Michael Bass, Mark Broussard, Amanda Thorn George, Maureen Coyle, Jim LaBumbard, Joanna Shapiro, Jaralai Christiano, Kelly Williams, Jacinda Ortiz, Michael Perrelli, and Kyle Van Fechtmann, plus the many helpful team public relations representatives.

Thanks to the players, coaches, executives, referees, and reporters who made the bubble possible, and to the NBPA's Michele Roberts, Ron Klempner, and Elle Hagedorn.

I am eternally grateful to Dr. Bretsky, Dr. Brara, and Dr. Hayes for their advice and care throughout the pandemic.

Shout-out to Andrew Sharp, Lou Pellegrino, and the GOATs. Play with a purpose. Thanks also to Michael Pina, the Open Floor Globe, and David Locke for regular conversations that helped keep me sane.

To my parents and siblings: I love you and miss you.

Finally, to the MVP, thank you for everything, always.